THE EVERYTHING
Guide to
FUNDRAISING

Dear Reader,

In the twenty-first century, fundraising has maintained its important role in American culture. In these uncertain times of economic woes and a seemingly unparalleled stream of natural disasters, people have taken stock of what really matters in their lives. They want to act on opportunities to assist others in their community and in the world around them. This is true at all levels, from community groups to public schools to corporations.

The Everything® Guide to Fundraising examines the world of fundraising as it affects us today, shedding light on the challenge of generating funds to support the causes that are important to you. From a school gift wrap sale to a golf tournament to e-fundraising efforts, there are many ways to raise money. This book explores the goal of reaching out and soliciting funds from donors, as well as various aspects of the fundraising process such as bookkeeping, accounting, taxes, communications, e-fundraising, and software.

While there are many facets to fundraising, perhaps the most important one is FUNdraising. Your enthusiasm is contagious, whether you are collaborating with colleagues, vendors, or donors. That element is bound to make a difference in supporting your cause, and it will serve as a great source of joy and pride in your fundraising efforts.

Sincerely,

Adina Genn

Welcome to the EVERYTHING Series!

These handy, accessible books give you all you need to tackle a difficult project, gain a new hobby, comprehend a fascinating topic, prepare for an exam, or even brush up on something you learned back in school but have since forgotten.

You can choose to read an *Everything®* book from cover to cover or just pick out the information you want from our four useful boxes: e-questions, e-facts, e-alerts, and e-ssentials.

We give you everything you need to know on the subject, but throw in a lot of fun stuff along the way, too.

We now have more than 400 *Everything®* books in print, spanning such wide-ranging categories as weddings, pregnancy, cooking, music instruction, foreign language, crafts, pets, New Age, and so much more. When you're done reading them all, you can finally say you know *Everything®*!

QUESTIONS?
Answers to common questions

FACTS
Important snippets of information

ALERTS!
Urgent warnings

ESSENTIALS
Quick handy tips

PUBLISHER Karen Cooper

DIRECTOR OF ACQUISITIONS AND INNOVATION Paula Munier

MANAGING EDITOR, EVERYTHING SERIES Lisa Laing

COPY CHIEF Casey Ebert

ACQUISITIONS EDITOR Lisa Laing

DEVELOPMENT EDITOR Elizabeth Kassab

EDITORIAL ASSISTANT Hillary Thompson

Visit the entire Everything® series at *www.everything.com*

THE
EVERYTHING®
GUIDE TO
FUNDRAISING

From grassroots campaigns to corporate
sponsorships—all you need to support your cause

Adina Genn

Adamsmedia
Avon, Massachusetts

I dedicate this book to my husband and partner, Michael, and to my children Alyssa and Ethan, who are unwavering in their support.

An Everything® Series Book.
Everything® and everything.com® are registered trademarks of F+W Media, Inc.

Published by Adams Media, a division of F+W Media, Inc.
57 Littlefield Street, Avon, MA 02322 U.S.A.
www.adamsmedia.com

ISBN 10: 1-59869-823-0
ISBN 13: 978-1-59869-823-7

Printed in the United States of America.

J   I   H   G   F   E   D   C   B   A

Library of Congress Cataloging-in-Publication Data
is available from the publisher.

*This book is available at quantity discounts for bulk purchases.
For information, please call 1-800-289-0963.*

Contents

Community Fundraising / 167

Grassroots Fundraising / 183

Fundraising with Kids and Teens / 193

Political Fundraising / 207

Odds and Ends / 219

All about Grants / 229

Acknowledgments

A very special thank you to those who work so hard in fundraising and who provided me with valuable information for this book: Jan McNamara in corporate communications at PBS; Natalie Canavor, a New York Metro–area consultant who helps nonprofits communicate more effectively; David Strom, a St. Louis–based technology expert, writer and fundraiser who cohosts "The Accidental Fundraiser," a podcast available at www.accidentalfundraiser.com; Ken Cerini, managing partner of Cerini & Associates, a Long Island-based accounting firm whose specialty includes the nonprofit industry; and Susan Hoffman, site director of JCCs Stiffel Senior Center in Philadelphia.

I would also like to thank my agent, Bob Diforio, who helps make opportunities possible, as well as Lisa M. Laing, managing editor of the *Everything*® series at Adams Media, for her guidance and support. And finally, I would like to thank my family for their enthusiasm and encouragement.

Top Ten Fundraising Tips You Will Learn from This Book

1. Networking is critical to your efforts. Have everyone in your group consider who they know that can donate goods and services to your fundraising activity.

2. Choose a locale for your fundraising event that reflects the members of the organization as well as the organization's mission and values.

3. Budget wisely. Some fundraisers, unfortunately, wind up spending nearly half of the income from an event simply to cover expenses. The better you budget, the better you can support your cause.

4. Join forces with organizations that have similar values and complementary missions. You may be able to accomplish more and share expenses.

5. Provide proper lead time when trying to garner media coverage. Magazines may need as much as three months or more, while newspapers and websites require less lead time.

6. Use technology to your advantage. Software programs can maximize efficiencies, and e-mail blasts are an inexpensive way to send fundraising appeals, invitations, information on upcoming events, and thank-you notes.

7. Participate in online social networking opportunities, which provide great tools for raising awareness—and ultimately funds—for your cause.

8. Solicit corporations. Studies show that corporate employees feel pride and loyalty when their company participates in philanthropic endeavors.

9. Build relationships. People are more likely to contribute to people they know who are dedicated to a cause.

10. Use *Who's Who in America* or the *Standard & Poor Directory* to find information on potential high-profile donors.

Introduction

▶FROM THEIR LIVING ROOM televisions, viewers around the world watched the importance of giving in real time, with Wal-Mart emerging as the impressive and organized leader, distributing much-needed cases of water to American storm victims in the aftermath of Hurricane Katrina. Wal-Mart demonstrated that the spirit of giving is not only alive and well, but also patriotic and necessary. Inspiring as the spirit is, however, one fundraising challenge remains: competition for donor dollars is fierce.

Money is fundamental to researching serious illnesses, fighting drug abuse and domestic violence, finding ways to stop global warming, supplying urban schools with necessary programs and equipment, sheltering the homeless, and helping those affected by violent crime and acts of terrorism. No matter what your cause, you will likely need to raise money at some point.

This book focuses not only on how the modern fundraiser goes about procuring money in a highly competitive world, but also on how to reach out and touch individuals in a manner that will provoke them to think, feel, and give.

Fundraising has become an art, and it can be very complex, involving software, advanced communications systems, marketing strategy, and corporate grant proposals. At the root of it all is the same basic need—to raise money for your cause, whatever that may be. Keep in mind that the most comprehensive fundraising software program or websites still have not matched the success of ninety-plus years of Girl Scout cookie sales.

It is important, therefore, to take a simplified approach to raising funds, no matter how creative or complex your upcoming fundraising plan may be. This book takes a practical, hands-on approach that can meet the needs of both the multimillion-dollar nonprofit organization and the local twenty-two member PTO. When everyone is playing by the same set of rules, there is no right or wrong means of fundraising, only the means of being successful in reaching your goals.

The key to successful fundraising is not whether you sell wrapping paper or scented candles; it's your inner desire to make a difference. If you have a passion and can convince others that you are working for a worthwhile cause—be it finding a cure for asthma or supporting orphaned children—you will inspire others to step forward and pitch in with goods, supplies, volunteer hours, or money.

This book highlights examples of many small-scale fundraising efforts and builds on the theme that fundraising is doable at any level. The focus is at the local level, because fundraising really begins when a child asks his mom to buy candy or wrapping paper to help raise money for school, or when the Key Club offers to wash cars for the local community. Perhaps that's what is meant by the expression, "Charity begins at home."

CHAPTER 1

Fundraising Basics

Whether it's to fix a leaky roof on an old church or help keep the homeless warm this winter, you have identified a need. But what next? How do you go about raising money to do the good deeds you want to do? This chapter introduces you to the world of fundraising.

Why Have a Fundraiser?

Fundraising can encompass a wide range of possibilities, from raising several million dollars for a new hospital wing to raising a few hundred dollars for new costumes for a high school performance. The idea of fundraising, however, offers a community, school, or organization more than just a means of raising money. It can also help your team develop cohesiveness, provide a place for individuals to use skills and talents they may not use in their everyday lives, and create a sense of community.

Your fundraiser may be the starting point for members of your neighborhood to meet other likeminded individuals and start discussing various community issues. It may also be a way of generating support for a cause you believe in.

Today, it is common to find schools encouraging students from grade school through college to engage in fundraising activities. While the parents could raise substantial amounts of money without the help of their children, these activities provide young people with a sense of teamwork and civic responsibility. Of course, there is also the personal satisfaction you get from involvement with a cause that you want to help.

Support and Involvement

When a group or organization, whether fraternal, charitable, or political, holds a fundraiser, they take some of the burden of financial support off of their membership and gain the support of a wider audience. This can help spur public involvement and promote public awareness.

For example, when individuals pledge money to PBS, they are becoming involved, in a small way, in the work of that organization. At the same time, they demonstrate their support by donating money to help the organization. Not unlike showing up at a stockholders meeting, they can become a small part of something larger, something they find meaningful. Many people are involved in fundraising for the dual purposes of helping others and socializing. Helping to organize and run the annual book fair at your son's middle school not only raises money to help the school, it's also a great way to meet other parents and get to know more people in the community.

Good Public Relations

While raising money for a specific goal is the primary objective, fundraising objectives also highlight and promote the work of your group or organization. Often, while promoting a specific fundraising effort, you will also distribute literature and tell others by word of mouth about the goals and mission of your group and the cause behind your fundraiser.

For example, representatives from the American Lung Association collecting money at a street fair will probably distribute fliers and data so the public can learn more about what they do, as well as provide health-related news and information. Fundraising often provides a means of educating the public by providing pertinent information gathered by your organization.

To run a successful fundraising drive or event, you need to introduce your members, volunteers, and everyone involved in the activities to one another. You want to establish a cohesive team for a successful fundraising effort.

Setting a Goal

Before you can start the process, it is important that you, and everyone involved in the fundraising efforts, are clear regarding what the money will be used for. Determining your primary goal can often be the cause for great debate in groups or organizations. You must establish priorities for your organization—does the school need new textbooks more than it needs a new gymnasium?

Establishing priorities requires careful examination of the available data. For example, the purpose of your organization may be to fight the HIV/AIDS epidemic. There are many ways to support this cause—you must look at the data and determine what will allow you to be most effective. Is there a greater need in your community to raise funds to help HIV/AIDS patients or to support researchers at a medical facility who are seeking a cure for this disease?

Preliminary research, polls, and analysis of existing programs can help you determine which needs to prioritize and establish and fine-tune your goals. Studies in your community may show money has been pouring in to support HIV/AIDS research, while little money has been donated to local housing for patients.

ESSENTIAL

Even when the purpose seems obvious, such as raising money after a natural disaster, make sure you are clear regarding how you envision the use of the funds. After Hurricane Katrina devastated the Gulf Coast, many groups specifically raised funds for victims and their families, while other groups sent money to help the relief workers.

Having a clear goal keeps your organization on track and inspires confidence. The more clearly you have stated your goal, the more easily you will be able to convince others to spend their hard-earned money to help your cause. Do your homework. The best way to convince others to give money toward achieving a specific goal is to have the data to support your need for funding.

Setting a specific goal will help your organization structure its fundraising plans. A larger-scale goal, such as building a new auditorium, will require a more detailed, larger-scale plan of action. Conversely, the goal of buying new volleyball uniforms will require less involved planning. Nonetheless, the goal should be clearly communicated to everyone involved, directly and indirectly, in the fundraising effort.

Targeting an Audience

It is important to establish your target audience even before you plan the details of your fundraising events or activities. Your goal is to raise money, but someone needs to be on the other end of that equation, writing out checks or handing over cash. Can you profile potential donors? Do you know who will be interested in helping you meet your goal? Can you reach these people?

It is in your best interest to establish who will be donating money. This way, your fundraising project is more likely to be successful. It will help you establish the magnitude of the project and determine whether your goal is feasible. If, for example, you are going to try to collect funds from students at the local high school, it is highly unlikely that you are going to raise the cash needed to build a new gymnasium. You will need to either establish a fundraising plan that attracts the corporate leaders in your community or scale down your goal to converting the old auditorium into a part-time gymnasium, rather than having a new structure built from the ground up.

ALERT!

One of the biggest downfalls of local fundraisers is not knowing the target community. Lofty goals and inappropriate fundraisers are a bad combination. Determine who comprises your target audience, what will attract it to your cause, and whom you may realistically tap for funding.

It is also presumptuous to expect everyone on campus or in the neighborhood to get involved and donate money. A large, high-profile organization such as the Red Cross has arms that extend nationwide and even worldwide. It can expect a large return based on calculating percentages and maintaining a database to track the number of people that donate money annually. The majority of local fundraising efforts have neither such a database nor such a far-reaching network. Therefore, you need to do some preliminary research and look into the potential donor base for your project.

If, for example, you are raising money for a sports program for underprivileged kids, you might want to tap into the local athletes and sports enthusiasts in your area. Studies show that women will more readily donate to a school-based, education-related fundraiser than men. College students have a greater passion for environmental and ecological concerns. Minorities have a greater concern for social and human rights issues.

Rallying Some Troops

"I wish I could, but I'm just too busy." That's a phrase you will hear all too often when trying to rally troops to work on your fundraising efforts. But there are many people out there who will be ready to give some time and effort to support a good cause—you just have to find them.

Reasonable Goals

Set attainable goals. This may seem obvious, but it is important to consider how much work can reasonably be accomplished by the number of volunteers you have. Trying to do too much will only frustrate everyone and may even drive away some volunteers.

It is also very important that you rally people behind the idea in a positive, but not pushy, manner. You need to gather prospective team members and promote the reasons behind the need for funding. In addition, you want to emphasize the idea of FUNdraising, or having a good time.

Getting others involved in a fundraiser can be very easy if the cause, or need, is obvious and touches the members, students, or community personally. The less informed your audience is about an issue, the more you need to be prepared. Gathering facts and figures isn't very difficult if you utilize the library, town records, and the Internet. Your enthusiasm for a cause may very well spread among your circle.

Show Them!

A simple example of winning over an audience with research and presentation comes from a father of two young children, who went before a local town board in his New England community to propose a fundraiser for new and better playground facilities. Many of the people sitting before him were elderly and had no idea what was wrong with the current playground. His idea didn't get off the drawing board.

At the next town meeting, the father brought documented proof of several injuries that had resulted directly from the old equipment. In addition to a polished proposal with facts and figures, he also brought a few of the local kids, including one who was injured on the playground. He got the town behind him and they offered their assistance for his fundraising efforts.

You should prepare appropriate literature that supports your fundraising goal or goals. Such literature should clearly illustrate your mission to potential contributors and volunteers. It should also address the urgency behind your goal and the history or background of your group, association, organization, school, or other affiliation. Remember that the people collecting the money, which includes you and your volunteers, also need to present themselves in a credible manner in your presentation.

FACT

It is estimated that more than 75 percent of people involved in fundraising activities are in some manner touched personally by the cause. A person who has a sister with breast cancer might participate in the Avon Walk for Breast Cancer; another might simply enjoy the programming on PBS. The point is the same: Most people donate their time or money to a cause they have a personal connection to.

Formulating a Plan

Many different elements factor into how you choose a fundraising event. Your fundraiser will become a project, and, not unlike starting a business, it will need to grow and incorporate the skills of various people whom you believe can help you reach the goal. New technologies can help improve your efficiency by monitoring goals and tracking progress.

FACT

Individuals give more than $222 billion per year, or about 75 percent, of all contributions to charitable organizations, according to *Giving USA*, the publication for the American Association of Fundraising Counsel. Foundations, bequests, and corporations combined give the other 25 percent.

You will need to create a time frame; an open-ended project is not really a project at all, but a process. While established fundraising organizations will always accept donations, a specific fundraiser is just that—specific—with a time frame indicating when sales or services end and totals are added up. Part of your goal will be to raise money to complete such a project by a desired date. The date may be selected for you by the nature of the project. For example, a fundraising drive to buy Christmas presents for underprivileged children will necessarily be time sensitive.

You will also find that, when you first start the wheels rolling for a fundraising project, it is very likely that your school, group, association, organization, or company has done something before to raise funds for a project. Therefore, you need not reinvent the wheel. While you are planning something unique that will achieve this particular goal, you can get rough ideas from project outlines that may already be sitting in your files.

In the end, there are many elements you will need to consider in your plan. Ask yourself the following questions:

- What is the primary need for funding?
- How much money do you want to raise?
- Who will be donating the funds? Who is your target audience?
- Who can you rally around yourself to help put this plan together?
- What is your time frame?

Online Tools

Online applications can boost your team's efficiency, making tracking and coordinating easier than ever. These applications provide tools for sending out targeted letters, e-mails, and faxes, organizing the efforts of volunteers, and issuing reports to help ensure your organization is meeting specified goals.

Online tools also enable you to measure a fundraising campaign's progress. With e-mailed newsletters promoting an upcoming event, for example, you can track how many recipients open your e-mail, the e-mail's click-through rate, and, if your organization has a web page, whether the promotion is driving traffic to the site. Through online applications, you can also schedule frequent automated e-mail reminders to your target audience as the date of your event approaches.

Two popular providers of online applications include Convio (*www .convio.com*) and Kintera (*www.kinterainc.com*). While both offer tools for success, individuals fundraising for various causes may be best served by developing a good list of e-mail contacts from which to solicit donations. So says David Strom, a St. Louis, Missouri–based technology expert and active fundraiser, who co-hosts the podcast *The Accidental Fundraiser* (*www .accidentalfundraiser.com*). Both applications allow individuals to import addresses to the program and personally connect via e-mail with several hundred people, many of whom will want to help. However, you cannot rely fully on e-mail. As Strom points out, "There are people you can't reach by e-mail who want to give you money."

There is an abundance of fundraising software, from off-the-shelf products to customized applications. When you are shopping for a program, be sure to select one that meets your organization's budget and needs. Discuss your organization's requirements with a software sales rep. Before purchasing an application, ask the rep for three references from organizations similar to yours to gauge their satisfaction.

Technology makes it easier than ever to track and measure the success of your events both during and after the event. Look for software programs that enable users to create custom reports in order to analyze progress on critical areas such as the number of registrants for an event and the amount of revenue raised. You may also want a program to track volunteer assignments, attendance, scheduling, interests, qualifications, and availability so you can match each volunteer with the most suitable role. There are numerous products available, including Sage Fundraising 100 and Blackbaud's Raiser's Edge. Before you invest in such software, look for one that complements your existing technology and consult an expert when necessary.

If software applications are not an option, simply get a notebook and start writing. Be prepared to cross out, erase, delete, or edit often, as even the simplest garage sale advertisement may require numerous revisions.

Social Networking

Encourage your supporters and volunteers to direct attention to your cause on social networking sites such as Facebook and MySpace. They can provide links to an organization's website so that their friends can learn more about it and even make a donation.

FACT

When selecting a software program to help you track and measure the results of a fundraising event, look for one that lets you not only run reports, but also e-mail them. This can be a handy feature when sharing information with board members, colleagues, and other stakeholders.

Honing and Presenting Your Plan

Your initial plan will take shape as you research the need for fundraising in greater detail. However, your idea won't become a full-fledged plan until you have gained support from your own organization, membership, student body, or association. Unless you can pull off a fundraising activity on your own, you will need to convince others to come on board with you and listen to their input and suggestions.

ALERT!

Don't fill in all the blanks. Make your initial fundraising plan one that captivates and draws attention to your issue. However, you should leave room for other people to provide their ideas. It's much easier to get people to join a work in progress than to try to fit them into predetermined positions.

Your idea needs to tell a short story. Remember, you need to rally internal support for the basic fundraising plan before you can start talking about details and fleshing out the plan. It is essential that your cohorts feel the same sense of passion for your cause as you do on a practical and emotional level.

Sometimes this is very easy. For example, if your organization is already dedicated to a specific cause, such as a foundation to fight diabetes.

First, be ready to present your plan. This can be an informal pitch to a small group of fellow students or a prepared statement in front of the board of a long-standing, 5,000-member nonprofit organization.

Second, be prepared to answer questions. How much money will we need to raise to build a new roof? Do we have a liaison to help us distribute the funds and any donated items to the local homeless population? Who will we hit up for funds? Your answers should be based on your research.

After you've presented the problem that exists, present your specific plan to solve it. Show the group what your organization will be able to do specifically to make a difference. Here's where you'll tell them what your project is—replacing old textbooks or funding a soup kitchen.

You may need a show of hands to let you know how many people are with you, or a vote by the board to move forward to the next step, which would likely answer the question, "What type of fundraiser did you have in mind?" We explore some of the answers to that question in Chapter 2.

CHAPTER 2

Selecting the Fundraiser for You

There are a host of effective fundraising options, many particular to a sector of the fundraising population. Girl Scouts traditionally sell cookies, religious groups may sponsor a carnival, and schoolchildren are very likely the reason why you have more rolls of wrapping paper than you will ever need. Your methods of fundraising should reflect a number of factors. By examining your group and looking at the potential donor base, you can determine which kind of activities will best help you achieve your goals.

Group Dynamics

The makeup of your organization or association will play a major factor in your fundraising choice. Consider the age and sex of your members, their interests, lifestyles, economic status, and level of commitment as you evaluate the kind of project to undertake. A group loosely formed without organizational ties or bylaws may choose to take on a less complicated project for fear of a loss of interest. It's easier for one of several friends planning a project to just walk away if he is dissatisfied than it is for a board member of a long-standing nonprofit organization.

In addition, look to the resources available to your group. Someone may know retail sales, have experience in running an auction, or be familiar with staging a local theater presentation. Take advantage of members' skills and talents as well as their connections. Whom you know is often just as important as what you know.

FACT

Organizations that select a fundraising vehicle together tend to experience a greater level of volunteerism than those that utilize one that was predetermined from previous members or an outside consultant or marketing firm. Studies show that volunteers work best when they have a sense of ownership stemming from being part of the decision-making process.

Finally, the overall assessment of your group or organization and how you wish to be perceived by the community should factor into your selection. The Hell's Angels could hold a biker rally and beer bash to raise funds and no one would blink an eye. If, however, a conservative neighborhood association held such an event, some people might question their credibility. Keep in mind the overall image you're presenting to the public.

Researching Your Target Audience

Who are the donors? Chapter 1 discussed learning about your potential audience of supporters. If you want to convince your audience to donate money, you'll need to find something that grabs their attention. Donations in the modern world of fundraising are driven by market research.

ALERT!

You've probably heard the expression "Give the people what they want." Take heed. One of the biggest failures of fundraising efforts is not taking the audience into consideration. Too often, groups get caught up and go full speed ahead with ideas they love but that don't necessarily appeal to their potential donors. Don't let this happen to you!

By doing preliminary research, you can characterize those individuals you expect to donate funds. If, for example, you are doing a fundraising event for a sports team, then you know players and their families are most likely to attend. What would interest the students and draw them and their parents back to the school in the evening or on a weekend?

The worthiness of your cause is the number one reason people will donate. Others include:

- A personal involvement in the issue or cause
- An enjoyment of the activity or a need for the services offered
- Support of the group behind the fundraiser
- Support for the community
- The good feeling derived from giving
- A tax write-off
- The simple fact that they were asked

These are among the major reasons people donate money to charities and other nonprofits.

Acting Locally

Although your first tendency may be to find an activity the entire town or city might attend, the reality is that fundraising efforts receive the bulk of their support from a nucleus centered closely around the group running the activities. Initially, the people involved will reach out to those they know, and those people may then take it one step further and reach out to people they know. People within a small circle (three degrees of separation) will provide the bulk of your funds, unless you are able to build a large-scale marketing campaign. From kids selling magazine subscriptions to executives looking for players for a fundraising golf tournament, the first people members turn to are family, friends, neighbors, business associates, and social contacts.

Driving Causes Home

The phrase, "Think globally, act locally" is appropriate when planning your activity. Perhaps your goal is to effect positive sweeping changes for the environment, especially at a time when Arctic icecaps are melting rapidly thousands of miles away. However, it is primarily the friends, family, and neighbors of your membership that will attend your "clean up the environment" fundraising dinner on Friday night.

Your cause, the activity you are planning, and how well you have promoted your need for money and the fundraising activity will determine how far you branch out to the target audience.

Establishing a Time Frame

Three other factors influencing your decision on a fundraising activity will be time, money, and resources. An urgent need such as raising money to help the victims of a hurricane will present a time element that limits your ability to do much advance planning. In such cases you will think, "What can we do tomorrow?"

In nonemergency situations, however, you will need to set your goals and plan your activities based on a variety of parameters. You will be able to control some of these, but others will be set for you by the nature of your organization, by available resources (including a site), or by those individuals helping you plan the fundraiser. For example, the time frame for building a roof on the community center might be three months because winter weather will delay construction. You will need to plan your fundraising activities with enough preliminary time for contractors and builders to assess the situation and work on the problem. The status of the current roof will also factor into your planning. Is it a potentially dangerous situation that needs to be addressed before a disaster occurs, or a matter of touch-up work and sealing to repair an old roof that's still sturdy?

Consider every possible factor when determining how much time you will have to stage a fundraising event or activity. It's better to have too much time than too little. However, planning too far in advance may cause you to lose the momentum and support of many of your members.

You will build a time frame around what warrants your attention. Ultimately, you would like to plan a fundraising activity with enough time to rally your membership, handle all the details, make the necessary arrangements, and spread the word. The complexity and scale of the activity you are planning will factor into your time frame. No, it doesn't take months to launch an effective bake sale. On the other hand, a bikeathon through the city of Los Angeles will take more than a few days of planning and promoting.

Costs to Consider

There will be some expenses associated with most fundraising activities. Numerous online fundraising websites promote and sell items from candles to jewelry in bulk quantity to resell at fundraising events. Renting a hall to stage a banquet will incur a fee, as will costs for decorations, not to mention the food, service, and entertainment involved. You will need to carefully consider the costs before venturing into a fundraising activity.

Network! One of the best ways to eliminate unnecessary cost factors is to have everyone in your group consider who they know who might be willing to donate goods and services to your fundraising activity.

One of the most important aspects regarding overall cost is determining what you can get for free. Donations of time, space, skills, and even tangible goods for sale or auction can make or break your profit margin. Take advantage of what other members of your group can offer. One organization had a member whose business was dealing in sports collectibles. She had staged collectibles shows and auctions in various locations and had already established contacts in the field. Therefore, the organization was able to run a successful collectibles auction to raise money with little outlay of funds.

Resources

Another key factor that goes hand in hand with money and your budget is your resources. Remember, whatever you need may cost you.

Materials

What can your group provide beyond the space and, in some cases, goods? Remember, you need resources behind the scenes, beyond what you are selling or auctioning off. For example, there always seems to be a need for tables and chairs, no matter what you are planning.

Behind the scenes, you may also need:

- Computers
- Vans or trucks
- Tables or display cases
- Ledgers and notebooks
- Paper goods
- Linens
- A sound system
- A/V equipment
- Cleaning materials
- A cash register or cash box

The availability of larger items and the items you need the most will factor into your planning. For example, if you need 300 chairs for a sit-down dinner and no one has access to inexpensive chairs, you might opt for a cocktail party where you can get away with having fewer seats for guests.

You should also consider what resources the group or organization already has. Many established clubs and associations have materials from meetings, parties, and other gatherings readily available for use. Don't forget to send out a wish list to supporters. For example, the PTO at one elementary school printed a wish list in its monthly newsletter requesting supplies needed for upcoming fundraisers.

Human Resources

Even after you've rallied the troops behind your need for funding, you still have to determine how many people are willing to roll up their sleeves and actually do the work to make your fundraising drive or activity a success. It does not take great numbers of people to launch and execute a successful fundraising activity; however, you will have to select an activity within the scope of the human resources available. Often, groups use a rough ten-to-one ratio when planning their events. Therefore, if you are holding an auction and expect 200 people to attend, you should probably have twenty people ready to handle the event.

ALERT!

Be careful not to let one person take on too many tasks, as he may be overloaded and either unable to complete them all or simply suffer from burnout. Spread the tasks and responsibilities according to experience, strength, and capability.

You will need to consider the strengths and weaknesses of your membership and try to determine whether you, as a group, have the skills necessary for a particular undertaking. Often, groups rally behind an idea assuming everyone will get involved. Think again. In a group as small as twenty members, if 50 percent of the group participates, that's an excellent percentage. The reality is that despite your members' best intentions, active participation in your fundraiser will generally boil down to a small number of people doing a large amount of the work.

Try to bring a variety of individuals into your activity from the planning stages through execution and post-activity cleanup and/or evaluation. A wide range of individuals involved in the project can provide various skills, spawn a wealth of creative ideas, and even attract a greater diversity of the population to donate.

Quality and Customer Service

Goods and services auctions are a very popular method of fundraising for schools, clubs, and various other organizations. People will bid on items donated by retailers and service providers. While people may bid more than an item is worth, they will still expect quality.

Before you stock up on 500 pairs of sunglasses from an online fundraising vendor, do your homework and make sure you are getting quality products. Simple common sense tells you not to plan a fundraising meal without tasting the food. Likewise, you should not plan a fundraising picnic without first ensuring that the location is free of yellow jackets. Always provide quality.

ESSENTIAL

You need to know what the laws, regulations, and zoning ordinances permit in a given area before you select it. This includes county laws and restrictions regarding advertising, alcohol sale and consumption, crowd control, parking, noise levels, and the soliciting of funds. While nonprofits may get favorable treatment in some respects, rules and ordinances will dictate what you can and cannot provide at your fundraiser.

Good customer service means that, just like any good retailer or service provider, you need to be sensitive to the needs and concerns of your customers, or in this case your donors or contributors. Yes, you are all working for a good cause, and no, you are very likely not receiving any salary for your hard work. This does not excuse rudeness or inadequate service. Be prepared to deal promptly, and in a courteous manner, with any complaints people may have. Be flexible. The same goes for your volunteers; you want them to continue their good work, so a little courtesy will definitely go a long way.

Fundraising Options

So, what's it going to be—a barbeque, a golf tournament, or art auction? Or will you be selling chocolates, candles, magazines, or used cars? If you use your imagination, you can ponder all sorts of unique and interesting fundraising possibilities.

Among the most popular fundraising options today are auctions, walk- or bikeathons, carnivals, and the always-popular sale of magazines, candy, wrapping paper, or other easy-to-manage (and transport and distribute) low-cost items. Benefit dinners, banquets, wine-tastings, and golf outings are more popular among the business and corporate crowd. Comedy nights, bowling events, and elegant fundraising house parties are also effective methods to raise funds. While fundraising outings are widely held, do not discount the "nonevent event" where supporters simply send a check within a certain time frame and expect nothing in return.

Auctions

In recent years, auctions have become a leading type of fundraiser for schools, associations, charitable groups, and religious organizations. The competitive nature of winning an item lends extra excitement to spending money. People are often willing to spend more than the value of the item, knowing it is for a worthy cause.

Auctions are a good choice for almost any kind of group or organization because they can be run on many different levels. By determining the economic level of your prospective attendees, you can get a feel for how high end you want to go. Usually, a cross section of reasonable goods and services works well for a club, association, school, or community/neighborhood group.

Kinds of Auctions

Traditional auctions need to be carefully planned so that the pace maintains a level of excitement. Items need to be displayed before the auction begins, and methods of bidding must be clearly explained. It is important that there are written rules and guidelines regarding how the auction is run so that final sales are not contested later. A program listing the items also needs to be carefully prepared in advance and distributed to everyone in attendance.

Silent auctions can be handled in one of two ways. Bids can be written down and placed in a bowl next to the item—the highest bidder then wins the item. Another way is to have everyone purchase tickets at the door for a set amount and place the tickets in bowls next to the items they are interested in bidding on. Then a lottery-style drawing occurs for each item. This is called a Chinese auction.

Planning an Auction

An auction committee of fifteen people is ideal. Members of the committee will handle such areas as securing donations of goods and services, cataloging or listing all donated items or services, picking up and storing auction items, transporting items to and from the auction site, preparing and printing up the list of items, publicizing the event, and staffing the auction.

While traditional auctions provide more excitement and can run the bidding up higher on popular items, a silent auction can allow the shy attendees to get involved, which is likely to increase the number of participants. Many people think of auctions as a means of buying valuable paintings or antiques at auction houses and are intimidated by the idea of bidding. Nonetheless, either type of auction—or a combination of both—can prove highly successful, as evidenced by the popularity of fundraising auctions.

If you are running a silent auction and know your event is short on time, try this approach. Print out a sheet of the winning numbers and distribute them to the tables of guests. Those who win can quickly claim their prize, and the rest of the audience can call it a night.

Soliciting Donations

The key to a successful auction of any kind is having the goods and services of value to auction off. Parameters need to be set up regarding the range of items you are looking for. In some cases, auctions have a theme, such as sports or cooking, but most often schools, charities, and community groups auction off a wide range of items of reasonable value.

It is up to those staging the auction to tap into the community donations of items or free services to be provided. A letter, brochure, and/or flier describing the specific need for funding will be necessary to attract donors. The mission and background of your group or organization must be clearly explained in print and in your sales pitch. Credibility on the part of those handling the auction will make or break your number of donations.

Of course, celebrity donations have a nice cache. A-list items such as Joe Frazier's boxing gloves or a jersey signed by Mia Hamm are bound to bring in big bucks. Again, find out who your inner circle knows or can access. Some experts recommend expanding a committee to as many as thirty-five people in order to broaden the possibilities.

ALERT!

Coordinate who is soliciting which vendors, merchants, or service providers. You don't want to annoy the very people who are donating items by having multiple people approach them after they already made a donation.

When soliciting, it is important to talk to the owner or manager and get a firm commitment in writing. Have a very basic agreement to be signed by someone in a responsible position in the store or business. Also, find out how and when you can pick up the item or display the service they will provide. Sometimes, a restaurant will give you a menu or a service provider will have you display her card and a brochure.

The items don't have to be expensive. One popular trick of the auction trade is to put smaller items together into a theme package. For example, a "Night on the Town" package might combine dinner at a nice restaurant, theater tickets, and free babysitting. Food baskets and handmade items or baskets of goodies put together by children can also be very popular and fun prizes. And don't discount free items that may hold value to members, such as a parking spot in a busy area.

Finally, don't forget to give credit to all of the people who donated goods and services at the auction as each winner is announced, and thank the donors at the end of the evening.

Sales

Selling items has always been a simple and effective means of raising money. From candles to grand pianos, the variety of items sold for fundraising purposes is quite vast. The Internet now serves as a valuable resource for finding bulk quantities of candy, candles, key chains, T-shirts, or thousands of other items for fundraising purposes. In fact, many one-stop-shop fundraising websites (see Appendix A) serve as portals to numerous vendors and merchants.

ALERT!

Before ordering from an online vendor, try to find out which vendors other nonprofits have used. Call and get shipping terms, a timetable, and a return policy, and ask questions before ordering from an online vendor.

While door-to-door sales are mostly a thing of the past in today's environment, children and adults have found that networking through friends, neighbors, coworkers, and relatives is an effective manner of selling goods. Wrapping paper, magazines, cookie dough, and other gourmet items have become favorites with schools and youth groups. Given the popularity of annual magazine subscriptions, it is a safe bet that your group could also sell a few subscriptions.

Before you start out, do some canvassing to see if any similar fundraising drives are taking place in your community. The third magazine drive of the season is likely to be a bust in a small town. Be prepared to counter other sales trends. For example, if every school in town is selling magazines, then be the first in the neighborhood to sell items like light bulbs or toilet paper (everyone needs them, right?). In fact, one elementary school had great success selling compact fluorescent light bulbs, raising funds for the school and raising awareness for the environment at the same time.

The keys to successful selling for a fundraiser are:

- Selling an item that provides you with a high enough markup to reach your goal
- Having a realistic sales campaign in a realistic time frame
- Making sure the buyer knows which group, school, or organization you represent (have literature and a badge or some type of identification)
- Staffing with convincing, but not pushy, salespeople
- Being able to describe the value of your product to the consumer
- Keeping accurate records of sales and making sure buyers receive their goods in a timely manner

A sales drive can be effective for a wide range of fundraising groups. The choice of item and means of selling will depend on your target audience, so research their buying habits.

Carnivals

Another popular fundraising activity is an age-old favorite, the carnival. Youth groups, schools, synagogues, and charities have all run successful carnivals. A carnival takes meticulous planning and preparation because it is a one-time event with numerous details involved.

Scheduling a carnival requires looking closely at other activities and holidays on the calendar to make sure there is no conflict, and that you will be able to draw a crowd. It requires that you have a secure, accessible location and available parking space. Games and activities should be carefully planned so they are safe for children as well as adults. Prizes must be distributed fairly. Rides need to be carefully inspected to make sure they are safe. Police and fire department officials need to know what is taking place and will generally provide support, providing, of course, you have any necessary permits or licenses to run a carnival. Look into local licensing and permit requirements well in advance.

Games and activities like ring toss, bean bag races, baseball pitching, shooting baskets, rope climbing, bowling, face painting, dance contests, and numerous others can be initiated with little expense and without bringing in major carnival rental equipment. The use of professional carnival activities should be decided well in advance in conjunction with your budget and funding needs.

Carnivals require a significant amount of preparation because there are many tasks involved, including finding the site, promoting the event, setting up, selling tickets, manning activities, and cleaning up. Plan a carnival well in advance and always have a rain date.

QUESTION?

Where do you get initial funding to kick off an event like a carnival or fair?
To run a carnival, a group or organization will need to either dip into its treasury or seek sponsorship to cover the costs of the activities or the whole event. Vendors or sponsors can set up their own booths or rides. Activities can also be donated by members or from existing resources. Be creative and resourceful.

Athons

Bikeathons, walkathons, bowlathons, danceathons, and similar events are very popular with charitable organizations looking to raise money. For example, the annual Walk for the Cure is a walkathon designed to raise money for cancer research. The need to determine where this activity can take place is paramount in planning such a fundraising activity. You will need to secure, often with local police and municipal authorities, a safe route for bicycles or walkers to follow. Promotion, prizes (hopefully sponsored), and security and safety measures need to be addressed well in advance.

You also need to print pledge sheets and give participants a reasonable amount of time to get pledges from friends, neighbors, and relatives. Such activities can be excellent fundraisers because they have low initial costs. However, they require a lot of planning, promotion, and manpower.

Online applications can help a group maximize results. Convio's Team-Raiser, for instance, enables volunteers to create web pages linked to an organization or event. Volunteers can also e-mail their contacts about their event participation and measure and display their fundraising progress. They can post photos, links, progress reports, and other content options, making the web page a destination site for their family and friends. What's more, they can use the site to manage secure online and offline donations. This is just one of many software programs on the market, so research the market before selecting the application that is most appropriate for your group.

Remember that the stars of your event are the walkers, dancers, bikers, or bowlers—the people who are doing whatever activity you've come up with. Therefore, it is important that you meet the needs of all of your participants. Water, towels, healthy snacks, rest areas, and even medical attention should be available, and encouragement and support should be provided.

These types of events don't end when the event is over. One of the biggest aspects (and occasionally headaches) of the event is collecting the money from pledges. Most people will be forthright and prompt about paying what they pledged. However, there's always one person who takes forever to send you the money. Be persistent and try to collect all pledged money.

Events with a Twist

Host a comedy night with up-and-coming comics providing the entertainment, and a panel of local celebrity judges or well-known personalities in your community. Try to get a professional comic to MC to keep the evening moving along. With this kind of event, you will be helping area talent build an audience and supporting your cause at the same time.

If your organization attracts the patronage of wealthy contributors, host a dinner in the spectacular private home of one of your supporters. With this kind of function, the more elaborate the home, the better. Your event will attract a big audience, for instance, if the home is filled with original art or is adorned by beautiful gardens. When you are scouting for locations, be sure to thank anyone who offers his home, and use tact when selecting one over another.

Try a bowling event, and up the ante by selling sponsorship rights for individual lanes, the way a golf outing might sell sponsorship rights to holes or flags. It's the kind of event that brings new meaning to the phrase "bowling for dollars."

The Nonevent Event

The nonevent usually consists of a mailing asking supporters for contributions to a cause within a specified time frame. This "unevent" is in lieu of running the traditional gala or golf outing, and it may appeal to donors who are plagued with event fatigue. There's an added plus: The nonevent gives donors the peace of mind of knowing the majority of their contributions go directly to their favorite causes, rather than paying for caterers and staff resources.

The nonevent event is a perfect way to let contributors know you appreciate their donations—and their time. Use this opportunity to thank them by inviting them to relax at home, send a contribution, and know that on this particular occasion, they don't have to attend yet another outing to support an important cause.

CHAPTER 3

Getting Started

Just because you came up with the brilliant fundraising idea doesn't put you in charge—or does it? Every fundraising project needs a leader to take charge. The leadership role will require a significant time commitment, and the leader will need the support of the members of the organization to get things moving.

3

Selecting or Electing a Leader

It is often assumed a good leader must possess the ability to tell other people what they need to do. In reality, however, the mark of a good leader is learning and listening. To lead effectively does not mean guiding a group of followers, but taking in data from various sources and utilizing it effectively to persuade others to work for a cause. After all, unless you are leading a military command post, people can simply quit—especially volunteers. A good leader knows how to communicate what it is that he hopes to accomplish effectively.

Once the membership has been sold on the idea of raising funds, an effective leader makes the people she is leading feel good about themselves, enjoying the work they are doing. The success or failure of a fundraising project can be influenced by the enthusiasm of the workers involved, because they are at the heart of the project.

Nonprofit Organizations

Nonprofits, once led by social workers who were passionate about their cause, are increasingly run by professional MBA types who can get more bang for the buck in areas such as administrative costs, with an emphasis on delivering services in the most cost-efficient manner. Still, their mission and doing good works must remain paramount in order to achieve fundraising success and best serve the causes. Meanwhile, as the baby boomers retire, the search for nonprofit talent will become more competitive, as candidates may gravitate toward better-paying professions. In short, the time to grow and develop future leaders is now.

Nonprofit leaders today must be able to work graciously with boards of directors, government bureaucracies, foundations, donors, volunteers, clients, and their service community. Those looking to develop leaders should look for individuals who:

- Understand an organization's mission
- Plan for the long term while simultaneously resolving any immediate crises
- Possess excellent communication skills to work within the organization as well as the media

- Inspire staff and volunteers who receive little or no pay
- Initiate collaborations
- Serve as a role model by pushing up their shirtsleeves and securing donations

People Skills

Perhaps the most significant set of skills you will need as a leader are people skills. After all, you can be an expert at setting the budget, following your calendar, and lining up the resources necessary to pull off your fundraiser. However, if no one follows your lead, you are not a leader.

Whether you are dealing with volunteers or donors, you will need to be encouraging and show a degree of patience and flexibility, even more so than in the office or at your workplace, where levels of seniority and internal politics may dictate protocol. You will also have to be accessible so you can address concerns, answer questions, and solve conflicts that may arise. To do this effectively, it helps to have all of your homework done in advance. Know as much as possible about the cause, your fundraising goal, and how to produce and promote your choice of fundraising activity. Have all of the FAQs answered ahead of time—in your mind or on paper.

Important people skills include:

- Listening when others talk
- Conducting research so you are well versed on your fundraising cause
- Delegating work to others clearly
- Giving people latitude to utilize their skills—don't micromanage
- Seeking out the opinions of others
- Monitoring people's work closely, but from afar
- Keeping others apprised of the progress of the fundraiser
- Remaining calm under pressure and getting along with various personalities
- Knowing when you need to ask for help
- Providing encouragement and showing appreciation

People skills are always a work in progress. You never know whom you are going to meet and what that person will be like. Whether you are working within an established nonprofit organization or orchestrating a grassroots fundraiser for a school or library, you will meet many different personality types, and your people skills will be tested repeatedly.

Other Important Skills

While the bylaws of your nonprofit organization may indicate how leaders are officially selected, the most important attributes for heading a fundraising project are people skills. Whoever assumes the role of leader should also possess various other skills, including:

- Organizational skills, such as planning and tracking tasks and activities
- Communication skills, both verbal and written
- The ability to persuade and motivate
- Flexibility, in case you need to shift gears or try new ideas
- Decision-making skills, including the tendency to listen to various points of view before making a decision
- Listening to the needs of others and considering suggestions or opinions

ESSENTIAL

Even if there is no required time frame for your fundraising effort, you should impose one. By setting a time frame, you establish parameters and inspire people to work harder. An open-ended fundraising campaign can drag on, and the people involved may lose their motivation. Deadlines, even soft ones, spur action.

Not unlike the old circus act where the clown tried to keep all the plates spinning at once, as the leader you will be asked to handle a wide range of responsibilities, even on what may initially seem like the simplest of fundraising efforts.

The size of your organization and the number of people involved in the fundraiser will largely dictate whether you will be a hands-on leader or an overseer. As a hands-on leader, you will be doing plenty of in-the-trenches work, such as putting up tents, driving the van, or manning the loudspeaker at the carnival. As an overseer, you will be in the position of having committee chairpersons do the necessary work. Your job is to see that each committee is getting the task accomplished within the constraints of your budget and time frame.

Who Is On Board?

Following your heartfelt pitch to raise money for the Children's Hospital of Miami, you received applause from the members of your nonprofit organization. You then gathered to discuss a fundraising drive to be launched within the next several weeks. The enthusiasm generated a flurry of excellent ideas, and ultimately you agreed to run a community golf tournament, since the activity of choice among many of your neighbors is golf.

FACT

Studies show that participation in a fundraising project drops by nearly 50 percent in the first two to three weeks. Most often, people realize they cannot devote the necessary time and effort. In other cases, individuals lose their initial enthusiasm for the cause.

However, within the next few weeks, the number of volunteers began to diminish. Who was really on board? Who was ready to pitch in and get involved in handling the workload that comes with staging a successful fundraiser?

Gathering human resources is only part of your equation. Actually seeing the results of their efforts is another. At some point, the old saying, "Put up or shut up" comes clearly into focus as you question the dedication of those people whom you initially thought would be involved. Emphasize to volunteers that you appreciate any time they can give to help the fundraising effort.

Match tasks to the specific time parameters of your members. Not everyone has to put in the same amount of effort; every little bit helps.

Concepts such as fun, togetherness, teamwork, team spirit, and "a good cause" need to be emphasized to rally your troops. Incentives can be used to lure volunteers, but these can open a can of worms unless the parameters are very clearly predetermined. You need to spell out what needs to be done to receive such an incentive. The incentive should help convince someone to work a little harder, but should not be so big it overshadows the real reasons for getting involved. Remember, the best incentive for volunteering to be part of a fundraiser should be the special feeling of satisfaction one gets from doing such a job. However, prizes and verbal or written recognition are right up there on the list.

Unless you are hiring a paid fundraiser, it is very hard to ensure that anyone will stick it out. Therefore, it is in your best interest to evaluate the skills, characteristics, and level of commitment of everyone who has pledged their time, and get your list of tasks together quickly.

As you begin planning a gala, expand your fundraising potential by inviting people within your circle of contacts, or the contacts of the person being honored, onto the gala committee. Let them know about the goals of committee members, including financial support and ticket sales. Also, mention how many planning meetings they will need to attend.

In fact, you should already have a list of what needs to be done from your time spent researching the fundraising possibilities. Asking people to take on specific tasks in accordance with their interests and skills is a far more effective means of getting the help you need than posting a general call for help.

Evaluating Your Personnel

So, who can do what? That may be your first thought as you look out at an enthusiastic crowd of potential volunteers. Nonprofit organizations often have members with skills in various areas that can facilitate the success of your efforts. If you tap into what people enjoy and what they have experience in and an affinity for, you can get a feel for who will be best at a given task.

While you may want to utilize an accountant to help with your books and people in other professions to employ their business skills, you should also consider people's hobbies and interests. Someone who crunches numbers all day may have no desire to look at your budget on the weekend or in the evening. However, she may be a marvelous auctioneer, having run auctions for a civic group or in college. Remember, one of the reasons people work hard in nonprofits and for community and charitable fundraisers is because it allows them to use their other skills. Tap those interests and skills and you'll find great enthusiasm!

Newer and Older Members

Include newer members of your organization and have them work alongside seasoned members and even board members. Working together allows the senior members to help train the newcomers. It is also very important to let new members of your organization run with the ball on occasion. While they may fumble, they may also score a touchdown with a new idea.

ESSENTIAL

Define tasks very early in the process and assign them quickly. The longer you wait to explain what people need to do, the greater the opportunity for volunteers to lose interest and slip through the cracks. Also, this way you can gather alternate volunteers in case someone changes his mind about being involved.

Tackling Tasks

Defining and assigning tasks is an important step in any fundraising activity. Each task should be written down and delegated to someone who feels comfortable handling that responsibility. This can be tricky because individuals may not have a realistic view of their own strengths and weaknesses. Personalities and character traits come into play, yet as a leader, you walk the fine line of not hurting anyone's feelings while finding the right person for the job.

For example, if the individual in charge of finding and securing the golf course for the tournament is known to be a procrastinator, then everyone else's tasks may be delayed until she completes the job. A good leader will assess, in advance, who might be skilled at doing a particular task and how the person goes about getting things done. In addition, you need to establish an open line of communication. Even if someone is doing a marvelous job, if no one else knows what she is doing, others may duplicate those efforts. Communication is key.

Selling is everything! If you say, "I think Michael would do a marvelous job at finding the site for us," you have a better chance of getting Michael to take the job of site coordinator than if you say, "I guess that leaves site coordination to Michael" or "Mike, you're stuck with finding the site."

Unity and Teamwork

When rallying the troops, you want to capture the initial enthusiasm and direct it into an activity before it fades. As the project takes shape, you will want to harness new ideas to maintain the enthusiasm and keep the tasks fresh for the people who are putting the fundraiser together. You can build on the unity the group feels by having tasks that overlap at various points. This will often be the case in your fundraiser, whether you make a concerted effort or not. By overlapping tasks, one group or committee will need to communicate with another to complete its work. Often, the programming and planning committees need to coordinate with the site committee to complete their tasks. All of them will also need to be in constant touch with the promotion and advertising committee.

By limiting stand-alone tasks, you increase the unity within the group, and you make people responsible to each other. This will often encourage someone to get the job done, if only to not let someone else down. Of course, this can be a double-edged sword. If one person, such as the procrastinator, has a task that affects the work of other individuals or committees and doesn't do the job, it can trigger a domino effect. However, if you are monitoring the work as it progresses, this can be avoided.

As the leader, you'll need to keep tabs on the work as it progresses. For this reason, it is also advisable to have a committee rather than one person handling key tasks. Therefore, if there is one weak link, the chain will not collapse and the work will still get done. Unity is also the result of frequent meetings and even social gatherings to discuss the progress of the fundraiser. Show your appreciation for the work the volunteers are doing as often as possible.

The Board Members

Board members of a nonprofit organization are usually senior members who have been involved with the organization for some time or high profile individuals in business or corporate America who have contacts in various industries. All board members should have a strong grasp of the overall goals and mission of the organization and be dedicated to meeting those goals.

The board also provides guidance and oversees the financial well-being and fiscal responsibilities of the organization. Board members should help provide access to resources for the nonprofit organization to meet their intended mission.

Whether you are talking about the board of a national fundraising organization such as the United Way or the five people who make up the board of a small nonprofit group, you should expect the board to contribute to your fundraising efforts. By giving their own money, they are setting an example and sending a message that they are committed to the fundraising drive or event. Increasingly, studies show more organizations are requiring board members to contribute funds, rather than simply seek contributions from their inner circle, as in the past.

Boards should be at the forefront of the organization, even if they maintain a low public image. Board members should:

- Help identify and contact contributors
- Help in the promotion of the fundraising campaign and the work of the organization

- Provide specific resources for fundraising campaigns or events
- Offer knowledge and guidance based on their background in the organization or in the for-profit business community

Multimillion-dollar fundraising organizations may have board members who are CEOs of major corporations. Their time is limited, but their high-profile positions and access to resources and funding are quite significant to the organization. Small nonprofits rely more heavily on their boards to oversee daily operations and, in some cases, to handle a portion of the fundraising activities.

FACT

Large organizations often use board manuals. A board manual serves as an orientation handbook and details the board structure and operations. It also includes listings of fellow board members and staff and provides general information about the organization.

Organizations with limited funds, however, often do not garner much buzz and are challenged to recruit potential board members. Boards-By-Design, started in 2005 at Duquesne University's Nonprofit Leadership Institute in Pittsburgh, was created to address this concern. Following the speed-dating format, Boards-By-Design puts together interested individuals and nonprofit organizations. Boards-By-Design hosts these events several times a year at a Pittsburgh restaurant, giving both sides five minutes to meet before moving on to the next candidate. The program has helped unite fifty organizations with board or committee members, and the concept is now gaining ground across the country.

The First Meetings

Now that you have a team together to kick off the fundraising drive, you need to decide how it will work. Whether you are about to launch a direct mail campaign, a beauty pageant, or a car wash, you will need to hold fundraising meetings. Even in this day of e-mail and conference calls, nothing beats the face-to-face, in-person meeting.

ALERT!

Keep the momentum going! Once your committee, group, or posse is formed, get together within two weeks. Don't give volunteers a chance to lose interest. Always have something planned for the meetings; you don't have to have a massive agenda, but make sure there is a purpose.

It is essential to keep people returning to subsequent meetings, maintaining the level of interest and enthusiasm for the fundraising goal. You want to make sure that people feel at ease in meetings. If people feel good and are in a comfortable setting, they will be more likely to participate in the discussion.

Meeting Preparation

Prepare and distribute an agenda for each meeting that includes a clear purpose for the meeting beyond the obvious: to discuss the fundraising efforts. Be as specific as possible!

Prior to your meetings, set some basic rules of procedure to maintain a sense of order and keep things running smoothly. Many nonprofits use Robert's Rules of Order—a precise format for running a meeting—to handle meeting protocol. Depending on the size and nature of the group, you will adapt your own version of this antiquated, but still widely accepted, method of governing meetings.

Meeting Tips

Make sure you have allowed sufficient time for everyone to know about the meeting. Send your letters or e-mails a couple of weeks prior to the date. Invite only the people who need to be there. Follow up with people who have not responded as the date approaches. Set a start and an end time, and keep track of the time as you go. Do not allow one agenda item to dominate the meeting unless it is considerably more important than all others.

It is important to try to involve everyone present in the discussion. If new members are present, make sure to introduce them or have them introduce themselves. As the meeting progresses and more people participate, try to keep the discussion from going off on tangents, and limit unnecessary side chatter.

ESSENTIAL

> Have someone record minutes at your meetings. Key decisions and a clear list of who is responsible for which task should be on paper—or archived electronically. Electronic minutes can be distributed to members so that everyone remains on the same page.

Finally, have refreshments! However, try not to let refreshments get in the way. Position them away from the main meeting area or set a specific time for a refreshment break.

Even an informal group should run the first meetings with some sense of structure and a touch of formality. It sets a tone that will be helpful once everyone has become more comfortable with one another. Frequently, once the members of a group get to know each other, more socializing or non-productive discussion dominates the meeting. As a result, not much gets accomplished. If you start off with some formality, a separation of "meeting" and "socializing" has been set.

Running a successful fundraising meeting also means keeping one eye on the goal at hand and the other on the clock. Remember, if people leave a meeting feeling like they have gotten something out of it besides cake and coffee, they will come back for the next fundraising meeting—which should be planned before you adjourn the present one. If people leave shaking their heads because the meeting ran until midnight, they won't return.

To keep the meetings interesting and the members coming back, you may try varying your meeting place. Sometimes, small nonprofits and other groups engaged in fundraising efforts will meet in people's houses. This alone can draw people who are curious about seeing each other's homes. If your nonprofit or school board has a standard meeting place, you might try a variation by having a lunch or dinner meeting. A new twist on an old theme may keep people coming back.

ALERT!

It is important to schedule both a start and an end time for the meeting. This way, you let everyone know the meeting is carefully planned around the agenda and you are cognizant of people's need to end at a reasonable time. Two or two and a half hours is a good length for a meeting.

Goals of the Meeting

Your first fundraising meetings should set the plan in motion. If you are seeking donations for an auction and no one has gotten any donations by the third meeting, then the approach is wrong, the cause has not been clearly identified, or your members are going after the wrong donors. Likewise, if you are embarking on a phone or direct mail campaign, you can get early feedback from those doing the calling or receiving the return mail. Early in the planning process, meetings can provide a chance to evaluate and remedy unproductive situations before they continue.

When you are planning a fundraising event, the early meetings give you an opportunity to establish a timeline to work toward the specific fundraising dinner, auction, or bikeathon. Again, you will be able to evaluate your progress from meeting to meeting and see how you can get back on schedule if you have fallen behind.

Finally, schedule enough meetings to maintain enthusiasm and keep everything running on time. However, do not hold meetings for the sake of meetings. Many groups meet again and again without rhyme or reason out of force of habit. This is not productive.

Motivation

Start motivating your team by establishing a level of communication and trust between members. People are motivated if they feel the cause is important and others whom they care about are relying on their efforts.

Enhance your abilities to motivate by first introducing the project team to one another. Next, make sure everyone understands the goals and objectives of the project and each person is clear about the tasks that need to be done and how they are integral to the overall fundraising objective. You'd be surprised how setting the wheels in motion properly from the very beginning will help you motivate people later.

Numerous books have been written on motivational techniques. Some emphasize rah-rah team spirit and others have more detailed theoretical insights into what motivates an individual. While such books may come in handy over the long haul, the simple approach is to look at who is working on your fundraiser and what piques their interest and enthusiasm. Children may be motivated by an incentive or prize at the end of the road—so might many adults. However, adults may also be reaping cognitive benefits such as advancing their education, learning new skills, or making new contacts that may come in handy in their professional lives.

The Truth about Motivation

Motivation is usually not rah-rah speeches from a podium, but pats on the back, thank yous, certificates, and, most importantly, a feeling of accomplishment after raising funds for your cause.

FACT

Professional motivators have been proven successful in nonprofit situations only if they are active in the cause the group is working toward. For that reason, a nonprofessional speaker who has a good story to tell involving the cause at hand will usually be far more effective than a professional motivator.

If you can research and find results in the field in which you are doing work, such as a decrease in student dropout rates, then you may hit the motivational nail on the head. For instance, consider volunteers of the Kenya Fund, sponsored by the Ethical Humanist Society of Long Island, a

New York 501(c)3 charitable organization. These volunteers help raise funds for Sema Academy, a school that once hosted only twenty children and now educates 400 in Kenya. In a land plagued by droughts, heavy rains, malaria, and war, Sema Academy is making strides, and students are performing above the national average. Whenever morale among fundraising volunteers is low, the leader points to sixty-plus students, receiving free tuition, who can help lead Kenya in the future. People are excited when they learn small efforts can bring big results.

Motivating from Year to Year

If you've had a relatively successful fundraiser in the past, you can motivate both your membership and outside attendees to come back next year by building on your theme. If one year you hold a dinner with entertainment, the next year you might add an auction as well. Then toss in a raffle the following year and add a dance contest. Once you have an audience that enjoyed a fundraiser one year, you can motivate them to return the next by building on, or leveraging, your fundraising event.

If you can become known as the organization that holds the best annual golf tournament, you can distinguish yourself in a hurry. Think outside the box and come up with twists on tried-and-true events. For example, one nonprofit that supports area charities hosts an annual masquerade with a new theme (*Arabian Nights, The Great Gatsby*) and different honoree each year. The new themes keep the event fresh, making them a night that attendees and volunteers look forward to every year.

If a fundraiser was only marginally successful, invite members to build a think tank and find new ways to build on a theme. People love being asked for input and having a say in the building process of any project or fundraiser. Taking something and making it better is the perfect way to pull people together. Building on a theme is an effective way to motivate people to step up for an annual activity.

Motivating others is an important leadership role, and the best way to do that is to stay motivated yourself. Keep one eye firmly on the project goals and the other on everyone involved.

Fundraising Consultants

Consultants have become a fixture in our modern world, prominent in many fields. Do you need to hire one for your fundraising efforts? Perhaps. The size and scope of the nonprofit organization is one determining factor. Another factor is the success or failure of recent fundraising efforts. Finally, there is the magnitude of what you are trying to accomplish in conjunction with the resources and manpower you have.

FACT

According to the Association of Fundraising Professionals, organizations increasingly retain consultants for a range of services from special-event coordination and targeted fundraising campaigns to administrative functions. It is important to work with professionals who are both cost efficient and who help your organization meet its goals. To that end, get references before hiring a consultant.

If you want to take on a fundraising activity much larger (or much different) than any other you've done before, some professional advice might be very welcome. In some cases, an organization is pressed for time because they have ongoing work to do in conjunction with the fundraising activities—this might also be reason to meet with a fundraising consultant.

ALERT!

Find out if a consultant has worked with your type of organization in the past and with your kind of fundraiser. Some consultants deal with government grants, while some deal with day-to-day operations, and others deal with special-event planning. Make sure to get the right consultant on board. Always check references.

Some fundraisers will ask for a percentage of the profits. This request, on top of a flat salary, should not be granted. However, if it's a choice between a set rate or paying a small sum plus a percentage of your profits, then you join an ongoing and sometimes heated debate. There are staunch opponents of the idea of paying a fundraising consultant based on the success of the event. They believe the costs should be fixed and the dollars raised should go to the cause, not to a vendor. There are others, however, who feel such a percentage-induced arrangement provides incentives for the consultant to work harder.

Do keep in mind that the people contributing to a fundraiser are contributing to a cause or goal that is posted. As soon as money goes for something else, whether it is to pay a consultant or to cover some internal cost of the nonprofit group, you may find the donors very unhappy. After all, they pledged $50 to help abused children, not to see the money go to a highly paid consultant.

Of course, the other side of the argument is that paying on commission is fair. That way, you spend more money only if the results of the consultant's preliminary work bring in benefits. This is a choice you will have to make if you decide to hire a professional consultant.

CHAPTER 4

Where and When? The Details of Your Fundraiser

You know why you are raising the money. Now you need to establish the details of your fundraising event, activity, or drive in conjunction with your planning committee and your board. This chapter looks at what you need to do to fill in some of the key aspects of your project, including locating a site and selecting the date or dates on which you run your fundraising event or campaign.

4

Location Selection

The choice of location for your fundraiser obviously depends on the activity, but it also depends on your resources and the location's accessibility.

Whether your planning committee is choosing a park for your 5K run or a restaurant for your fundraising breakfast, you must make all considerations to accommodate the projected turnout. Special consideration may be afforded to major contributors who must attend. List all factors prior to selecting a location and discuss them with one or more board members to ensure you have addressed all key concerns. Then, conduct research to make sure a similar event isn't taking place the same day.

ALERT!

Double-check the availability of the location as the day approaches. Confirm that the site is reserved for your group—a mistake (on your end or theirs) can be costly if it means you don't have a site the day you need it!

Some fundraisers have seen low turnouts due to closed roads, detours, or heavy traffic. While these factors cannot always be avoided, they are also worth exploring. Find out as much as you can ahead of time. The more difficulties you can avoid, the better off you will be. Stay on top of the situation by being proactive.

Donated Space

One of the biggest expenses of your fundraiser may be in renting a hall, restaurant, or other location. If a member can donate a location or you can use a facility that is owned or leased to the organization, you can cut down on expenses dramatically. Therefore, the more networking your planning committee and board members do to secure a free location, the easier it will be to meet your financial fundraising goal.

You can also try to negotiate a deal with a site. For example, you may get a room in a restaurant free, or for a minimal cost, in exchange for mentioning their name in all of your advertising literature and promotions. Caterers often appreciate the additional exposure a venue gets when their site is selected for an event attended by prominent people in the community.

Location Hunting

Go in groups. A simple rule of thumb says you will never remember all the questions to ask when you are scouting a site for your fundraiser. Even if you are in your son's school and deciding whether you should use the gymnasium or the auditorium, have another set of eyes and ears to take in the surroundings. You'd be surprised at what another person might point out that you may have missed. It can be helpful to snap digital photos of each location to refer to later.

To find the best site for your fundraiser, first consider the size of the expected turnout. You will then need to compare rental rates—and remember, always inquire about what is included in the rates and what restrictions they may have. For example, can alcohol be served? If so, what are the additional costs? Can you bring in a DJ or a band, or will you receive a discount by using the house entertainment? Do you have to use the catering facility of the hotel, or can you bring in an outside caterer? If you find a location that suits your needs, confirm available dates and find out how far ahead you need to book. You should also ensure there will be adequate parking.

A site coordinator acts as a liaison between your organization and the owner or manager of the site. You need to know how the site is run, and who can help you handle any problems. She will have a vision for how you can make a location work best. Choose your site coordinator wisely; look for someone who has planned activities or events.

The more familiar the location is to your members and prospective attendees, the better chance of a successful turnout. A fundraiser for the library held in the library courtyard, or a school fundraiser held in the school gymnasium, can help set a meaningful tone for the fundraiser.

Many owners or managers of sites are willing to give discounts or special deals to nonprofit organizations or grassroots groups. The more in step with your cause the owner or manager is, the more likely you'll have a low-rate, or even donated, facility.

The "Right" Date

Selecting a date for your fundraising event or a week for a fundraising drive can be a frustrating task. You'll need to factor in numerous variables, including holidays and the availability of key players in the organization. In addition, you will need to consider what time will draw the most attendees or attract the most donors. While you are at it, check the calendars of other nonprofits so you can avoid competing events—no matter how different the events may be.

Seasons to Watch

The peak times of year for fundraisers are typically in the spring and prior to the end-of-year holiday season. The spring affords you good weather and lets you get your activity in before the end of the school year and the start of summer. The holiday season is a time of giving, and also ends the tax year for individuals who are looking for an extra tax writeoff. People may be more receptive on the phone or by mail as the holidays approach. On the other hand, it is also the time in which thousands of other fundraising campaigns are in effect, so there is more competition.

Start by choosing dates that allow your group or organization enough time for proper planning. The bigger the undertaking, the more time you are likely to need. One nonprofit that hosts a gala where auction items are donated by professional sports stars—and where the sports celebrities themselves attend—spends a year planning the event to iron out all of the details.

Weather Considerations

Obviously, you will want good weather when planning a carnival or golf tournament. However, you may also need to consider factors such as hay fever and allergy season. Of course, if the premier golf course in the area can give you a specific date free of charge, you may abandon many of your other considerations—but not all. Don't take a date if it really won't serve your purpose. After all, you can play on any golf course in the Northeast in December, but you probably wouldn't want to—although being unique sometimes works. One school held a very successful beach party in January; they just imported sand and held the event in the gymnasium.

Organizing and Record Keeping

There are popular software programs specifically designed to help you track fundraising, but you can use any organizational software or simply keep records in a notebook or ledger. There are two primary areas you will want to keep track of. First, make sure you have accurate information on everyone who is involved in working on the fundraising campaign. You need to have an idea of what everyone is doing and have accurate contact information readily available.

FACT

As of 2004, there were more than 1 million 501(c)(3) organizations, according to *The NonProfit Times*. Many people expect the number of new fundraising groups to continue to rise. That means there is a lot of competition out there for donations!

The other key records are those of sponsors and donors. You want to know who donated money, how much they donated, and when. You then want to be able to send thank-you letters and follow up with these donors in the future. Make sure you have adequate contact information. You need to build your valuable database of people and businesses you can tap into in the future. If you can set up your records so they can be accessed from a number of different fields, you will be able to look up donors by location, past donations, and other characteristics.

By keeping accurate records of all procedures and money transactions, you can also update your sponsors and donors on the success of the program. Major sponsors should receive updates on how much money is coming in and what the money is being used for. This keeps them in the loop and serves as good public relations for your organization.

Setting up a Schedule

No matter what you call it—schedule, timetable, plan, or program—a successful fundraising activity or event needs to follow some kind of defined schedule. The larger the program or event you are planning, the more complex your plan needs to be.

Not unlike managing any other type of project, you will need to list various tasks and, based on the completion date of your fundraising efforts, include a timetable that indicates deadlines for completing tasks. Schedules need to be comprehensive yet not so complicated that other people cannot follow the plan of action. There should also be room for any adjustments that need to be made.

FACT

Hold a pre-event dress rehearsal or at least a walk-through. Prepare a script or action plan for the event that spells out what is happening when and who is participating. Have a pre-event conference with all the key players and review the action plan. This is an excellent way to confirm who is doing what, identify concerns, and address them in advance.

Mapping a Timeline

If you are planning a fundraising drive for six months from now, you should map out what needs to be done during that time and how long it should take to complete the various tasks. You may plan by working backward from your completion date in accordance with how many weeks it will take to finish each task. Don't forget to consider the timing of publicity for your event. You will need to time the release of publicity to appear several weeks, or even months, in advance of your fundraiser. Include deadlines in your schedule for getting the word out about your event.

The dates that appear on your timetable, also known as baseline dates, are the initial dates for starting and finishing a task. You will use these dates along with your ongoing schedule to compare all tasks' expected completion date with where they currently stand. Your timeline should be tied in to your budget (more on budgeting in Chapter 6). You will need to watch the budget in conjunction with the timetable to see how much money you are laying out in advance and how much you are spending as you progress. It is critical to keep in mind that if you are spending $2,000 a month from a $10,000 planning budget, you will run out of money in five months. If the big push for your event is scheduled to begin in six months, you will be out of funds by the time you get there.

Schedule the most important tasks early on. For example, you would want to find a location before deciding on a local caterer or determining how many tables and chairs to order. Reserve your location six months to a year ahead of your event, if possible.

Keep in mind that just because a job can be completed in six or seven hours it does not mean it will be completed in one day. Elapsed time is how much real time is needed to complete an activity. Someone working on a specific task may need twenty hours to complete the job. However, because he will not put in twenty straight hours, you will need to determine how much time he can put in on a daily or weekly basis before determining when that job should be completed. For example, a commitment of five hours per week will mean the job will be completed in the twenty-hour total but over the course of four weeks.

Printers' Schedules

Printing is a very time-sensitive aspect of your fundraising project. You will need to know well in advance when the printer you choose to work with needs final copy for advertising and promotional materials as well as day-of programs and organizational literature. Background materials on your nonprofit may already be available, but this may be the ideal time to update such material and run more copies.

High quality digital printing enables programs to be designed with variable data to customize each piece for its intended recipient. For example, if you wanted to reach out to a strong supporter, you could thank her for her past support and suggest a donation reflecting an incremental increase over the prior donating period. Meanwhile, in that same variable print run, an inactive recipient from your database could receive a solicitation mentioning how much her support has been missed. Experience has shown that response rates from variable printing projects are higher than with traditional offset printing, where identical pieces are mailed to everyone.

FACT

One of the biggest errors that is made during the planning phase of a fundraiser is not allowing sufficient time for concept development and design as well as printing, assembling, sorting, addressing, and mailing. Efficient project planning and management is essential. The additional cost for a rush turnaround by the printer and the mailing house can reduce your net revenue.

Ensure consistency between your printed materials and your website so your branding remains strong. This will help your charity stand out as a well-run organization, inspiring confidence from your target audience.

Tracking Your Progress

You need a way to follow the progress of your fundraising project. Therefore, you want to have each task clearly displayed on a schedule or matrix. You should be able to see multiple tasks and their relationship to one another. You also want to be able to see who is responsible for handling each task. All of this should be part of the software program you are using or part of the notebook in which you are writing your schedule of activities.

Volunteers can run reports and share them, as well as progress updates, with others in the organization through online software programs. If they are soliciting donations, they can share that information with friends and families via e-mail or on their individual websites. This strategy can help an organization build enthusiasm for a cause, either within the organization or with an external audience.

You can track progress on a monthly, biweekly, weekly, or daily basis, depending on the nature of the project and the number of tasks and people involved. Frequently, a fundraising project is tracked less often in the beginning and almost daily as the end of the project nears. Milestones should be marked off as they are reached.

Schedules can be hard to follow, especially when an organization is largely comprised of volunteers or needs board approval on key decisions. Therefore, you should leave some slack in your schedule so tasks have a little extra time to be completed beyond the "on paper" completion date.

Don't assume you know how long a task will take. Talk to whoever is going to do the work to find out how long it will take him to complete it. If the time frame sounds unreasonable, research how long it takes someone else to do the same task. For example, if a printer says he can have the job in five weeks but you want it in three weeks, comparison shop with other printers and see what they can offer you. If two other places can do a quality job faster and at a similar rate, you should go with one of them. Getting a consensus is a good way to determine how long it should take to complete a job and at what cost.

Contingency Plans

Always have backup plans. One of the most important reasons for keeping track of the ongoing progress of your fundraising campaign is to have a Plan B or even a Plan C in the event you need to switch gears. For smaller projects where you do not stand to lose money, you may just shrug your shoulders if all goes wrong and say, "We tried. We'll try again next time." However, if your organization has invested time and money and put its reputation behind a fundraising campaign or event, it is important to have some last-minute tricks up your sleeve.

Reduce the Risk

There will certainly be unforeseen developments along the way, but there are ways to reduce the probability of problems that might occur. Look at risk factors surrounding your fundraiser that could directly or indirectly impact your goal. Are the highways leading to the golf course closed for repaving? Is there a for sale sign on the catering hall you just booked for your fundraiser? You cannot anticipate all possible scenarios, but if you have backup plans, you can reassure donors they will receive goods and services or, in the worst-case scenario, have their money returned. It always helps to remind people, when calamity strikes, that their donations are for a good cause.

Coming Up with a Plan

A contingency plan may be as simple as securing a rain date for a golf tournament or calling FedEx to overnight an important item to the auction.

FACT

You may want to take out insurance to compensate your organization in case your event has to be canceled because of bad weather or other unforeseeable circumstances. While this can be costly, it can ultimately prove valuable.

The bottom line is to think about what your organization will do to shift gears if all is not going as planned. It is also important to have someone in charge of determining when to make such a change in plans so you can start the process of notifying everyone involved.

Inviting Special Guests

Okay, you have the place, the date, your timeline, and a contingency plan in case anything goes wrong. Now, what can you do to put this fundraiser over the top? How about a special guest? Let's assume Julia Roberts and the governor of your state are both busy. How about a local celebrity? Chances are between your board and your members, someone has access to a well-known personality. In some instances, a personality can detract from the matter at hand, but in most cases, she will help attract a crowd and generate support for your fundraiser.

To find a celebrity of any stature who will be effective, you should first look for someone who believes in your cause. Then find someone who will be in town or accessible when you are having your fundraiser. You might also seek out someone who fits the theme of your event. For example, a professional golfer to launch your tournament or present the prizes to the winners would be a fitting choice for a golf tournament.

Dealing with Celebrities

If you have a celebrity of any magnitude coming to your fundraiser, you should carefully plan exactly what he is expected to do (and not to do). Chances are, his time is limited, so if there are photos to be taken or an award to be presented, make sure you can schedule it to take place when he shows up. Celebrities are prone to the same scheduling snafus as the rest of us, and they may be late or even have to cancel their appearance. Double-check that he is coming, and do not center your event around his appearance unless he is already a major player for your cause.

It is often to your advantage to invite a local media personality or celebrity who is more in touch with the community and the people than a big-name celebrity, who may only disappoint when she arrives late, has little to say, and can stay for only five minutes.

Use Your Auction

A nice way to work a popular figure into your fundraiser is through an auction. The daughter of a chef in one of New York City's finest restaurants was a student at a local grade school. Dad offered to cook a dinner for eighteen people as an auction prize. Another school had the brother of a professional basketball player in attendance. Big brother agreed to come by and, as a prize, give a twenty-minute basketball clinic to five lucky kids. These are major ways to boost an auction while letting a personality do what he does best.

If someone has a contact that isn't a household name but is a star in a field of interest, that contact's services can be utilized in your auction. Golf lessons from a pro or a makeup demonstration by a top Hollywood makeup artist are ways to increase the bidding. Determine whom your membership can reach. If you get a talent to donate her time to perform at your fundraiser, you should then make a concerted effort to see everything is taken care of, from sound checks to refreshments to transportation. Anyone who is going out of her way for you deserves to be treated well.

ALERT!

Don't hand a celebrity or politician a microphone and ask him if he wants to talk. There are many stories of celebrities going off on tangents or monopolizing the time with their own agendas. If your celebrity guest is willing to speak, politely indicate that you'd be thrilled to have him talk for a few minutes about your cause.

Media Representatives

Part of your publicity campaign, discussed in detail in Chapter 10, will include inviting the media to your fundraising activities in an effort to gain some valuable press. While this is wonderful in theory, it can present problems. The media is usually kind to nonprofits, but not always. If members of the media are present, you will need to have someone guide them around and answer their questions properly. There are plenty of cases of reporters putting a negative spin on their stories or getting facts and figures wrong.

Should the media be there to interview people running your fundraiser, try to point them in the right direction. You will want the most knowledgeable, well-spoken representatives of your organization speaking to the press.

Staging Repeat Performances

"We did it that way last year." That statement can be positive or negative, depending on how well the fundraiser went the previous year. A successful fundraising effort certainly bears repeating. However, how much you should repeat becomes a question that is often debated by fundraising committees and boards. The tendency to fall back on tried-and-true plans can sometimes diminish the opportunity for forward thinking and new ideas. On the other hand, repeating a fundraiser, sometimes with only a few changes, may bring in even more money than it did the year before.

QUESTION?

Why host the same fundraiser year after year?
Good events are worth repeating—and something your supporters may look forward to annually. What's more, your organization will have conducted much of the legwork already and now you can work on building the event's branding and following instead.

Points to Consider

If you repeat a fundraiser, plans, organizational materials, and contact numbers for sponsors, special guests, vendors, and donors should all be easily available in your database. People who handled specific tasks last year will have a running start this year.

But there are also compelling reasons to change direction this time around. New members might have new ideas, additional resources, and contacts to more significant donors. And times change; what was in last year may be out this year. In addition, you may not have access to the same resources, site, number of volunteers, or budget to work with.

Expanding for New Ideas

Ultimately, the best answer is often a variation on a theme. A successful golf tournament one year might be a tournament with a dinner the next and a tournament with special prizes for side activities (like sinking the longest putt) the following year. Building on a theme or changing certain key elements is often the manner in which fundraisers become annual events.

CHAPTER 5

Organizing the Troops

You have a goal to work toward and a group of people who are excited about helping you achieve it. How do you utilize your human resources in the best possible manner to reach your fundraising goal? You will need to set up guidelines for volunteers or staff members, form committees, divvy up responsibilities, and shift the work force from one task to another whenever necessary.

Setting Guidelines

Establish the procedures for fundraising activities. Even if you are not part of a larger umbrella group, you will need to draw up guidelines before you set up your fundraising campaign, activities, or events. This is especially critical for future leaders who may run a fundraising campaign at a time when there is frequent turnover.

The level of formality of such guidelines and the protocol you will follow will depend on the size and structure of the organization and the fundraising activities you have in mind. Obviously, five kids running a lemonade stand to raise money for new basketball uniforms will require far less structure than twenty students on a college campus orchestrating a twenty-mile bikeathon for several thousand riders.

Be Succinct and Clear

Guidelines should serve as a roadmap for carrying out the fundraising plan in succinct and clear language. All primary activities should be included, such as promotion, programming, administrative duties, and so on. The responsibilities of the individuals or committee should be outlined with details included to avoid confusion. While you don't want to pigeonhole people, you do want to provide them with a basic job description to follow when they are doing their tasks.

The guidelines should set the tone for transactions and interactions with other people, including donors, as they shape the overall parameters of the fundraiser. For example, areas to be addressed might include:

- How to explain information about your goal to a prospective donor
- How specific concerns or complaints are addressed
- The procedure for moving to a contingency plan, and who makes such a decision
- What to do if someone is injured or gets sick during your fundraising activities
- Who is in charge of ordering from vendors, and what procedures to follow
- What does and does not need to be presented to the board for approval

- If there is no board, who makes the decision on each aspect of the project
- Who can call a meeting, and the procedure (and how many people are required) for taking a vote

Documentation

Having written guidelines from the beginning can come in handy if anyone questions how you are handling certain procedures or if you are accused of treating a certain volunteer or group of volunteers unfairly. It assures everyone knows the rules and how things should be handled. Having general procedures and guidelines written down can also serve as a guide to future fundraising efforts. Such guidelines will help next year when you start planning your fundraising efforts.

ESSENTIAL

Have a separate set of guidelines for specific fundraising activities that differs from your organizational code of conduct or bylaws. While you might not have separate guidelines for selling candy versus selling wrapping paper, your rules for making sales calls should be outlined on a separate page and e-mailed or handed to everyone involved in the fundraising project.

Finding Volunteers

Whether you are the executive director, a salaried employee for a nonprofit, or a volunteer yourself, you will likely be working with a variety of volunteers as you plan a fundraising event.

Recruiting People

Nonprofit organizations often find volunteerism goes in cycles. Many organizations report that for several years they will have plenty of volunteers, and at other times they will be busy recruiting. The nature of the organization, the economic climate of the times, the needs of the community, and various other factors may determine how many volunteers you have at any given time.

Most volunteers will come through your membership and word of mouth. Often, people who are attending meetings but are not yet volunteering only need to be asked if they can help run events or activities in a small way. When a school runs a fundraiser, word spreads and announcements in the school papers or on posters let others know about the upcoming event. E-mail blasts and phone chains are a great way to recruit volunteers. These efforts will attract attendees and will also draw people who are interested in getting involved in making the fundraiser a success. The ongoing fundraising campaigns of major nonprofit groups such as the Salvation Army encourage donations and also attract additional volunteers.

Similarly, when people express interest in volunteering, try to engage them immediately, even if there is no immediate task that needs action. Drop them a note, thank them for their interest, and let them know when you might need their skills or the date of the next general meeting. Keep the lines of communication going by e-mailing newsletters. Good volunteers are not always easy to come by, so consider this opportunity a gift!

High schools and colleges are often a good place to find additional volunteers. Students are often looking for community service credits, or they may simply be interested in your cause. Make it easy for them to get involved!

The baby boomers can serve as a valuable resource for organizations looking for volunteers. It is anticipated that by 2010, many of the nation's 77 million baby boomers will near retirement—and will have time on their hands and a lot of expertise to offer. Highly educated and experienced, boomers are well versed in law, medicine, education, management, entrepreneurship, and other key areas. Studies show that boomers who volunteer engage in their community, stay active, and feel personally fulfilled. Matching their skills to your needs can prove beneficial to any organization, and perhaps increase their level of contribution, both in expertise and dollars.

Keeping People

Volunteers will get involved because they:

- Are passionate about the cause
- Want to give something of themselves
- Want to hone or apply skills they may not get to use often
- Are looking for experience to add to their resume
- Want to do something worthwhile for other people
- Are looking to meet people and socialize while doing something constructive

These are among the key reasons volunteers will come on board. They will likely be turned off and back away if they feel their reason for helping is not being met or feel they are engaged in an unpleasant or stressful situation. Unlike a job, it is easy to walk away from an unpleasant volunteer experience.

FACT

Between 26 and 29 percent of Americans volunteer. These percentages are at an historic high, with more people volunteering today than at any point in the past thirty years. With increased concerns about crime, gangs, poverty, disasters, the environment, illiteracy, and homelessness, Americans volunteer to make a difference.

With this in mind, you need to accentuate the positives and ever so gently find ways to correct the negatives. Starting new volunteers off with specific, nonthreatening tasks can indoctrinate them to working on the project without throwing them to the lions. For example, you don't want to have a brand-new volunteer talking with potentially major donors unless he is the main contact point for those donors. You will more likely ask new volunteers to help with promotional materials or join the committee in charge of gathering resources or refreshments. The new volunteer will probably feel more comfortable starting off this way than suddenly being responsible for a major chunk of the contributions.

Training Tips

If volunteers are ready to work, you will need to make sure they are versed in what they need to do. Not unlike a paying position, job descriptions should be prepared, and volunteers should be trained in how they can best complete tasks. Keep it simple so you don't intimidate new volunteers. Remember, you will also find some people who will go beyond the call of their duties.

It is also important to try to assess the skill level and ability of your volunteers in advance so as not to insult anyone or appear condescending. Find out what they have experience in and, more importantly, what they enjoy doing. For more specific or specialized tasks, such as maintaining the budget or handling the accounting procedures, be selective from the start and find someone with both the necessary experience and the ongoing dedication to the organization or the cause. Switching treasurers midway through a fundraising effort is not easy and lends itself to errors in accounting.

If you are working with a nonprofit organization, board members should be encouraged to help find someone with an accounting background. If you are running a school fundraiser, you need to network through teachers and school administrators to see if they have someone in mind. Volunteers with experience in a particular area may need training in some aspects of your organization and its goals, but don't try to dictate the job to her. Rely on her expertise in the area—that's why you're bringing her on board.

Present the big picture; don't just train volunteers to do a specific task. Get them acquainted with the overall work being done by your organization or group so they have a better understanding of the group's goals and feel a part of the overall group.

Online Training

Online tools bring fundraising to new heights, including training. Training modules or handbooks for volunteers can be posted online. By posting a manual online, an organization can save money on printing costs and ensure volunteers have access to the latest updates. What's more, an organization can provide critical information to virtual volunteers who contribute to your cause from around the world and stay connected through their Internet connection. Some organizations also train volunteers via e-mail. However, online documentation or training by e-mail can sometimes get lost in translation. Phone conversations can serve to clarify instructions and help ensure volunteers fully understand their roles.

Creating Schedules

It helps if volunteers know when they will be needed. It helps even more if you know when they will be needed. Therefore, a volunteer schedule needs to be set up and carefully maintained. Volunteer schedules often require great flexibility for many reasons:

- Volunteers often need to change their schedule around.
- You may need to change the schedule based on the completion or lack of completion of tasks.
- External factors ranging from the weather to political snafus are a reality.
- You may have over- or underestimated your need for volunteers.

Schedules should be works in progress. Start by estimating how long it will take to complete a task, but realize things may happen more quickly—or more slowly—than you expected. You can reassess your time frame and adjust it to be more realistic once the activity is under way. Always estimate on the long end.

Schedules should be flexible not only in terms of the amount of time needed to complete tasks, but also in regard to the amount of time any one volunteer can put into the effort. Someone may be available for three hours one week, four the next, and seven the week after that. It is an inexact science, so try to have your bases covered with the phone numbers or e-mail addresses of a few extra volunteers on hand at any given moment. It's also a good idea to appoint a volunteer coordinator to handle the responsibility of finding backups or fill-ins for specific tasks.

Working by Committee

A committee is a group of people officially delegated to perform a function such as investigating, considering, reporting, planning, or acting on a matter.

Whatever the makeup of the group or organization running the fundraiser, committees will break down the responsibilities so that smaller, manageable groups can handle them. Even if each committee is composed of only two or three people, it lets everyone involved know who is focusing on and responsible for each particular aspect of the overall fundraising project. Committees, or even individuals handling tasks alone, will report their progress at meetings.

Fundraising committees often include:

- A planning committee handling the major details
- A site committee, in charge of finding and securing the location and making sure all of the details are worked out
- An administration, finance, or budget committee, which is in charge of monetary matters
- A security committee in charge of safety (usually for a larger-scale fundraiser such as a carnival or conference)
- A programming committee, in charge of developing the program of activities and speakers
- A sponsorship committee, in charge of making a list of potential key sponsors and reaching out to those sponsors
- A publicity committee, in charge of spreading the word about the event or fundraising campaign with a promotional and advertising campaign

Most often, all committee members are asked to seek out donors. However, there may be a specific committee finding and talking to major donors.

The need for all of these committees depends on the size and structure of the group running the fundraiser. Very often, even in large membership organizations, there will be only a few people handling these important tasks. In smaller organizations, there may be a fair amount of overlap. One person may sit on several committees, or a committee may serve several functions.

Committee Relationships

A committee is usually formed among people with similar skills who want to do a specific job. For example, someone in the printing business and a couple of people with PR backgrounds might all join the publicity committee. It is important to establish a general mode of operations for each committee at the onset. Someone will chair the efforts and each person will have specific tasks.

QUESTION?

Can you fire a volunteer?
In a manner of speaking, yes. While a volunteer is not receiving a salary, you can politely ask a volunteer to step down, but only with just cause. If someone is not doing a task well, help her do a better job. However, if she is doing something unethical or illegal, you may need to "fire" her. Have positive proof of what she has done before speaking to her; otherwise, you could be sued.

If you are heading the fundraiser, you will need to get reports from committees on a regular basis so that you can look at the overall schedule or time-line and see if the work is getting done in a timely and cost-efficient manner. If a committee is languishing, it may need help. You can offer to work with it, add an additional committee member if possible, or simply make suggestions. While you don't want to overstep your bounds or insult anyone, you might be able to find a way of helping the committee stay on track. You may also be asked to play peacemaker among committee members.

Committee Reports

Committee reports can be as elaborate or as simple as necessary. The intent of a report is to update all key individuals involved in the fundraiser or in the organization with the latest accomplishments of the committee and where the work stands in relation to the schedule and budget. A committee report should restate the goal of the committee and provide an update on various tasks. Include necessary expenditures and the need for additional resources if necessary. Also, include expectations such as when tasks will be completed and what else the committee plans to do.

Showing Appreciation to Volunteers

Volunteers' hard work and time commitment should always be acknowledged. Don't let the volunteers who are working hard for your cause feel their efforts are going unnoticed. There are several ways to let them know you appreciate their efforts and to say thank you for a job well done.

If your nonprofit organization has a newsletter, you might mention the individuals who helped. If you have numerous volunteers, you can at least thank the committees. If this was a grassroots fundraising effort for your school, temple, church, or community center, you might send out thank-you cards.

Be extra mindful to show your appreciation to your virtual volunteers. Thank them for each accomplishment, and let them know specifically how their work is helping your cause. Because you most likely will have little if any face-to-face time with these virtual volunteers, thank them for the good work they do so they remain engaged with your organization.

FACT

Large nonprofit organizations often have annual dinners or banquets where volunteers can be acknowledged from the podium and asked to stand. In some cases, plaques or pins are handed out in recognition of a job well done. This kind of dinner can also serve as a successful fundraiser if the honorees invite guests who pay to attend.

A simple and frequent show of appreciation following a school or similar community-based fundraiser is to take everyone out for coffee and dessert. It's a small dip into the profits to pick up the tab for a mini party to make sure everyone feels good about the job he has done. Such a gesture will go a long way when lining up the volunteers next year. No matter how you do it, it's important volunteers know their work is appreciated. Saying thank you is part of the pay rate for volunteers, and it is an important part of the job.

Hiring Professionals

If you can get the job done with volunteers, do so. If, however, you are pressed for time or cannot find someone to handle a specific (and necessary) task, go ahead and hire someone, requesting some consideration because you are a nonprofit group or simply a group of people staging a fundraiser.

ALERT!

You should not work out a deal offering to pay someone based on the success of the event or fundraising campaign. Professionals are doing a job for you—they should be paid for the service you hired them for, regardless of factors out of their control (such as a low attendance rate).

Most often, a professional—whether it's a clown to entertain children or a lawyer to handle a major lawsuit—will be paid through your organization's treasury, regardless of the success of the fundraiser. When retaining professionals who are interested in your cause or mission, you will likely find they will be more accommodating with their fees.

The bottom line: You need to be able to justify paying someone for services. Can this person bring you closer to your goal? Do the policies, bylaws, guidelines, and, most importantly, the members of the organization support the hiring of a professional? Whatever your answer—and your final decision—use it to set an ongoing precedent for the future.

CHAPTER 6

The Big Bucks

Fundraising is all about—what else—money! How will you convince people to open up their checkbooks or wallets? This chapter looks at how to successfully make money and secure donations for your cause. But you will have to spend some money before you can start making any.

Assessing Your Costs

In the ideal fundraising scenario, there would be no costs—everything you need would be donated or sponsored. While this can occur in some cases (usually smaller activities or events), it is likely you will need to spend money to make money. Whether that means buying refreshments, hiring a professional auctioneer, or catering a dinner, you will need to determine the amount of money your organization can put up as seed money, or what percentage of the proceeds from ticket sales can go to planning and running the fundraiser.

Raising money is a costly endeavor. Don't forget to maintain your base of past supporters, or your fundraising efforts may wind up suffering. One study showed charities may lose more than half their revenues from "downgraded and lapsed donors."

Some of your expenses may include:

- Site rental, including not only the facility, but also maintenance and security personnel
- Food and refreshments, including servers and bartenders
- Promotion and advertising, which may include printing, mailing, e-mail blasts, and website costs
- Travel and lodging for special out-of-town guests
- Microphones, speakers, and A/V equipment
- Special personnel such as musical performers, an auctioneer, a golf instructor, or a casino dealer
- Items to be sold (don't forget shipping costs)
- Telephone bills, including internal calls between committees as well as calls to prospective donors
- Miscellaneous items, from paper clips to raffle prizes

These are just some of the things that will cost you money and reduce your revenue. The more you can get donated or sponsored, the greater the revenue available to benefit your cause.

The trick is to make sure you have budgeted enough for each item that will not be donated. Also allow for the likelihood of unanticipated expenses, which will inevitably occur. Try to get as many goods and services donated as possible. These contributions will go a long way in paring down expenses and supporting your cause in the long run.

Budgeting Expenses

Understand how much money you are starting with and how much you must raise to meet your fundraising goal. See the big picture by listing both the money you'll spend and the money you'll make.

Depending on the activity or event, you will have a variety of ways in which you can raise funds, including:

- Selling tickets or admission individually or to groups
- Selling refreshments
- Holding a raffle or offering a door prize
- Selling ads in the program or journal accompanying your event
- Teaming up with a known goods or service provider or vendor to get a piece of its sales

Often, you will find ways to utilize several of these methods and others to generate additional income for your fundraising activity. For example, a golf tournament can generate money from greens fees (or admission) and/or selling refreshments, raffle tickets, and advertisements in the program. Holes, holes-in-one, and flags can raise additional sponsorship dollars. A pre-event dinner can also add revenue. What's more, people can buy items at the pro shop, with a percentage going to your cause.

Look for as many moneymaking ideas as possible, but stay within the spirit of the event. After all, you want to provide value, and not cause supporters to feel they are just being hit up constantly for more donations. People will buy more and give more if they believe they are receiving quality goods and services.

FACT

It is common for 50 percent of your income from a fundraiser to cover your expenses. Some organizations strive to keep fundraising costs at or below 15 percent of their total income. You can do this through generous donations from your organization's members or supporters.

Typically, a nonprofit organization may spend 10 to 40 percent of its budget on fundraising activities; with that in mind, don't spend the entire year's fundraising budget on one activity. Also, stay within the boundaries of any start-up money you receive and do not spend any potential funds before you see them. Yes, you may raise $50,000, but if your budget is only $10,000, you are asking for trouble if you spend $30,000 and hope to make up the difference with revenue.

If funding is coming in from advance ticket sales to your banquet or talent show, you can increase your expenses as needed, but do not build a budget on speculation. Also, remember not to build up your budget based on pledges for participants who will be engaging in an activity. While most people mean well, someone will inevitably pledge $10 a mile for your forty-mile bikeathon when she only has $300 in her checking account.

The Ever-Changing Budget

You may be a little more liberal in spending anticipated income if you have staged a similar fundraiser in the past and earned substantial revenue. However, you never know if the night of this year's auction will be the night of a major rainstorm that keeps everyone at home.

Your budget may change as you plan and conduct your fundraiser. Perhaps there will be unexpected costs that will need to be added to your plans. Or perhaps you will add to or adjust your budget as you incorporate new ways to make money. In addition, you may scrap plans that don't look cost efficient or that are beyond your budget. Flexibility is key as you work with a budget.

Sponsorship

Getting significant portions of your upcoming fundraiser sponsored is one of the best ways to get adequate funds to cover your initial expenses. If you're having a golf tournament, you can have a different company sponsor each hole. You can then put their names on the scorecard and have signs by each hole.

You can also have sponsors for the lunch you provide or for a demonstration given by the resident pro. You can display their logos on banners or screens. Everything can be sponsored—you just need to let people know you are looking for sponsorship. Call for sponsors through e-mail blasts and posts on your website. Newspapers are another great source; some sponsors may sign up as media partners and donate ad space, enabling you to announce your event and call for sponsors simultaneously.

In addition to helping you achieve your fundraising goal, sponsorship from a major corporation bodes well when you are seeking additional sponsorship from other companies or grants from foundations. When a major company sponsors your activities, it lends credibility to your event, so aim high when seeking sponsors.

ALERT! Most sponsorship is provided in exchange for signage or some sort of mention of the company, which is usually mutually agreeable. However, if a sponsor begins asking for any kind of control over your plans, you may have to say no. Remember, your organization needs to maintain control.

Finding Sources of Funding

The key to your success will be finding fundraising sources and tapping them for donations. After all, this is what your fundraising efforts are all about. Whether your fundraising goal is $5,000 or $5 million, you will need to develop a list of prospects—potential contributors. Your list of potential prospects may include individuals, businesses, civic organizations, government agencies, foundations, and trade associations. Another prospect? Community banks, which may set aside dollars to support local efforts that improve the region and help them get their names out to a local audience. For every prospect, you will need to compile information for your database.

Keep in mind that some volunteers will give time instead of money, which they might not be able to part with at present. Don't alienate hard workers by making them feel guilty if they don't hand over a check. They may well be future donors when their financial circumstances improve.

Choosing Prospects

How do you develop a list of prospects? Your first list of prospects will be the people who you already know are committed to your cause, your board of directors if you have one, committee members, and all of your current contributors. One way to quickly develop a prospect list is to have people you already know, specifically your board, fundraising committee, or others working on a grassroots fundraiser, write down the names of three to five people they know. These people can be from all areas of their life: family; business or work; civic, religious, or recreational activities; neighborhood, and so on.

Build your list, expanding from a narrow list of people to a wider, broader cross section of the community. You might segment your list as follows:

- People involved in the group or organization, such as board members, general members, and everyone working for your fundraiser.
- Contacts, including families, friends, neighbors, work associates, and others.
- People who benefit from or have an inherent interest in the work of your group. For example, someone who has a hearing-impaired

child will be more likely to give to an organization raising money to help the hearing impaired.

- Community supporters, including business owners and political figures. While some people may not be as knowledgeable about your cause, they may understand the value of giving as part of a larger community effort.
- The community at large. This can range from your school district to your city, depending on your budget, resources, time frame, and volunteer base. Reach out as far as you can without jeopardizing your fundraising plan.
- Previous donors. Never forget your database. Go back to those who have given before, thank them, and ask them if they will donate again.

The reality is that anyone can end up on your list and in your database. It is in your best interest, however, to start close to home and branch out.

FACT

Age, income, education, and employment status are all factors in who gives money versus time, according to a national study released by Thrivent Financial for Lutherans in 2008. The majority prefers to give money, but young adults often say it's easier to give time, while pre-retirees and retirees prefer to give money.

Know Your Prospective Donors

Who are your prospective donors? It helps to know this information. It is also to your advantage to note the characteristics of your prospective donors. Area of residence, occupation, marital status, and other considerations will help you narrow down a target audience. If, for example, you are raising money for a summer drama performance program for the local youth, parents of school age children are more likely to see the need than the young singles crowd. Therefore, you should advertise and put more effort toward promoting your fundraiser in venues that attract families. There are issues that are nearer and dearer to the hearts of women, seniors, singles, and people of various minorities and ethnicities. Baby boomers may be more concerned about ecology issues, whereas working women may respond more quickly to women's rights issues, and minorities may respond more favorably to raising money for civil rights causes. Know how to tap into the community that will be most interested in your message.

Individual Contributors

Most small nonprofits dream of those five- or even six-figure contributions from corporate sponsors. Yet in reality, the vast majority (90 percent) of the billion-plus dollars raised each year from fundraising campaigns stems from individual contributions. Receiving gifts of varying sizes from individuals and maintaining relationships with those individuals form the foundation of successful fundraising. One of your goals, besides raising money, should be building a base of donors for future fundraising efforts. An auction that drew 125 people and generated a modest $4,000 may not seem worth all the hard work that went into the planning and staging. However, you now have 125 names to send thank-you notes to and solicit for your next fundraising venture. If you see to it that they have a good time, they will be the first people to attend next year, and you can throw in entertainment to make their evening even better and draw an additional 125 people!

Fundraising efforts generally grow over time. Whether you are working for a nonprofit group or pulling together community fundraising drives, you will be able to build on your initial efforts through your database. Those attending your June event should receive a direct mail letter in November letting them know about your upcoming March fundraising drive. The small activities that raise funds for a school when your child enters kindergarten may have grown into big fundraisers by the time she is in sixth grade. Keep the ball rolling by maintaining contact with individual contributors, no matter how small their donations may be. Never say, "That person gave only [x amount]." Each little contribution adds up.

It is critical to nurture relationships with existing supporters by letting them know how their efforts are helping your cause. To do so, record the positive aspects of your fundraiser and then spread the good news to your base. This will serve as a major selling point when soliciting people next year.

What causes do households support? A 2007 Center on Philanthropy at Indiana University study found that religious charities top the list. Additional nonprofits that generate support include those providing the basic needs of others, those with combined purposes (such as United Way, which redistributes funds to a variety of recipients), health causes, and relief efforts.

Studies show income plays a big role in how people contribute. While those with high income give more frequently, they tend to give a lower percentage of their incomes than those who are less affluent. At the same time, in tough economic times, contributors often scale down donations when bracing for downsizing and other financial worries.

ESSENTIAL

A study by the Center on Philanthropy at Indiana University found nearly three out of every ten households alternate giving and not giving every year. Because a good percentage of households do not make the same kinds of contributions year-to-year, you'll want to grow your roster of supporters while also maintaining relations with an established base of supporters.

Alternative Ways of Fundraising

Charities can also benefit through nontraditional means of giving that extend beyond the writing of a check or the contribution of one's time. Consider, for example, life insurance policies. Typically, people buy life insurance to provide for the ongoing financial security of their families. However, once their children are grown, they may have little need for that policy. Instead, they can contribute to their favorite causes by donating that policy so the proceeds benefit the nonprofit. This strategy can appeal to donors who wish to continue their support of an organization well into the future. What's more, these donors can reduce the amount of their estate tax at both the state and federal level.

Other alternatives include investments such as hedge funds, real estate, and private equity. As the *Chronicle of Philanthropy* reported in June 2006, Purdue University, which used to have the majority of its assets invested in stocks, had put nearly a quarter of its assets in alternative investments, including real estate, by 2002, enjoying an 11.9 percent return on a $1.34 billion endowment. Smaller nonprofits, however, typically find these alternatives too risky, experts say.

Make an ongoing pitch for alternative ways of fundraising on your website. With this strategy, you can educate supporters about strategies to support your organization that they might not have considered otherwise.

Nonprofits can also work with an investment advisor to help the organization grow an endowment. Many large financial institutions, including Wachovia and Merrill Lynch, offer consulting services specifically geared to help nonprofits grow and manage their investments. Choose one that understands your organization and its needs, goals, and any regulatory requirements.

Foundations

You may turn to a foundation for a portion of your funding. A foundation is either public, receiving support from multiple sources including individuals, private foundations, and government agencies; or it is private, deriving money from an individual, a family, or a corporation. Foundations are usually nonprofit and are set up to provide money to worthwhile causes and activities, including educational, scientific, environmental, political, and charitable needs. To retain nonprofit status, they usually must donate a specific portion of their funds each year.

FACT

Foundations typically provide funding for special projects that help a specific cause; they generally do not fund the ongoing operating expenses of a nonprofit organization. To find foundations, you will need to do research. The Foundation Center (*www.fdncenter.org*) offers many resources to help you get started.

Seeking a grant from a foundation will require not only research on your part, but a well-honed grant proposal in accordance with the guidelines of the foundation. While grants can be a major step for a small nonprofit, keep in mind there is great competition for grants, and they are designed to provide a portion, not the majority, of your fundraising needs. Chapters 17 and 18 have more information on grants.

Corporations

Corporate donations can add significantly to your revenue. Such donations are usually the result of a connection between one of your board members and a corporate executive. With the passing of the Sarbanes-Oxley Act in 2002, a public corporation is more accountable than ever to its shareholders and must report where their money is going. Therefore, before a corporate check will be written to your nonprofit, it is likely the corporate donors will want to know:

- The goals of the organization and/or specific fundraiser
- The background of the organization or individuals looking for funding
- Exactly how the money is going to be used
- What contingency plans are in place if the fundraising plans are not proceeding on schedule
- How realistic your fundraising plans are and what your budget looks like
- How the efforts of the fundraiser will be monitored and evaluated
- How the company can be showcased in a positive manner

While a wealthy individual may choose to give money and remain anonymous, a corporation will want its name attached. The public relations aspect of funding a good cause is a plus for the company, and its concern is focused, in part, on its public image. Companies often sponsor events such as golf tournaments or bikeathons that can help them feature their products or their name in conjunction with your cause and/or organization. Corporations tend to support causes related to health and human services and education. Studies show that the biggest corporate givers are typically pharmaceutical companies.

One of the biggest problems you'll face in trying to get donations or sponsorship from a corporation is finding the right person to talk to. Often, you'll make a strong appeal to an executive who has no real decision-making power. He will then need to take it through channels to a series of other executives who will then convene with more executives who will forward it to yet more executives, and so on. By the time your appeal for funding reaches the right channel, the cause may be miscommunicated, as in the old game telephone. ("It wasn't to help save Crystal Gayle; it was to help save a whale!")

To avoid this difficulty, inquire about a corporation's guidelines for grant applications. Sometimes this information is readily accessible on a company's website. Again, the Foundation Center (*www.fdncenter.org*) is a great place to start. Bear in mind that corporations—just like individuals—are vulnerable to economic downturns. At a time when there is concern about a recession, corporations may find it prudent to give less than in previous years.

Other Major Donors

Most major donations stem from wealthy individuals who are passionate about your cause. You should approach them carefully, and court them in person. Naturally, the definition of a major donor may change from one place to another. For example, a $5,000 donation from a Wall Street executive in response to a direct mail campaign might be a modest donation for an organization that frequently receives six-figure contributions from multimillionaires.

However, if you are thinking of tapping a major donor in a small suburban town for $5,000 when most of the other donations are $50 to $100, then you will treat this donor in a very different manner. Larger donations for most nonprofit groups are generally accepted to be those of $500 or more.

Research potential major donors before you approach them for money. The more you know about a person, the better your chances of receiving a sizable donation. When courting such donors, come prepared with backup literature and materials supporting your cause and describing your organization. To impress a major donor, you should have information readily available highlighting your mission statement, board of directors, and fundraising team.

Following up leads is important. Sometimes, through researching names and potential donors' backgrounds, you will discover a connection that results in an additional donation. Play detective and look for commonalities between the potential donor and yourself, your organization, or perhaps a board member.

Tapping Your Sources

Yes, "tapping your sources" is just another way of saying, "asking for money." Let's face it, you will need to ask for money, whether it is asking people to buy something, take part in an activity, or simply donate.

While much of this book focuses on planning your special fundraising events or activities, there are other means of raising funds, most of which are standard practice for nonprofit organizations. Established and even newer nonprofits use three methods regularly: direct mail, telephone soliciting, and Internet contributions.

Direct Mail

Think of direct mail, and you'll immediately think of the junk that fills your mailbox every day. The reality is, however, that direct mail works. If it didn't, you wouldn't be getting piles of junk mail every day. While most of it may be tossed, an occasional item may catch someone's attention. People do respond to a small percentage of the so-called junk mail, and that percentage makes direct mail economically worthwhile for most nonprofits.

While only a small percentage—perhaps 2 or 3 percent—will respond, direct mail works because you are dealing in volume. The more you send, the more that 2 or 3 percent return amounts to in revenue. In addition, you are spreading the word about your organization and your cause to a mass audience.

If your direct mail piece is related to an upcoming event, make sure it is sent out with a sufficient amount of advance notice. Include all pertinent information (time, place, admission price, and so on). Last but certainly not least, retain a dependable mailing house that can get your mail out quickly and professionally. There's more on direct mail in Chapter 7.

FACT

One of the biggest factors in the success or failure of a direct mail campaign is the quality of your presentation. Look to professionals who have written direct mail pieces for some guidance. Your message should be clear, concise, and attention-grabbing so that it stands out from other mailings.

Telephone Soliciting

Telemarketing, as you probably well know, is still alive and well, but it has drawbacks. It can potentially alienate prospective donors. So why do people still consider telephone solicitation? It can work if it is done effectively and to the right people. This is where knowing your target audience can help an organization reap big rewards. Volunteers from a school calling at 4:30 in the afternoon and then apologizing for interrupting a parent's day is a better start than making a random call at dinnertime and launching into a sales pitch. Your telemarketing method should be based on research, personal attention, and honesty.

The telephone has become less personal over the past decade because of the widespread, unauthorized use of mailing lists. People no longer answer the phone expecting to hear a friendly and familiar voice. Instead, they often do not answer the phone at all if they do not recognize the phone number on their caller ID. If they do answer, it is often with a "Who is this?" attitude, bracing themselves for another solicitor.

The bottom line is, telephone solicitation can work only if it goes against what has become the norm—impersonal, scripted (even automated) cold calling. You need to be personal; call people who are involved in your cause and talk to them like real people. Chapter 7 covers soliciting by phone in more detail.

ALERT!

There are guidelines established by the Federal Communications Commission (FCC) regarding the time periods in which you can call, and what constitutes harassment or inappropriate conduct in such solicitations. Get a copy of the FCC regulations and any local laws governing phone solicitation. For more information, visit *www.fcc.gov*.

Websites

Websites and other online strategies enable fundraisers to cast a very wide net for an increasingly broadening audience. A website is a most effective tool to communicate information about your organization and even to provide a link where supporters can donate money easily and securely. Some hesitation about donating money may exist on the part of the public, especially if they are unfamiliar with your group. Obviously, the bigger the organization, the more confidence people will have in the security provided by the site.

FACT

While the Internet has become increasingly popular among nonprofits, the old door-to-door solicitation approach has diminished greatly. It has gone from one of the leading methods of raising funds to last on most listings. Safety issues, the time involved, and the ease of getting donations through the Internet have all but eliminated this once viable means of solicitation.

On your site, make it obvious where the donations can be made and make the contribution process very easy. In fact, it should be possible to contribute from every page on your site.

Web fundraising is becoming more prevalent as online security measures become stronger. A website should also serve as a place where people who learn about your organization can then send a donation via snail mail. Fundraising over the web is covered in more detail in Chapter 7.

Giving Something Back

For a $50 donation, you get a T-shirt; for a $100 donation, you'll receive an umbrella; and for $200, you'll get a tote bag. This is typical of the fundraising efforts of PBS and similar organizations. You donate money and get something in return.

Giving people an additional incentive can spur contributions. Having a sponsor who can provide you with T-shirts or some other giveaway item makes this added incentive work. It also raises public awareness about your organization. Bumper stickers, T-shirts, caps, mugs, and tote bags featuring the name of your organization are all very visible items. One fundraising group gave a jacket to everyone who put in three hours of volunteer time at its annual conference. This created a professional, united look among the volunteer staff and served to promote the organization.

One of the simplest things to do is give recognition. It costs little, if anything, to acknowledge somebody's generosity and it makes people feel good when you do so. Consider mentioning volunteers and donors in the monthly or quarterly newsletter.

CHAPTER 7

Honing Your Skills for Effective Fundraising

Let's face it. Many people find it difficult to ask friends, neighbors, and strangers for money. But if you don't ask, you won't receive. This chapter will help hone your asking skills, whether it's verbally or in writing, providing strategies to help you put your best foot forward. All it takes is effort, a passion for your cause, and respect for potential contributors.

Fancy Phone Techniques

Telephone solicitation is both a successful and highly annoying method of raising funds. Most telephone solicitation is done poorly, and the organizations paying telemarketers often receive a low rate of return for the time and cost invested. In some instances, such campaigns reflect poorly on the image of the organization. The question is, how do you do it right? Most people do not want to talk with telemarketers, so you immediately have one strike against you.

ALERT!

When it comes to phoneathons, some callers give more than others. Contributors tend to give more than the average donation when told about a big gift just made by a previous caller, according to one study. Contributors, however, did not up their donations if the previous gift mentioned was greater than $1,000.

Some tricks to doing telephone solicitation successfully include:

- Use a targeted list generated in-house.
- Pronounce names with care. People are more likely to contribute if you don't butcher their names.
- Plan to follow up with a mailing about the fundraiser. People usually want to see something in writing.
- Work from a flexible script, one that explains the need for funding but also allows you the leeway to converse on the subject intelligently and answer questions.
- Prepare in advance so that you are well versed in your subject and organization's history. (This is where paid telemarketers often stumble.)
- Listen. Too often, solicitors are so eager to sell that they do not hear what the other person is saying.
- Determine suitable calling times, which exclude dinner hours and weekends. Don't call people repeatedly.

- Keep in mind that people may not be interested (or may even act rude). Shrug it off and move on to the next call.
- Seek a common denominator. What brings the potential donor and your cause together?
- Ask for a specific contribution and then have a backup amount or two ready.
- Maintain a polite and courteous demeanor.

QUESTION?

How do we comply with the Do Not Call Registry?
Make calls only between 8 A.M. and 9 P.M. Promptly disclose the charity and all information about the solicitation. Never misrepresent what the charity does, how the donation is used, or how much is spent on programs and costs. Visit *www.ftc.gov* for more information.

It's hard for most people to muster up the enthusiasm to do random calling, even for a good cause. It is in your best interest to hone a list of good prospects and maintain a database of people who have given in previous years or have sounded enthusiastic about your cause. You can gather names at events, seminars, conferences, or even in schools and universities where the issues you are working for are being discussed or taught. One nonprofit group gathered names for its environmental cause on a college campus outside the environmental studies classrooms. Members asked if the students minded being called or e-mailed.

Don't Call Us

In 2008, the National Do Not Call Registry became permanent. It permits calls from charities and political organizations. Those who retain third parties to phone on their behalf should know call recipients may ask not to receive calls from the third party on behalf of that charity again; otherwise, those third parties may find themselves subject to an $11,000 fine for each violation.

Handling a Telephone Campaign

Give volunteers a portion of the list to call and schedule them for reasonable periods of time to make their calls. There is a high burnout rate in phone solicitation. Encourage phone-calling volunteers to take their time, learn the basic script, and speak clearly and in a friendly manner. Anyone doing phone solicitation should take frequent breaks, as it can become very tedious.

Make it easy on your potential contributors. If you send follow-up materials in the mail to someone to collect pledges, include a return envelope. Don't forget to include a thank-you note.

Remind volunteers not to get frustrated if they do not generate many pledges. Letting people know about your organization and your cause is a start. Perhaps the next time the person hears about the work of the organization, she will have enough knowledge and will want to contribute. By calling, you are planting seeds.

When callers do get pledges or requests for written materials, they should take down the name and address of the person and double-check all of the information before hanging up. Remember to say thank you.

Direct Mail Campaigns

Direct mail fundraising activities are conducted by nearly every nonprofit organization and political campaign where there is a diversified need for financial support. Such programs have been proven to be effective.

Direct mail is a great way to solicit donations, and it is effective in introducing a large number of people to your organization—potentially garnering their financial support in the future. Through direct mail, organizations can secure new contributors and boost their base of ongoing contributors.

It's a strategy that enables both small groups and large organizations to quickly and simultaneously ask hundreds or even thousands of individuals for their financial support. A typical direct mail response is 2 percent of the total number of pieces sent. Three percent is considered a good response, and upward of 5 percent is terrific. Therefore, if you mail out 1,000 pieces and get donations from fifty of them, you are doing great.

Drawbacks

Direct mail does have its drawbacks. For starters, recipients often do not think twice about discarding direct mail pieces. People often would sooner toss a letter than turn down a friend who personally asks for a donation. There is no guarantee that the recipient will even open the envelope, let alone read the letter and take action by writing a check. Furthermore, you may know your good buddy is in a position to make a substantial contribution—and would do so simply because you ask. However, when responding to a general direct mail letter, that same person may make only a nominal contribution, assuming they actually save the letter. The lesson here? Asking personally for a contribution still garners the best results when you are dealing with people you know well.

Another drawback of direct mail is the competition. Even in this age of high-tech communications, people receive a wealth of direct mail, and yours is likely one of many.

Plan of Action

You will need a strategy if you want your direct mail campaign to succeed. To achieve that good response of 3 percent, you must first address the following:

- Who is to receive the mailing
- How often you will send letters
- The contents of the mailing
- A plan for testing your solicitation materials
- A P.O. box or address where people can reply and someone in your organization can pick up the mail regularly

Too often, people mistakenly think that once the pieces are in the mail, the job is finished. In reality, it has only just begun. With any luck, you will begin getting responses within a few days of your mailing, and you will need to be prepared for such a response—which hopefully will be a good one.

FACT

Community organizations seeking to reach every household or business in a specific ZIP code can inexpensively purchase a list of addresses— ask for referrals from other trusted professionals or search on the web to find companies that sell mailing lists. You can find lists that simply indicate "Occupant" as the recipient. These lists are typically purchased for one-time use only.

If you are a grassroots organization and you know who your compatriots and supporters are, then you are in a position to create a mailing list in-house. The obvious advantage, along with the ability to personalize your mailing, is that you and your organization already have an existing relationship with the people you are asking for a contribution. Some organizations exchange their lists with other nonprofits—a strategy that some say results in further donations. Others, however, feel that exchanging lists can compromise the relationship they have worked so hard to develop with donors. See Chapter 8 for further discussion on this practice.

The contents of a typical direct mail solicitation include a letter, sometimes a brochure, and always a reply card and reply envelope. The letter will usually be one page or two sides of one sheet of paper if a brochure is included. When there is no brochure, you may elect to write a longer letter—up to four sides.

Bulk Mail: Pros and Cons

Another key element of direct mail is using bulk mail. Organizations pay a one-time permit imprint fee of $175, and an annual Standard Mail mailing fee of $175. There is a minimum of 200 pieces or fifty pounds of mail presorted by ZIP code required for a bulk mailing. Bulk mail has its benefits: It is less expensive, and the indicia, a code that appears in place of stamps on your carrier envelopes, can save your volunteers the time of sticking stamps onto envelopes.

The major drawback is that bulk mail can be very slow. Depending on the size of the town or city you are mailing from, as well as the time of year and the number of states and ZIP codes your mailing is going out to, it might be two to four weeks before all of your fundraising letters are received. Therefore, you must consider your time frame carefully and allow for those extra weeks until the bulk mail is delivered. Plan direct mailings with enough time to prepare your own mailing list, write effective copy, and have your mailing materials edited and proofread. Also, allow enough time for the printer to do the job and for you to proofread the materials in order to catch and correct any errors before sending. Finally, take time to select a good mailing house. Ask for references and find out if the mailing house is reliable at getting the mail out in a timely manner.

If your entire mailing is within one ZIP code and you can deliver your letters to the post office that serves that ZIP code, you may do better than a mailing house would. Experience shows that bulk mailings sent from suburban or small town post offices to a single ZIP code might be delivered the next day if not within the week.

FACT

One community organization in Pennsylvania led a successful direct mail campaign—increasing its membership by nearly 20 percent while it promoted its cause. It sent its first mailing to 300 households in its 2,000-member mailing list. When it received a positive response, it fine-tuned the letter and sent it to the rest of the list. It ultimately had a 5 percent response rate.

Fundraising Letters

Effective fundraising letters get an organization's point across in a clear, concise, and heartfelt manner. Catch the attention of a potential donor with a letter that provides facts as well as a personalized appeal. Never beg, and don't confuse people with details of a problem that they do not understand. Instead, feature a compelling statement about your activity or organization that will prompt people to take the time to send in a contribution. Generate the kind of letter that lets people know how their contribution will help you reach your goals.

To be effective, make it as easy as possible for people to donate money. If you have a website, you should include the URL so that your audience knows where to go to find the latest information as well as how to contribute online. Be sure to include clear instructions. Finally, people should know what they get for their contribution and if the organization has 501(c)(3) tax-exempt status so they can claim a deduction on their personal income taxes.

Determining the demographics for your mailing is very helpful. Writing to a business community will be very different from writing to students in a college town. Phrase the letter so you get your point across clearly and in a manner that appeals to your readers. In some instances, you may have a different letter for each of a few specific target groups.

You will also need to consider who in your organization would be best suited to write such a letter or letters. Seek out someone with writing experience. Also, look at mailings from other organizations—don't throw out the ones you receive in your mailbox—and use those as inspiration.

Test Marketing

How will you know if your letter is compelling? Use test mailings to determine the strength of your letter. If you anticipate a mailing to 5,000 households, test your letter by sending it to the first 500 names in the database. If your response rate is 2 percent or less, you might consider rewriting the letter and mailing it to another 500 households. If your response is good (say, 4 percent), then you will send it through your mailing house to the other 4,500 households. You might even send out two different letters to 250 households each.

ALERT!

If you send two versions of a letter, be sure to keep track of which letter went to which households. This may be as simple as sending "Version 1" to the first 250 names and "Version 2" to the second 250 names. But write it down clearly so that you are certain later which version generated the better response rate.

Building Your Web Presence

The Internet is an important tool for generating income and gathering signatures for petitions in support of your nonprofit. It is also a tool to promote your organization and your cause to the world. Social sites such as Facebook and MySpace as well as podcasts and blogs are popular forums in which to generate interest in a cause. These tools will be examined in greater depth in Chapter 9.

FACT

According to the Association of Fundraising Professionals, the Internet is a great way to develop a roster of online volunteers who can lend their expertise. These volunteers can help with everything from research to database construction. Because online volunteers are often out of sight, take care to nurture relationships with them so they stay committed to your organization's goals.

Most organizations build their presence through a website. To build an effective site, you need professional help, which may or may not come from within your organization. Most organizations usually have at least one person who is a computer professional or at least savvy in creating a website.

What are the characteristics of an effective website? A website must be appealing to the eye, informative, enlightening, and easy to navigate. It is also an important branding tool for an organization, so make sure your logo, taglines, and other materials correspond with those in your printed material.

A good website has quality content on readable, concise webpages that allow people to learn about your causes and concerns, read your mission statement, get background information on your organization and board members, and donate money in a safe and easy manner. "Safe" means providing online protection so people know their personal information is protected, and "easy" means simple to navigate. People should be able to donate with a few clicks of the mouse—and then receive a thank you (which is very important); look for applications with auto responders that send a thank you to a contributor after each online donation.

ALERT!

If you are going to include links to other sites, make sure the links work and are in line with the mission of your organization. Links may lead to surprising places you do not want to be associated with. Check out all links before allowing them on your site.

You also need to have a good web developer to help you create your site and a server through which to post it. Many services provide both development and access to a server. Otherwise, if you have someone in your organization able to develop sites or you have access to website development software, you will need to find a site hosting service to get your site onto the web. You may want to invest in a backup server (or retain a web host that offers this service) in order to keep your site up and running should the system crash. Keep in mind that the bigger the site, the more it will cost. A powerful website can be money well spent, particularly when it offers reporting features, enabling an organization to see a site's click-through rate and streamline its fundraising efforts by collecting and organizing data.

Whether you build your own website from software or have a professional website designer come in and do the job, you need to carefully navigate and read through the site to make sure it works. Don't be afraid to alter the site or even tear it down and start it again from scratch. Many computer programs make it easy to input all the changes you will need. WYSIWYG (what you see is what you get) programs are fairly easy to learn. These have the benefit of showing you how the page will look on the Internet while you're working on it.

Those with a better understanding of the computer may want to learn some basic HTML to fine-tune your webpages. When shopping for website-building software, know your needs ahead of time and look for a program that meets those needs—don't get carried away buying a program with numerous new features that don't meet your specific needs.

Also, do not let your website get stale. Update your content often, or people will not return. Take it easy on the graphics; too many graphics can bog down the site, causing it to load very slowly. As a result, viewers may click on another site if yours takes too long to download.

As more people gravitate to the web, online fundraising has become part of most nonprofits' repertoire. Yet despite the fact that online giving makes donating easy for supporters, many organizations still say it is the least effective means of generating funds. Therefore, do not bank on your website as your primary means of fundraising. Let your website be just one of several means of fundraising but a major means of providing information.

E-Mail

You can use e-mail effectively to communicate with members of your organization and better establish relationships with donors. Sending information about what you are working on, updates and reminders of your upcoming fundraising events, and thank yous for contributions or volunteer work are all great uses of e-mail. One New York organization that supports women and girls sends periodic e-mails to supporters to invite them to view the latest picture gallery—a tactic that also drives traffic to its website.

Keep in mind that people do not read e-mails that go on endlessly, so think brevity. Also, don't send random e-mailings, as people delete unwanted e-mails and this does not ingratiate you to these individuals. Make sure that the recipient consents to your having his e-mail address, and don't just add to your e-mail list from other sources.

You should also:

- Maintain an updated e-mail list and add or delete new or old members. Always delete someone who has asked to unsubscribe.
- Respond to e-mails within one or two days of receiving them.
- Avoid jumping at the chance to ask people for money—build a relationship. It costs nothing but a few minutes to send an e-mail, receive an inquiry, and send a response. Build a relationship first, and then ask for a contribution.
- Avoid sending attachments. Computer viruses have made many people leery of opening e-mail attachments.

Public Speaking

You're at the banquet you've been working on for months. Everything is in place, and everyone is seated. You've already helped raise money for the organization, and now it's your turn to get up there and say something and . . . you drawing a total blank.

Public speaking is not easy for most people. Making a speech about your organization or a cause that is near and dear to you is certainly no exception. Whether you are asking people to make a contribution or thanking everyone for the fine job they've done putting the activity together, you need to be prepared.

Some people work from a written script, whereas others are comfortable with a rough outline. You can also use index cards, but always spend some time gathering and practicing your materials in advance. Remember not to hide behind a written script.

Other pointers for keeping your audience interested in your speech include:

- Build a little story to pique interest
- Emphasize key points
- Make them laugh
- Give them something to think about

- Speak long enough to get your point across but not long enough to prompt them to look at their watches
- Remember to pause to let them digest information
- Vary your tone as you talk—do not speak in a monotone
- Don't fidget with your hands or shuffle your feet
- Make eye contact with the group as a whole
- Talk to all the people, not just one corner of the room

Don't hit people over the head, asking them for money in your speech. There's a fine line between requesting and badgering. A heartfelt and personal request, perhaps using a true story as an example of the need for funding, can often be your best tool.

Annual Campaigns

The keys to a successful annual fundraising campaign are consistency and your database. Supporters may not be consciously awaiting your call or letter, yet in all likelihood they know you will be contacting them around the same time each year. The Muscular Dystrophy Telethon, Girl Scout cookies, and many mail campaigns take place at the same time each year and in the same (or a similar) manner—and people have come to expect them.

ALERT!

Maintain the integrity of your database by only making changes from information provided directly by the donor, not off of other lists or information supplied by third parties. Make sure your data is updated and accurate by verifying it directly with the donor.

While you may alter your methods, it is important to keep the basics similar from year to year so people recognize your letter or pencil in the date of the fundraising dinner on their calendars. Naturally, if your fundraiser was not successful last year or you've found a major way to improve on your results, you'll want to implement some measure of change. Do so without changing everything at once. People like a sense of familiarity. Leave some key elements, such as logo, location, type of event, and time of year.

Your database should tell you who donated last year, how to contact them, and how much they gave. This is very important for next year. Keep good records of donors and update such data as it changes, including new street addresses, phone numbers, and e-mail addresses.

Annual fundraising drives can be a staple for your organization and, if done correctly, will grow over time. They are a feature of a majority of non-profit groups today.

Annual fundraising campaigns:

- Provide ongoing donor support
- Provide a basic blueprint of the fundraiser
- Establish your organization as an ongoing presence
- Are anticipated by donors who may already be prepared to give
- Are easier to run because there are blueprints from previous years

People look forward to annual events or activities, and your volunteers will know when it's time to gear up for putting in more time and energy in order to make the campaign a success.

A Public Relations Primer

Effective public relations efforts take some careful planning. The goals are to present your organization in the best light, keep the media informed about your ongoing activities, and dispel any negative press or misconceptions about the work that you do.

Getting Started

To build your PR campaign, consider the best way to present your organization and your mission. This involves carefully determining which stories are worthy of media attention. Be realistic; don't make up a story or try to interest the external world in internal affairs that don't belong outside of your newsletter.

The best place to start is with stories illustrating your involvement with the community and highlighting activities related to your cause. What role have your efforts played in making a change? What is forthcoming that can draw attention to your organization? Press releases should talk about your latest news and key activities. Perhaps your organization has a program offering job skills to those with disadvantages, giving them new opportunities for personal growth and improved economic standing.

This is the kind of story that might interest reporters. Use this information as a launching point to tell people about the positive change your organization brings. See if a newspaper might highlight the new CEO in a profile. Perhaps some big-name celebrity has agreed to appear at your upcoming carnival or your fundraising idea was so unique and innovative it was covered by the local news. Take notes and don't forget the digital camera. Always look for opportunities you can use to develop a press release that will benefit your organization with positive publicity.

Awards programs are always a good way to generate positive buzz about your organization, and the possibilities are limitless. Conduct an online search for awards programs. Winning organizations will generate new headlines to media outlets, as well as new reasons to spread the word about the good work you do.

Crafting a Press Release

Here are a few tips to follow when you write a press release:

- Use a short, attention-grabbing headline, but one that is not misleading.
- Include the who, what, where, when, and why of your story in the first paragraph.
- Make sure your facts and figures are accurate—double-check.
- Try to keep the release to one page, two tops.

- Include a general paragraph about your organization.
- Make sure to include contact numbers for more information.
- Keep quotes short and to the point.

Media List

Names, mailing addresses, e-mail addresses, and phone numbers of key contacts for newspapers, television and radio stations, wire services, and websites should all be included on your media list. The list will grow over time, and you'll need to update it frequently since editors and producers change jobs often. Check with the local chapter of your region's press club and inquire about obtaining a media guide listing the most current contacts for reporters and editors in your area.

Put your media list together so you can access contacts by type of media, region, or subject. This way, you can easily locate all local radio stations, media outlets pertaining to education, or local newspapers in your county or city.

To build your own media list, you need to conduct research, which includes using the web, visiting the library, and digging for sources. References such as *Publishers Weekly* (*www.publishersweekly.com*) or *Broadcasting & Cable Yearbook*, among others, can help you put together your list. Also, use simple methods such as scouting the local magazine racks and reading the mastheads, checking your local TV and radio guides, and searching the web under your topic of interest.

Working with the Media

Press releases are one way to get the attention of the media. You can also invite the media to attend events you are holding. You might also pitch stories about your upcoming activities to reporters and freelance journalists.

If you are just establishing yourself with the media, start with simple, concise information and build from there. Editors and producers have little time to read extensive details, so they won't get to page two of a release from a group they've never heard of unless the story is extremely compelling. If you do not have a blockbuster story off the bat, you can get them acquainted with your organization and what it is you do. Once you have reached the media, follow up, and follow up again. The news media are busy, so you must—politely—stay on top of them if you want to get coverage.

Also, look for people in the media who have supported your cause before. For example, if a newscaster has been very active in raising money for autism, that's the newscaster to contact and invite to your fundraising event to raise money for autism research.

Before an event, prepare a press kit. This should include some background information about your group or organization (compiled into a document called a backgrounder) plus recent press releases, brochures, or newsletters you have pertaining to the event. You should include all recent stories about your organization that have appeared in the press.

How's this for a match made in heaven? You want media attention for your organization and newspapers have pages to fill, especially on slow news days. Take digital photos of momentous occasions, including a sizable financial contribution from a local donor, or perhaps a celebrity MC who hosted your event. Media outlets often print these kinds of photos.

You can also write and record public service announcements (PSAs) to distribute to radio stations. Unless they are for a specific event, try to make them as timeless as possible so they can run indefinitely. Either way, keep them simple, to the point, and about fifteen or thirty seconds long. If you do not have the facilities to record a quality PSA, then get a short script in the hands of an announcer. Some stations are okay with using prerecorded PSAs, whereas others want to have their announcers record them. Talk to the stations in your area.

Media Sponsors

You want to publicize your upcoming event, yet you lack the funds to run an ad. That's where media sponsors come in, donating valuable commercial airtime or print ads. These kinds of sponsorships benefit nonprofits in promoting their events, enabling organizations to draw bigger crowds and hopefully more money. Media outlets benefit, too; these sponsorships enable them to raise their stature in their market by supporting an organization that helps the community. In this arrangement, the sponsor's logo or company name is typically listed or mentioned in all advertising, including any electronic ads, which will have links back to the sponsor's site.

Damage Control

It doesn't happen often in the world of nonprofits and local fundraising, but there are some times when you might find yourself the target of negative press. This is when you have to exercise damage control. For example, if someone says your recent fundraising activity was a bust because it did not raise much money, you can point out that while it did not raise the funds you had hoped for, you are pleased with the turnout and are encouraged that the event helped present your organization and raise the community's level of awareness of your cause. You can add that you are looking forward to building off of this start next year, and you anticipate much greater success. It is important to address the problems or accusations and explain what the situation really was. Try to put a positive spin on such activities, and always point out the highlights of your activity, event, organization, school, or group.

CHAPTER 8

A Lesson in Ethics

Fundraising depends on the support and generosity of the public. For this reason, it is vital that those involved in such activities perform their tasks with integrity and earn the donors' respect. In fundraising, ethics comprise a very broad spectrum of how you conduct business, not only financially, but also with regard to morality and fairness.

8

Establishing a Code of Conduct

A code of conduct is a manual to guide the actions and activities of the organization's members in their ongoing activities, including fundraising. This code need not be elaborate, but it should clearly explain the fine line between activities that are acceptable for a nonprofit organization and those that are not.

A code of conduct should outline the manner in which the fundraisers will act in various situations. It should cover monetary and accounting practices as well as practical concerns regarding how to represent the organization when communicating with donors. Furthermore, a code of conduct will identify who is responsible for overseeing specific problems and activities.

FACT

Your volunteers may be eligible for tax deductions. They should keep track of any expenses they incur that are directly related to their work on your fundraiser. Remind volunteers that they can deduct out-of-pocket expenses such as travel costs and include items such as clothing (e.g., a uniform) purchased specifically for the purpose of the fundraising activity.

Money Matters

One primary concern of most organizations is the handling of money. In nonprofits, money raised from donors is not to be used for individuals to profit from unless it goes to salaried employees or administrative costs. Nor can it go toward nonorganizational activities, such as backing a political candidate (unless, of course, yours is a political fundraising organization).

There should be no finder's fee, which means no payments or special consideration made to an officer, director, trustee, employee, or advisor of a nonprofit organization as compensation for successfully soliciting a donor. This is not to say you cannot reward the top salesperson in a fundraising campaign. Incentives for selling anything from Girl Scout cookies to the winning ticket in a raffle for a luxury car will encourage sales. In fact, one charity actually gives the seller of the winning ticket the same luxury car as the person holding the winning raffle ticket.

Awards and incentives are a great idea. To ensure transparency, explain these incentives in detail in advance and make the specifics available to every participant in the fundraising program. Make these specifics available to potential donors as well.

A code of ethics should also address the use of funds by board members, to ensure that funds are not used inappropriately. It becomes harder to raise money for a foundation if the foundation cannot show that it made sound use of the money it raised. Often, a well-intentioned group or organization loses sight of the overall goal in an attempt to compete with other fundraising groups or organizations. While there is a need to be competitive for donor dollars, it cannot be at the cost of the integrity and values on which the organization was founded.

ESSENTIAL

Make sure your organization can justify all expenses, right from the start. When launching a kickoff party for an upcoming fundraising gala, for example, make it clear the money is being used to jumpstart the fundraiser, not for excessive entertainment or valet parking.

Taking Risks

There is a fine line between misuse of funds and taking a calculated risk. For example, after much deliberation, one nonprofit organization voted to finance a film about a topic that shed light on the group's mission. This was new territory for the group, which had never financed a film before, yet because the intentions aligned with the goals of the group, they took the risk and gave a young filmmaker the chance to help spread the word about the work of the group.

Risks should:

- Align with the organization's goals
- Not result in funds going to a person or company for reasons other than those of the company's missions or goals
- Be calculated and decided on by the board or a vote of members and not be a unilateral decision

The fewer people who know about something, the more likely it will be open to scrutiny by others. Therefore, communication and consent by several members or the board of directors is important for the proper conduct of most organizations—at any level. This level of checks and balances applies whether a group of three children selling cookies is deciding who will hold the money or a multimillion-dollar nonprofit is earmarking dollars for the building of a new hospital in an underdeveloped nation. If many people know what is going on, there is less room for misuse of funds, whether intentional or accidental.

Taking Gifts

Like taking funds for personal use, accepting personal gifts should be forbidden. Enact a policy prohibiting the acceptance of personal gifts or the use of resources intended for the organization. This kind of policy can be hard to monitor, but numerous organizations fall prey to the mishandling of such contributions, so it is worth including in your code of conduct.

Establishing clear policies from the beginning can help avoid temptation later. Be as detailed as possible when setting up guidelines so people understand the level of conduct expected of them. This will go a long way toward ensuring the organization conducts itself with integrity long into the future.

In addition, a nonprofit group may be in a situation to receive special discounts, services, and other perks; these are not for personal use. Volunteers are not entitled to a car, computer, or other organizational resources because of the time they have put into the organization. This includes the $300 someone spent on personal long-distance phone calls made from an organization's headquarters.

Every organization will have situations where people take advantage—they're hard to prevent. One trusted employee at a nonprofit professional organization manipulated members' checks to make them appear as though they were made out to him, and then deposited them into his personal account. The organization instituted stringent policies for handling member donations, and of course, the individual stepped down from the organization. That said, experts say most organizations conduct themselves with integrity and spend the funds raised in keeping with the organizations' intended mission.

Conflicts of Interest

In one New York–based nonprofit support group, attorneys are permitted to be on the board of governors as legal advisors, but they are not allowed to hold highly visible positions as chapter presidents. In Pennsylvania, a doctor may sit on the board of a medical nonprofit organization but may not do canvassing for donors. Different organizations view conflicts of interest in their own way.

The general theme of such a conflict is that an individual's job or title puts her in a position to gain at a personal level while working for the organization. The question is, where do you draw the line? Can someone in a profession donate her time in a situation in which she could stand to gain business without taking advantage of the situation?

While people do make professional contacts during their work for nonprofits, a clear line must be drawn regarding how they deal with their personal business and the nonprofit business. If a potential conflict arises, it is up to the individual to step forward and present the situation to the board. Usually, the member knows if something he is doing professionally or personally is a potential conflict with the group. Don't let your organization get into a position where any members (or potential donors) may suspect one of the leaders is doing something for his personal gain rather than for the good of the organization.

Selling Mailing Lists

Mailing lists are very important to the success of a fundraising campaign. Today, mailing lists seem to travel from source to source at an alarming rate. No sooner do you sign up for a weekly circular at your local supermarket than you find ten other pieces of promotional mail in your mailbox. Despite antispam laws, you sign up for an e-newsletter and suddenly you're the recipient of junk e-mail.

Pros and Cons

Many organizations have their own membership lists. Members join most organizations and place their names on such a list with the understanding that you are keeping their information private. The more personal the information on the list, the more imperative it is that you safeguard it. If people lose their trust in your organization, you can lose members, and your prospective pool of donors may shrink. In short, this is a very strong reason not to sell your mailing list; many believe this practice is highly unethical and can even jeopardize your organization if your list lands in the wrong hands. The FCC and the postal service are cracking down on list-selling activities.

That said, some research indicates that the exchange of mailing lists can point organizations to future supporters. The debate continues about the practice of exchanging mailing lists, so consider the consequences before doing so.

Check any list you buy against your own list that you have generated in-house to make sure there are no duplicates. Sending two copies of your letter to the same household will not make a very good first impression.

Should You Buy?

Another option to consider is buying a mailing list. Some list-selling companies build their following by selling lists to organizations like yours in hopes that not only will you be a steady customer, but you will recommend them to others as well. Be warned, however, that not all list companies are alike. Some will sell you the names of 20,000 people who are not at all interested in what you have to say. Because many organizations have never purchased such a list before and are not familiar with the mailing list industry, there is still a learning curve that favors the sellers. Therefore, it is buyer beware. When buying a mailing list, it is usually for limited use, meaning you can only use it one time and by a certain date.

There are a few questions you should ask to ensure that you are getting the most useful list possible. First, find out how often the list is updated. Consumer lists age at a rate of 2 percent per month. In one year, 25 percent of the list can be outdated. Next, ask how the list was generated. It's important to know where these names are gathered. If this list is the reproduction of old lists that have been sold many times, the people on the list may have been inundated with mailings. Finally, in what ways can this list be categorized? Many lists can be broken down by various types of information to help you reach your target audience.

When shopping around for a mailing list, it's advantageous to get referrals from others who have used the company to purchase their list(s). Be sure to ask about what type of response they received and how current the list actually was.

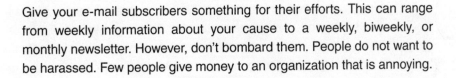

Give your e-mail subscribers something for their efforts. This can range from weekly information about your cause to a weekly, biweekly, or monthly newsletter. However, don't bombard them. People do not want to be harassed. Few people give money to an organization that is annoying.

E-Mail Lists

There are plenty of places to purchase e-mail lists. Here, too, you must take heed of what kind of e-mail list you are buying and from whom. It is easy for almost anyone to build up a random mailing list of thousands of people's e-mail addresses, and the recipients may very well become angered that they have received your "junk" e-mail. While there are some legitimate online list sellers, you may have better luck creating your own e-mail list.

Gather addresses by asking people who come to your website or communicate with you in any manner if they will give you their e-mail address.

It's unethical to take their e-mail address from another source. Also, have a privacy policy drawn up to guarantee them that their information is safe in your hands and will not be sold or distributed elsewhere. Post this policy on your website so that supporters are comfortable giving their e-mail addresses; by posting the policy, you will further enhance your organization's integrity.

One of the foremost complaints from Internet users is the inability to unsubscribe from a list. Make sure you allow people to unsubscribe easily if they do not want your newsletter or e-mails.

Another complaint from those who send e-mails is that there are times when server glitches cause an e-mail campaign to malfunction, and this prevents supporters from receiving your materials. In other instances, organizations do not get enough supporters to opt in to make an e-mail campaign effective. For this reason, it is important to track the results of your e-mail campaigns. Some programs even enable you to track how many recipients actually open your e-mails. You may find it is worthwhile to deploy a mix of strategies incorporating both e-mail and direct mail.

FACT

There is good reason to limit your e-mail correspondence to those who have expressed interest in your cause. Sixty-five percent of people who use e-mail consider unsolicited e-mails from nonprofits or charities to be spam, while 74 percent consider e-mails from political or activist groups to be spam, according to the Pew Internet & American Life Project.

The advantage of e-mail marketing is reaching people very quickly all over the world at little cost. You can also be quite current because they will get the message that very day, and perhaps they will be inspired to take action immediately. Too many people forget the immediacy of e-mail and send the same message month after month. Always add current information and updates so people know your correspondence is fresh and not something written months ago.

You can also use chat rooms and newsgroups to spread the word about your group or cause if the group is amenable. Some news groups have policies against solicitation, so be sure to read the forum's guidelines before posting. Even if there are no rules against it, you may want to feel out the situation. Don't just jump in with a sales pitch or solicitation or you might alienate everyone. Remember, it's unethical to use information you gather online without the person's consent, such as copying e-mail addresses from a chat room or other list. For younger generations, social networking has all but replaced e-mail. Social networking is examined in further depth in Chapter 12.

Credibility

Obviously, you will lose all credibility if you are caught falsifying records to make your organization appear more financially successful than it is. Receiving grants is at a premium today, and it's tempting to round off income or try to make your organization appear more credible by adding on funding sources that do not really exist. It's a big risk you should not take.

Tread Carefully

Besides money issues, making claims you cannot keep also puts your credibility in jeopardy. Like any business, a nonprofit must be able to deliver on a promise, just as donors who pledge money are expected to deliver on their promises. If you claim your organization has helped many children learn to read, be prepared to explain where, when, and through which program. It doesn't have to mean every child in the funded program will be reading at an appropriate grade level, but don't say your organization has taught children to read unless there are children who could not read before who can now read at some level.

Be Honest

On a more basic level, if you are selling something for the holiday season, you must deliver it before the holidays. Don't tell someone that by holiday season you meant Valentine's Day when she clearly bought wrapping paper for Christmas.

Make it clear how your organization spends money. Nonprofits may be hit hard by rising postage and other costs, so make sure the public understands any new economic pressures your organization may be experiencing.

ALERT!

Don't allow your organization or group name to be used in conjunction with commercial ventures, or vice versa. Nonprofits should take careful steps to remain independent. If a nonprofit organization is too closely aligned with a commercial company, it can erode the credibility of the organization and jeopardize its nonprofit tax status.

Activities to Avoid

There are a variety of activities your organization should avoid altogether to maintain integrity. Most are common sense, but it is worth pointing them out here so they are on your radar.

Creative Accounting

An effective organization will want to avoid what is sometimes called slippage. Slippage includes creative accounting, misleading results, overstating your case, marketing hype, deceiving to influence others, concealing of bad news, or claiming false credit for others' work. These are all unethical activities that cannot be permitted by a successful nonprofit.

Inappropriate Personal Conduct

Conduct and ethics will often come into play. This includes the way members behave within the organization and while soliciting funds. If someone has his own personal agenda, the functions of the group—including meetings, conferences, and fundraising activities—are not the place to carry out such personal aims. One woman, while putting together a fundraiser, slipped in that she was job hunting and used the opportunity to meet people to hand out her resume while collecting donations.

Advertising Plugs

Guest speakers may attend your function out of kindness and generosity, and to sell their latest book or services. If your organization approves of such activities, be sure to set the policies and procedures in place in advance so your group can monitor how these actions are to be carried out. Often, a group will have someone speak at a conference or seminar knowing he is also going to promote his work in some manner. As long as these kinds of plugs do not detract from the subject at hand, it is permissible. This is a judgment call your organization will need to make.

Misleading the Public

Fraudulent practices, such as telling donors there are plans in the works when in fact there are none, can get your nonprofit listed among the Internet watchdogs that monitor fundraising activities. Internet and charitable fraud has increased in recent years. Places such as the American Institute of Philanthropy (*www.charitywatch.org*), the Better Business Bureau (*www.bbb.org*), Charitable Choices (*www.charitychoices.com*), and Philanthropic Research, Inc., (*www.guidestar.org*) rate and report on the activities of nonprofit groups.

ESSENTIAL

Websites offer research tools that allow prospective donors to look up the mission, goals, financial information, and history of nonprofit organizations. While they do not recommend one nonprofit over another, they often provide grades that can influence people when they are searching for worthy charities.

Harassment

High-pressure selling techniques may also cross the line. These include ongoing phone solicitations or e-mails where solicitors won't take no for an answer. Let's face it—if you've called someone three times and she has politely gotten off the phone each time, she is not interested. In simple terms, there is no place for harassment in fundraising.

Donors have a right to choose whether to contribute, based on the honesty and integrity of your organization as presented by each member. Education about your mission and your organization should be readily available and used in place of high-pressure selling techniques. In fact, if you persist with a high-pressure appeal, supporters may begin to question your legitimacy.

FACT

Websites with privacy policies are more apt to generate trust among donors. Any website that collects personal information should post a privacy policy. It should be clear and easy to understand and should concisely explain how personal information is collected, used, and stored and whether it will be sold. Include an e-mail contact in case someone wants more information, and follow up within twenty-four hours.

Don't forget etiquette, an important part of any successful sale. It is worth pointing out that when you build up a good relationship with a contributor, that person may make another contribution during your next campaign. However, if you pressure someone into giving you money just so you will stop your persistent solicitations, you are not showing the organization in a positive light and will most likely not see further contributions from the individual. Your job is part soliciting or selling and part building up relationships and a positive image for the organization and the good work you do. Ethical practices and clear policies that demonstrate to members and donors alike the integrity of your organization are critical components to a successful fundraising effort.

CHAPTER 9

Communication Tools and Practices

Communication methods will figure critically in your success as you plan and launch a fundraising event or campaign. This chapter looks at internal communication between members of your group or organization and takes a more in-depth look at using the web to spread the word about your fundraiser. It also provides practical information about how to organize and store your communication records.

9

Your Communication Infrastructure

Whether you are calling people via an informal phone chain or launching a comprehensive e-mailing campaign, you must make sure everyone involved in putting together the fundraising activities is readily accessible. As early in the planning phase as possible—perhaps at the very first meeting—make sure you know:

- The level of technical knowledge of the group as a whole
- The manner in which people are most comfortable communicating with one another
- The type of technology available within the organization for communication purposes
- The budget (if any) and need for phone systems, cellular phones, or other communication tools that will be purchased or rented

Communicating During Planning

Because communication is vital to an effective fundraiser, you must determine which methods you will be most comfortable using. Next, find a common ground for the skills of your group. If, for instance, the members of your group are computer literate at only a basic level, then e-mailing and instant messaging will be appropriate; however, you may need to come up with a Plan B if people are unfamiliar with complex software or a spreadsheet program.

Most small to mid-level nonprofits have a skeletal full-time staff. Therefore, many of the people on a team may need to be contacted at their homes or offices or by cell phone. Mass e-mails are quick and fine for memos, reminders, or minutes of the last meeting—provided they are not extensive text documents.

More personalized messages or those of a potentially sensitive nature may need to be communicated by phone or at in-person meetings. Many organizations have seen strongly worded e-mails cause friction between members, though they were not meant to be confrontational. Remember, e-mail does not catch the nuances you can convey in a phone call, so try to minimize e-mail debates. Make e-mail part of your repertoire, but don't overdo it. People often dismiss and delete messages without reading them if you bombard them. That said, it can be useful to follow up a phone conversation with an e-mail reiterating the basic points discussed.

Assign someone the task of setting up the master list of names and e-mail addresses for the organization. If possible, include a section within the master list to note who does not want to be called after 9 P.M., who does not want to be e-mailed at work except in the case of an emergency, and so on. People have their own personal rules and habits concerning how they handle their communications. It is important to respect those wishes.

Once you compile an e-mail list of your membership, watch over the list and monitor what is being sent. It is not the place for jokes and other off-topic e-mails. Inappropriate e-mails can cast your organization in a bad light. What's more, people may begin to disregard e-mails from your organization if members deem them uninformative.

On-Site Communications

At events such as carnivals, conferences, or golf tournaments, cell phones and rented walkie-talkies may be necessary for on-site communication. Naturally, discretion is needed—don't call someone's cell phone when he is teeing off on the course. Individuals manning central locations should be the only ones making contact with one another during your fundraising activity; this minimizes cross talk.

Because some people frequently check e-mail while others do not, phone calling chains are also still a workable communication system for smaller and grassroots nonprofit groups.

Knowing Who to Contact

Call Samantha for information on programming, Fred for site-related questions, and Lauren for issues concerning outside vendors. A phone list or organizer can make life simple. The diversity of tasks and committees makes it important for everyone involved in your fundraising activities to know who is overseeing each aspect of the project and who to turn to for answers.

The smaller the group, the less formal the structuring of such contacts needs to be. A larger group, however, may need to set up a hierarchy of who reports to whom simply to avoid overwhelming any one person with phone calls and e-mails. Determine how many people are working within a committee. If one committee has forty people, it might be best to have more than one person overseeing the committee and fielding calls from all of these people. Think about subcommittees and redirecting some of the communications to other people.

Playing devil's advocate early on and anticipating as many potential problems as possible allows you to set up contingency plans and lets volunteers know who to contact or whom they can expect to hear from when there are problems. This strategy will enable you to set up a logical communication system. Some youth groups have local troop leaders who report to regional leaders who report to state leaders, and so on. You may not be involved in an organization of that size, but a line of communication can help make things easier nonetheless.

An Intranet Site

An intranet site is a secure website where staffers and representatives can collaborate and share information, an administrative tool that helps a nonprofit stay organized. It is the go-to site where members can find the resources they need, virtually around the clock and from any desktop, as long as they have a user name and password.

Intranet sites are advantageous especially when members are located in various parts of the country or the world. With an intranet site, an organization can post training modules, ensuring that all members, no matter where they are located, receive the same information. They can also be used to post forms—even extensive manuals and directories—members can download as needed. And they can feature calendars and articles to help members perform their duties. Organizations with local chapters can use the intranet to post flyers, banners, and other materials needed for fundraising.

There are a host of options from which to choose, including Basecamp (*www.basecamphq.com*) and Epiware (*see www.epiware.com*). When evaluating applications, consider how you envision using an intranet site. Also, find out if the programs have trial periods, and get recommendations from other nonprofits and tech experts you trust.

Information Storage

Most nonprofit and grassroots fundraising groups have limited resources and must get the most out of older technology for both communication purposes and data entry and storage. Because your members will likely have varying degrees of computer expertise, you will need to rely on a software system that meets all of their skill levels while also serving your organizational needs. Ask the person who is best versed in computers to select and manage your software. However, she must keep in mind that buying the latest software with advanced capabilities might not work for people using home PCs that may be two or three years old. Practical considerations and the learning curve of the people involved need to be taken into account before buying state-of-the-art equipment that no one can use.

Networked or Not?

Data storage and retrieval is a vital function of your software. Many small nonprofits have a few key people who handle areas such as membership and contributions. Access to these areas should always be limited to a small number of people, no matter how large your nonprofit grows. You can have separate databases that are maintained individually or a shared database with a system that can be accessed by several people. Ideally, a shared database allows various individuals to make changes so everyone can see them and others do not have to make the same changes to their individual databases. This can save time and allow everyone access to the same updated information. Not having duplicate information means you won't have to wonder which database has the correct phone number for a particular person.

Unfortunately, this does not always work. "The system is down" is one of the most common phrases heard today. A problem with the software or hardware means no one has access to the information—everyone is affected by it. In addition, just as one person can add data everyone else can read, one person can also make a mistake everyone else must contend with. In short, unless everyone involved is computer savvy, shared or joined systems are not recommended for most fundraising groups. If you do use a shared system, you'll need to use password identification. Otherwise, too many people (including unauthorized people) can gain access to your database and use it for personal reasons.

Even if shared or joined software does not seem necessary for your group at the moment, it is worthwhile to consider the purchase of a program that offers these features so you have room to grow and change as your organization expands or members become more proficient on the computer.

Determining Your Software Needs

Your database is your lifeline. Because the success of every nonprofit group is dependent on the involvement of various people, it is beneficial to have the storage and retrieval of all key data readily accessible. You will want to store and access information about the following people:

- Board members
- General members
- Contributors
- Major donors
- Volunteers
- Vendors
- Organizations similar to yours
- Government or neighborhood leaders
- Media contacts

It is imperative that your data storage software be easy to use and have the capacity to retrieve information from various data fields. When shopping for such software, you will also need to make sure the software you choose is compatible with your computer system and supports data from other popular programs, such as Microsoft Excel and Lotus. The more people working on the fundraiser, the more likely you will need to input information from a variety of programs.

Buy software that comes with an online tutorial or a clear set of instructions on how it is used, as well as technical support provided with a toll-free number. Gather opinions on which programs will work best for your needs. When shopping for software, ask if updates are free of charge or if there is a fee. This way, you can budget as necessary.

Financial Software

You may be using more than one computer program to handle both data and financial information. While both should be accessible by only a few key individuals, the financial software should be especially limited in usage. Password protection is vital regarding your financial information.

Keep your software needs in mind. Nonprofits may require software for:

- Data entry and storage
- Budgeting, bookkeeping, accounting, and maintaining financial information
- Assembling newsletters and publicity materials
- Project management

The first two areas are common for organizations of any size; the others will depend on the size and purposes of your organization. Also, always keep in mind the "garbage in, garbage out" mantra, which serves as a reminder that the computer is only as good as the people who input, understand, and know how to utilize the data.

Creating the Database

Information on shopping for fundraising software can be found at NPO-NET (*www.npo.net*), a service of the Information Technology Resource Center, a nonprofit organization based in Chicago that assists other nonprofits in computer and technology data. You might also look to the Nonprofit Matrix (*www.nonprofitmatrix.com*), an online guide to web-based services for charities and other nonprofits, or Coyote Communications (*www .coyotecommunications.com*), for resources and other information for mission-based organizations.

When setting up a database, think about how the information will be accessed and used. Always consider how data will need to be retrieved. Think about what information is most beneficial to the needs of your group. Review with others and get a consensus on what to include. Build on the categories as new ideas are suggested and your organization expands to new areas of interest.

Update your database often. Members will change, new board members will emerge, and committees will be formed and dispersed. Such information must be updated monthly or bimonthly. Also, frequently backup all data onto disks, flash drives, or hard copies so you are not at the mercy of a computer program that could become corrupt.

Updating Data

One of the most significant aspects of software is the ability to update information. You need a system that makes updating information a simple task and allows you to add categories as the information becomes available. Ideally, you want to add new information within a few days of receiving it. For example, if you had a sign-in sheet at your general meeting and five new members listed their names and addresses, you'll want to add the information to your database before the sheet is lost or misplaced.

Another reason for keeping your tracking and updating procedures simple is that, at some point, the task will be passed on to someone else, who may be less computer proficient than yourself. You don't want to discourage and scare away volunteers by making a job too complicated or intimidating.

Institute a system so you get updated information from members and others in a timely manner. The same holds true for your lists of media contacts and local politicians, whose information should be routinely checked and updated. Because it is unlikely the newspaper will contact you when it's been bought out, it is up to you to touch base every few months in order to keep track of what is going on.

Using a Website for Your Fundraiser

A website is a powerful and dynamic medium that allows you to spread the word about your mission, your upcoming events, and the good work your organization achieves. The American Jewish World Service, a New York organization, uses the web to post compelling three-minute videos shot by trained staff members who highlight the group's workers and volunteers helping people around the world. The group also posts clips on YouTube, where volunteers discuss their efforts. These highlights will also be featured in DVDs that are sent to potential contributors. This approach does not require expensive equipment—experts peg costs at less than $1,000 for digital video equipment and editing software. Vendors such as Entango (*www .entango.com*) and TransactU (*www.serviceu.com/transactu/index.html*) can set up customizable transaction pages that mirror your organization's website. They can handle back-end functions such as online donations, credit card fraud screening, and more.

Videos and Podcasts

High-ranking videos can be a great way to solicit donations or collect a database of prospective supporters who may grow interested in your cause and ultimately donate. Nonprofits also use their website to post podcasts— online audio broadcasts—where supporters can listen to interviews and stories about their favorite organizations either online or by downloading them onto their portable mp3 players. Podcasts are another inexpensive way to communicate a message. All you need is a microphone and software, which are both very inexpensive.

Blogs

Other nonprofits use blogs—online diaries—where an organization's members and volunteers can post noteworthy commentary about their cause and their organization to help raise public awareness and invite online discourse. You can set up a blog for free (check *www.wordpress.com* and *www.blogger.com*), and you can post a link to your blog on your site to drive traffic. Readers can stay up to date with your blogging by subscribing to a Really Simple Syndication, or RSS feed, which notifies them of new postings. However, all blog posts should be monitored and in keeping with your organization's mission. Have clear policies in place so blog posts enhance, rather than detract from, your organization.

Driving More Traffic to Your Website

When you post content to your site, think about the words visitors might use when they are web surfing for information about matters pertaining to your cause or organization. Think of these visitors as perspective supporters who might contribute if only they knew about your group. Once you decide on the words they might key into a search engine, be sure to weave the words into the content of your site. This is a low cost way to boost your rankings in the search engines. Of course, there are search engine experts who specialize in attaining high search-engine rankings, but hiring them can be costly.

Furthermore, you can drive traffic to your site by including a link to it in your e-mail signature, both for home and at work, if your employer allows it. Often, companies will agree because they like to support charitable efforts of their employees and their community; what's more, your employer may help you get further publicity by posting a link to your website from the company site.

Putting It All Together

Yet with all the bells and whistles—videos, podcasts, and blogs—it's important your website include some basics. For instance, it is advantageous to set up a separate page, linked to your home page, that provides information on fundraising activities.

Provide the details as they fall into place. Put someone in charge of updating material on the website frequently. This same person can fill in the data on your newly developed fundraising page. However, material you send this person needs to be carefully checked for accuracy. Establish a process whereby the planning committee communicates via e-mail with whoever is maintaining your database. Get confirmation that the material was received and posted. Double-check it to make sure it was posted correctly. Many non-profits are lax in getting timely material onto their websites because there are too many people involved in the planning and not enough communication with the webmaster.

ALERT!

Too many data entry people can spoil the website. Limit the number of people who can post on your site. The more you filter the material through one or two central people (unless you are working in a very large nonprofit), the easier it is to have a website with a consistent look and accurate information.

Try to make the fundraising activities stand out from other information on your website. Design the page in a manner that invites the user to check out the information. Graphics, entertaining and informative copy, and all the important details need to be clear. Make it easy for people to sign up in advance or even buy (or reserve) tickets to your event through the site or by calling a phone number or sending an e-mail to an address posted on the site.

Even if your organization does not have a website, you can develop a page for the upcoming event on one of the many free sites offered on the web. This will let you post information about your fundraiser and provide web users with an easy place to learn about what you have planned. Remember, communicating through your website is only as effective as the number of hits it receives—and this will happen only with good promotion, which will be covered in Chapter 10.

You are better off if you can keep the website design and data entry in-house and not rely on outside computer help. Several years ago, organizations relied heavily on others to handle all of their web needs. Now, technology has made it much easier to do the vast majority of web work in-house, including designing graphics and content and responding to inquiries. If you do require outside help, try to minimize your needs by learning as much as you can about how to manage your own website. Plenty of easy-to-use software programs are available, and you can find numerous websites offering build-your-own web page capabilities.

E-Fundraising

E-fundraising is gaining momentum, and no campaign would be complete without it. It is estimated 85 percent of all adults spend time on the web, and to reach this audience—especially younger generations—you need an online presence in order to build your database of supporters.

E-Fundraising Today

E-fundraising may be the most appealing of all strategies because it is a low-cost way to generate revenue, allowing for a larger share of funds to directly support a cause. Although it is a relatively new strategy, the future of e-fundraising is just beginning to reach new heights.

E-fundraising is picking up steam thanks in part to new partners. In 2007, YouTube launched an initiative in which nonprofits in the United States with 501(c)(3) tax filing status can register for a free nonprofit-specific YouTube channel. They can upload footage of their work, public service announcements, calls to action, and more. Through this channel, they can also collect donations with no processing costs, thanks to Google's Checkout for Non-profits. Other initiatives, such as JustGive (*www.justgive.org*), provide portals where people can find charities they find meaningful. The site reported it received $25 million in donations in 2007, up 45 percent from 2006.

Evaluating E-Fundraising

E-fundraising requires significantly lower expenses than other established methods, such as phone solicitation or direct mailings. It costs almost nothing to send mass e-mails, including fundraising appeals, invitations, information on upcoming events, and thank yous. Your organization can save money on printing, postage, and the services of a mailing house.

Still, some people remain skeptical about e-fundraising. Stories of stolen identities and fraudulent charities create uneasiness among potential contributors. Nonetheless, once a nonprofit has established its presence and reputation, the Internet can prove less expensive than direct mail campaigns for reaching a mass audience. The site should convince donors it offers web security, no personal information will be shared or sold elsewhere (include a privacy policy), and donors' money will be used for the reasons for which it was donated.

ALERT!

State and local governments have regulations and guidelines regarding what they consider charitable solicitation. In some cases, it may be necessary to register as a charitable organization in other states before you can solicit funds via the Internet. It is advisable to talk with a lawyer about this issue.

New Frontiers

Another growing trend has for-profit businesses providing space for nonprofits or teaming to offer ways in which to donate money to your organization through their websites.

Even if e-fundraising does not make up the bulk of your revenue, use your website to promote activities, raise awareness, and recruit new volunteers. It is also a beneficial tool in the event of emergency situations such as the September 11 terrorist attacks, Hurricane Katrina, and other devastating hurricanes or floods around the world. The Internet provides the immediacy that allows people to donate to help the victims of such disasters as quickly as possible.

Pros and Cons of Internet Fundraising

Advantages of e-fundraising include the following:

- Your organization can reach more people in less time than ever before.
- Costs are relatively low.

- If your e-fundraising capabilities are set up correctly, people can respond immediately to requests for donations.
- You can respond quickly to donors' questions and concerns through e-mail.
- You can update information on a daily basis and keep people abreast of the latest news and activities in your organization or regarding your topic of interest.

FACT

More people will find your site if you work to get your name in as many places as possible Get like-minded organizations to trade links with your site. People who are interested in one site can easily find other causes that inspire them.

While you certainly want to have a web presence, there are reasons why you should limit your time and efforts on e-fundraising. The disadvantages include the following:

- In general, people are still hesitant about giving money online unless they are confident you will receive it and their privacy will be protected.
- There is a tremendous amount of competition on the Internet for donations and unless you have major marketing dollars or a plan and the time to institute a grassroots marketing campaign, it is unlikely you will be able to stand out from the crowd.
- Hackers, viruses, and technical problems can wreak havoc with your site and you can lose data, including pledges or donations.
- It takes constant work on your website to keep it current.

Despite the disadvantages, it is worthwhile to establish a web presence and put a system in place to collect donations or at least pledges. If nothing else, promote your site as much as possible so people can read about the work you do and get information about the cause you are supporting.

Requirements for E-Fundraising

To effectively receive contributions online, you will need a service that allows you to process credit cards, a web page set up to accept credit card information, and a merchant services account with a bank or third-party provider. You should also make sure your Internet Service Provider (ISP) is equipped to help you set up a "storefront" for receiving donations. Some ISPs are more familiar with the needs of charities and nonprofit groups; others are more comfortable working only with for-profit businesses dealing in tangible goods, as opposed to online donations. Conduct some research before selecting an ISP.

Online contributions have rapidly become an essential component of political fundraising. Take the 2008 presidential campaign. In November 2007, Congressman Ron Paul raised $4.2 million in one day, while Senator Barak Obama's website brought in $28 million in the month of January in 2008. Online contributions allow campaigns to secure credit card donations twenty-four hours a day at minimal expense.

Another, more affordable, means of using the web to solicit donations is simply to post information directing people to contribute by mail or pledge by phone. This eliminates having to deal with credit cards or online transactions. You can certainly offer both options, but this way saves you from having to worry about online business transactions and may also eliminate legal questions regarding donations from other states or countries. You might even provide a printable online form. Many smaller organizations use the Internet in this manner to request donations; this method works well for some, but not all, organizations.

E-fundraising is tricky. Be prepared to handle donations as they come in and thank donors immediately. Though many organizations report it still makes up only a small portion of their revenues, e-fundraising is a growing area of fundraising and will continue to develop in the coming years.

CHAPTER 10

Spreading the Word

No matter how long and hard you've worked at planning a carnival, auction, or walkathon, if people don't know when it is going to take place, you won't make money. Advertising and promotion are key elements in a successful fundraising campaign. This chapter covers strategies to build buzz about your event or promotion in order to reach as wide an audience as possible.

10

Internal Publicity

Internal publicity means spreading the word throughout your organization. In a small group, this can be done via word of mouth, e-mails, and a reminder postcard or letter. Larger organizations, however, should make the most of their newsletter with a story about the upcoming fundraising activities in addition to a well-placed advertisement.

Flyers at meetings and other organizational events can be an inexpensive way to put the information in front of your members. If it's a school function, you'll want to distribute the flyers to teachers so children can bring them home in their backpacks. Use your computer to create a flyer that tells people who, what, when, and where, then make photocopies. Encourage your members to spread the word to friends, neighbors, relatives, and business associates. In a mid- or large-sized organization, you may need to establish an advertising and promotions committee. Each person should work on various methods of promoting your event, being careful not to overlap.

Remember, people give to people they know. The board of directors of most smaller 501(c)(3) nonprofits has a hands-on responsibility for fundraising. They also help put a name and face to a cause. The bottom line is that successful fundraising events typically have a high level of participation from the board.

Get Your Board on Board

Enthusiasm is contagious. Give your board of directors the details about the event and let them run with it. Along with generating excitement, the job of your board liaison (or fundraising chairperson) is to convince the board this event is being planned by a well-organized committee and has the potential to be a successful fundraiser for the organization. In the best of circumstances, the board president and the committee chair will have discussed how the individual board members can participate prior to presenting the information at the board meeting.

There are two ways board members can participate. The first is to buy tickets, and the second is to help sell tickets. The committee needs to create a mechanism to help board members promote ticket sales.

For example, on big-ticket fundraisers, members of the board are often asked to provide names so personalized invitations can be sent. Business colleagues, associates, and friends will be more inclined to write a check if they know the board member will also be attending. It makes a big difference if the president of the board will say that he is purchasing four tickets, plans on personalizing thirty or forty invitations, and intends to follow up with telephone calls; follow-up e-mail reminders from board members also prompt supporters to buy tickets. These kinds of personal action serve as promotion, and they sell tickets—lots of them—at all price ranges.

Get Your Staff and Members on Board

Before anyone can help you advertise and promote a fundraising activity, she must be well versed in the details. Everyone involved in your organization needs to know enough about the fundraiser to speak intelligently and enthusiastically about it and direct people to the appropriate contact person.

Don't tell everyone to spread the word until the word is clearly defined. One of the biggest problems any organization can run up against is telling people about an upcoming activity before the plans are confirmed, and then having to backtrack. Set a date for officially releasing the information.

Everyone working with the project should know in advance all of the details you plan to include in your upcoming advertising. Therefore, the planning committee should brief everyone on the details of the forthcoming fundraising campaign or event ahead of time.

After informing the core group who will be involved in the fundraiser, you will then reach out and invite your membership. Many groups find that mailing invitations is effective. This can range from a formal invitation to a postcard. Quite often, a well-designed postcard enables you to reach a large audience at a very reasonable cost, especially if it is sent out as bulk mail. Remember to give yourself enough lead time because bulk mail travels slowly. E-mail event invitations are another popular approach.

Defining Your Advertising Needs

Advertising and promotion for a neighborhood-based fundraising event such as a school carnival might be as simple as putting up posters and flyers in the display windows of neighborhood stores and restaurants; on bulletin boards at libraries, community centers, schools, and churches; and even in apartment buildings. Smart organizations will promote the fundraising event in their newsletter, and they will also try to get coverage in the newsletters of other neighborhood organizations. Sometimes you can trade postings with other organizations that are also planning upcoming events. The goal is to get your information in front of as many people as possible as often as possible.

FACT

You must always keep in mind the strategies you will need to ensure your event is financially successful. Selling ads in a program book requires a different kind of promotion effort than selling tickets. Furthermore, the advertising needed to sell $50 tickets for a dinner will differ from that used to sell $12 tickets for the circus.

Look closely at your target audience and select the most effective advertising and promotional mediums for your particular event. Research which means of advertising will reach your target group. For example, college students are more likely to see an online advertisement or article than an audience of seniors, who might be more easily reached by telephone or personalized letter sent through the mail. What's more, because the business community responds well to e-mail, you can send out e-mail alerts, detailing which sponsorship levels are still available and which have already sold out.

Radio

There are several ways you can use the air waves to get the word out about your cause. You could opt for a public service announcement, but if you have the opportunity, you could also get a member of your organization onto a talk radio show.

Public Service Announcements

FCC licensing often requires radio and television stations to include some amount of public service programming. As a nonprofit organization, you can run PSAs on radio stations. PSAs are generally fifteen to thirty seconds in duration, and occasionally as long as sixty seconds. Call the station and ask who handles PSAs and community affairs. Find out what restrictions the station may have and whether it wants PSAs submitted on CD or if it wants the script for its announcers to read.

Determine how many people you want to reach. You shouldn't reach out to 100,000 people to tell them about a silent auction that will only hold 200. Plan your advertising and promotional campaign in accordance with your size and space restrictions, as well as your budget limitations.

You may be able to coordinate your publicity efforts with a particular radio or television program. For example, one year the Philadelphia Old House Fair coincided with a local network's efforts to promote its own home restoration programs. A very short trailer mentioning the Old House Fair appeared after the home restoration shows for a couple of days prior to the fair. The placement was perfect for the audience the planners of the fair were hoping to reach.

Going on Air

Almost any city or town has its fair share of talk radio stations. An ideal way to get your message out there without spending money is to try to get someone from your organization, or a spokesperson for your cause, on talk radio. Television is another possibility, but unless you have a speaker who is comfortable in front of the camera, you may do better with radio.

A local celebrity can also be beneficial in promoting your upcoming fundraiser. Contact radio stations in advance, possibly ones that already know you from running your PSAs, and find out which talk shows might work for you.

ALERT!

Even music stations are generally required to have some time devoted to community service programming. Unfortunately, this may be at 6 A.M. on Sunday morning. Always consider whether an opportunity will let you connect with your target audience or whether it will be a waste of your time and resources.

You'll do better on an all-talk station, where you might fit into one of its daytime programs for a short interview. Most often, the program host will ask you in advance what you want to talk about. Prepare questions you have answers to and that feature highlights of upcoming fundraising activities.

A subtler way of getting your message across is to call in and talk about a topic on a primetime radio call-in show. Keep in mind that radio primetime is during the morning and evening rush hours when people are heading to and from work. Mention your organization or fundraiser in the course of the conversation.

The Internet and E-Mail

E-mail is a quick and inexpensive way to spread the word to your members. If you have e-mail addresses provided by previous contributors, then they, too, should receive an e-mail. Spam, or the mass distribution of e-mail advertising to an unsuspecting audience, is not permissible. It does not put your organization in a positive light. Use controlled e-mail lists of people you know are willing to hear from you.

If your organization has a website, post the information there. However, you must remember that posting material on a website does not help reach people unless the site itself is promoted. You will have to spread the word about the website for it to be an effective means of promoting activities and events. Make sure you include your website address on all of your literature.

FACT

Websites should make visitors want to come back for more information. Post stories about your programs and invite reader feedback. You also might include online polls and surveys. The more interaction, the more likely users will feel a connection to the site. In addition, you can better determine how many people are visiting your website and seeing your fundraising promotions.

Other ways to utilize the Internet are to send announcements to websites that support your mission, post messages on message boards, and mention your fundraiser in appropriate chat rooms. Often, community-based websites devote a calendar listing for nonprofits.

Online Newsletters

E-newsletters have become an important communication tool between organizations and the public. Numerous for-profit businesses and nonprofits have successful online newsletters. If you decide to publish one, utilize the technology to your advantage. Combine quality content with an easy-to-read layout and use headers and footers to offer subscriptions. Include information about ongoing programs and, best of all, promote what you have coming up. Be careful to have a reasonable balance between content and promotion. People will unsubscribe if you are overselling and underinforming, so keep the content compelling. Also, stay on top of current happenings in your area of concern.

The best place to get people to sign up for your e-newsletter is from your website. The less information you request, the greater the chance they will sign up. The minimum you need is the person's e-mail address and name.

Beyond that, keep it simple; long and particularly invasive sign-up forms turn people off, and you will lose them.

You should also include a table of contents at the top of the newsletter so people can see what is coming up before they scroll down. Use short, catchy headlines and post your fundraiser promotions in strategic, high-visibility locations.

ALERT!

Don't forget to link the newsletter back to your own website, and always make it possible to contribute with just a couple of clicks. Avoid sending slow-to-load files that discourage viewers from reading. Some of your recipients may not have state-of-the-art computers, and they may not bother to look at a newsletter if it takes too long to open.

The Print Media

Almost every newspaper has some listing of community activities in which you can be included. The print media also includes display and classified ads. Free weekly and monthly newspapers, which typically serve a couple of towns or neighborhoods, are filled with advertisements and classifieds. Phone calls to the advertising department should provide you with advertising rates. Display ads will be more expensive and prominent than classified ads, and you will need to consider your budgetary constraints before spending the money on a larger ad. However, some newspapers might agree to be a media sponsor, donating the ad space.

Looking Within the Community

Another print media group is newspapers and newsletters published by community- and neighborhood-based organizations outside of the immediate membership. Some may have been in the community for generations and have thousands of members in several neighborhoods. A listing in such a newsletter could mean reaching a wide audience within a small geographic area.

Utilize the local papers and look for specialty publications in your field of interest. Give papers thirty to sixty days advance notice and call to confirm that the ad or listing is running. Make sure to double-check that all spelling and information is accurate. Get a tear sheet from the newspaper once the ad has run to document your advertising expenditures.

When buying ad space, particularly classified ads, remember to be succinct, because classified advertising space is sold by the line or by the word. Advertising rates in local papers and circulars are usually fairly low. As a nonprofit organization, you can often get a discount, and you might be able to use your contacts to work out a favorable arrangement.

Magazines

Magazine advertising can be more expensive. Look specifically for magazines that cater to your target audience and inquire about classified rates. As with other print media, you should get a discount. You may make a tradeoff and let them distribute copies of the magazines at the fundraiser in exchange for a low ad rate. Remember, magazines usually have a three to six month lead time.

Articles can provide you with free advertising. Part of the public relations aspect of fundraising is trying to get articles placed in publications. Look for angles that would make interesting articles and pitch these ideas to magazine or newspaper editors. Make sure to get the name of the right editor for your type of story.

Signs, Flyers, and Posters

You'd be surprised at how cost effective simple advertising can be. A simple sign or well-placed poster can be seen by a significant amount of passing traffic and sell tickets. Unless there are specific warnings against posting such signs, you should seek out high-traffic areas where people who might be interested in your organization and your fundraising activities will walk or drive past.

Posting Etiquette

A college organization will post signs for an upcoming fundraiser all over campus and in off-campus establishments frequented by students—with the permission of the owner or manager. In addition, you'll see signs and flyers at bus shelters, on lampposts, on supermarket bulletin boards, and on the fences surrounding construction sites.

Don't forget to include your website on your sign, which can help drive contributions. After the event, remove the sign from lampposts, bus shelters, and the like; you want community support, so support your community after your event by tearing down the signs so they don't become litter.

If people can't catch your headline while walking or riding by, then your ad may not be effective. Keep in mind that white space serves a purpose. Don't overload printed advertisements. Too much copy turns people off, especially in a society where people tend to have short attention spans.

Unique Promotions

Handouts are also a popular way to spread the word among students or in areas of high foot traffic. Of course, this requires someone to be there to hand out the flyers.

Stickers and other forms of grassroots marketing can also be effective by simply putting the information in front of people. Stenciling or chalking information on sidewalks has become a favorite guerrilla method of advertising. Of course, it has also led to legal problems in New York City and other places where it is not allowed. Get an idea of the legal ramifications before you try guerrilla methods.

Posters, signs, and flyers should be easy to read and include all of the key points. Grab the readers' attention as they pass by and give them the details in an eye-catching manner.

Promotional Activities

Promotion essentially means spreading the word without buying advertisements. From T-shirt giveaways to launch parties to kick off your ticket sales campaign, there are plenty of ways of promoting your activities that won't cost you as much as advertising.

Promotions That Work

A promotional activity that helped one nonprofit organization increase single ticket sales was for something called the Lobster Pot, a fundraiser with a $30 per-person ticket price. Throughout the history of the event, the organization relied solely on its members to sell tickets. This method worked well for them; about 500 tickets were sold each year.

FACT

It never hurts to have a kickoff event to promote your upcoming fundraiser and draw the attention of the media. Another way to promote your event is to create photo opportunities with captions the print media might want to publish.

One summer, there was concern about the ability to continue to reach the goal of 500 tickets, let alone surpass it. Promotional activities were introduced for the first time to create awareness of the event before the ticket selling began. The two major promotion activities were press releases and letters of endorsement. Local newspapers ran photographs and short articles based on the press releases they received. The letters of endorsement were sent to businesses in town.

As in past years, members sold the tickets. They made sure to knock on the doors of the businesses that had received the letters of endorsement. The result was an all-time record, with ticket sales jumping to 630.

Being Clever

If, for example, you procure sponsorship for giveaway items, give them away in any number of methods. From a contest at a local high-profile sporting event to handing out freebies in a busy mall, giveaway items and prizes draw attention.

You may be able to tie in your fundraising activity to another local event. For example, one organization that was raffling off a boat arranged with a local boat show to have the drawing at the show.

Tie-ins with sports are successful in promoting charities. For example, a promotion might include a donation of $1,000 from a sponsor to a certain charity whenever the home team hits a home run or the high school football team scores a touchdown. These kinds of tie-ins are hard to get at the professional level but are more easily attainable at a local, minor league, college, or high school level.

A well-timed presentation of an award to a local celebrity or community hero is another way to promote your organization. Your budget will dictate how much you can spend on promotion. Your creativity can then stretch your promotional budget a long way.

A Little Help from Some Little Friends

Although you want to stay within the bounds of good taste and safety, you can create new and unconventional means of promoting your organization or upcoming fundraising activities. Consider North Shore Long Island Jewish Health Systems. In 1953, the entity was simply North Shore of Manhasset, and fundraisers got the community involved by collecting pennies—250,000 in total—from local schoolchildren. The hospital also had celebrity support from stars of the day, including Joan Payson, the owner of the New York Mets, and singer Perry Como.

Getting children enthusiastic about raising funds for a local cause is a great way to muster support from their families and generate buzz in the community. Over the years, publicity has sometimes manifested itself in bizarre ways. You don't necessarily want to try these stunts, but you can get your creative juices flowing by pondering some offbeat methods of promotion.

Cause Marketing

With nonprofits and businesses alike competing for mind share, organizations are finding success by building a presence where their audience and prospects gather, raising awareness for their cause.

For instance, on the grassroots level, one supermarket showcased posters made by schoolchildren whose artwork highlighted the merits of reducing energy consumption by recycling and choosing compact fluorescent light bulbs. Community-based organizations sometimes post signs in town squares showing the progress of their fundraising goals, generating a "We can do it" spirit among residents. By connecting with audiences on their turf, an organization can build a new league of donors.

Cause marketing is gaining in popularity. If you are partnering with one or more corporations to help spread your message and raise funds, be sure your organization and your corporate partners are clear about what each side hopes to gain from the collaboration. You get the best results when goals and roles are specified early on.

On a larger scale, celebrities and well-known brands made a splash in 2006 with (PRODUCT) RED, which uses 100 percent of the money raised for the Global Fund to Fight AIDS. With this campaign, participating brands such as Apple, Motorola, and Dell offer a special version (usually in the color red) of popular consumer products and a portion of the proceeds go to the Global Fund. The campaign has already raised more than $100 million.

Printing

If you are a small organization or grassroots group, you can use one of the many design and printing software programs such as Printmaster or Print-shop to create quality printed materials that attract attention. The key is learning the program thoroughly and having a good layout and some sense of design. Study the spacing, design, and layout of other brochures, flyers, and printed materials to see what stands out to you.

ALERT!

Whether it's a print advertisement, brochure, or web ad, one of the most common mistakes is trying to put too much information onto the page. White space can be very valuable and will make your ad easier on the eye.

Start with a prototype and show everyone at the committee meeting before mailing out any final products. If you are using a software program, it will be easy to make changes based on the feedback of others.

Hiring an Outside Printer

Nonprofits tend to select either photocopy or offset printing. Photo-copy uses photocopiers, which can be state-of-the-art machines that create excellent materials in a short time. Offset printing is more costly and slower but can provide higher quality, especially when photographs are involved.

Outside printers can be costly. Make sure you really need something to reach your sales or revenue goals. Have a reasonable budget for printing and stick to it. Keep in mind that once a printer gets started, running additional copies can be less expensive. For instance, 100 invitations might be $200, and 250 might be $300. A significant chunk of the cost is the initial layout and setup of the printer's equipment. Once the press is running, the cost to you is primarily paper, so it doesn't cost as much to run additional copies.

If you are using an outside printer for journals, programs, or newsletters, make sure to shop around and get several quotes before committing to one. Remember, the least expensive may not always be the best. Don't sacrifice quality for a quick job that may look amateurish. Ask several key questions, including:

- How long will it take to complete the job?
- Can you see proofs before the job goes to press?
- In what form does the printer want copy delivered? Does it need everything camera ready?
- Can you see samples of various kinds of paper?
- Are there less costly methods to achieve the desired result, for example, by selecting different paper stock or modifying the layout?

You will also want to see samples of products similar to those you are trying to create. Most printing houses will provide you with choices for everything from font to paper quality. Paper stock varies greatly in quality and price. Check out a few before making a decision. The more formal or high end the event, the more you need to spring for better-quality paper. Try to match the look of the materials—from content to paper quality—to the event you are planning.

Review proofs carefully. Proofs are the prototype of the printed work. Most of the work is done by computer, but there is still a person handling the typesetting process, and errors can always be made. The more people that see it, the more likely you will be able to catch errors.

If you have a program or journal, you might be able to work a deal with the printer, such as providing a full-page ad at no cost in exchange for a discount on the cost of your printing job. Look to see how you can promote any vendors in a way that might leave them inclined to give you more for what you are paying or offer you a substantial discount on your bill. Free advertising goes a long way if your product will also reach the printer's target market.

In the end, choose a printer with whom you are confident you will receive a good, quality product.

Visual Effects

Don't scrimp on the visual image when you are promoting your event. It is true a picture is worth a thousand words. In this day and age, when people are reading less and flipping channels more, the visual image has a greater impact. You want to make a strong first impression in the mind of your audience. Retain a good designer, hopefully through contacts within your organization. A good designer will create a visual image that can help sell tickets. Whether it is an invitation going out to fifty people or a flyer that you will make 50,000 copies of, it is important your printed product looks good.

Fit the graphics, design, and text to your organization and your fundraising event. If you are planning a trip to the circus for kids, you'll have a far different tone and more colorful design than if you are planning a formal black-tie dinner honoring a longtime board member. Plan the printing design and graphics accordingly.

Working with a Graphic Designer

Before a good graphic designer will go to work, he will ask you to provide the text. He will also ask if your event has a theme. Designers will use this key information as a starting point. The theme lets the designer know how you might address issues such as marketing, advertising, and decorating. He needs to know how much space the text will take up on your poster, flyer, postcard, or invitation. A good designer will also tell you if you have too much text or too many design elements in your planned presentation.

Be prepared to advise your designer accordingly if you plan to use the graphic design for everything that you print, which may include postcards, newspaper advertisements, flyers, posters, napkins, and more. It is advantageous to create a visual theme that carries throughout your advertising and marketing.

Assuming your intended audience will see more than one advertising or promotional piece on the event, well-designed printed materials will help contribute to the branding and identification of your fundraising event. After a while, people will need only to see the image, design, or logo to think of your organization; it will lend a sense of consistency.

Photos That Matter

Let's face it—a dozen photos of gray-haired bigwigs in business suits accepting awards is boring! Get photos of your group or organization in action, photos of your cause, photos of your neighborhood—anything that represents your group in an interesting way.

Visually appealing materials are those that say something to your audience or make them stop and think, smile, or react in some manner. The beauty and majesty of a whale is more appealing on a "Save the Whales" flyer than the face of a committee member who is not known to the vast majority of people reading the material.

If you are using photos, get permission from the photographer and let her know that you would like to feature the photo for a nonprofit mailing. The photographer may be inclined to waive a fee for the exposure and for a good cause. If photos are too expensive, you will need to use those in the public domain or those taken in-house by your own members.

Also, be sure to take plenty of photos of fundraising activities—not just people smiling, but people in action as activities are taking place. They look good in the newsletter, on the website, in slide presentations, and in brochures and other printed materials.

CHAPTER 11

Corporate Fundraising

Corporate America has served as a longtime supporter of nonprofits by both initiating and promoting
fundraising drives. Supporting nonprofits is part of a
strategy enabling them to give back to their communities and build strong ties with their employees, clients, and vendors. People want to do business with
those who give back, and that can be good for a company's bottom line. Studies show that in strong economic times, corporate giving increases. Yet when
there is economic uncertainty, some business sectors
decrease their financial support. This can prove challenging to fundraisers, especially when they must
compete with other causes for the same corporate
dollars.

The Role of Corporations in Fundraising

Corporations can play a key role in your ongoing fundraising efforts by sponsoring your events or specific programs. They can also provide grants, which are discussed in greater detail in Chapters 17 and 18, or team with your organization to raise money for a good cause through their product marketing.

As attractive as those dollars are, keep in mind that corporations typically do not lend support for purely altruistic reasons. Most are generally looking at the bottom line first—theirs, not yours. After all, they are responsible to stockholders. The motivation driving companies to get involved in charity is not completely selfless. Corporate donors are seeking some type of return on their investment.

Donations

Companies are not only able to help your cause with funding, they may also offer goods or services. For example, a beverage company might donate juice to schools and children's programs, knowing these students will likely request their parents buy the juice products at the supermarket. In another example, a corporation might sponsor a program or a series of programs at a nearby performing arts center, building goodwill with its community and helping make the region an enjoyable place to live for its employees. What's more, they are able to attract additional talent to the region by bringing the arts to the community.

Giving Back to the Community

While corporations do indulge in philanthropy in part for publicity and business reasons, most are dedicated to giving something significant to the community. The Ronald McDonald House Charities programs are an excellent example of the power of a global company to help seriously ill children in great need of love and support. Its Ronald McDonald Family Rooms provide play areas and computer stations near hospital neonatal and pediatric intensive care units so that families of children undergoing treatment have a place to relax during a stressful time. There are many other ways a company such as McDonald's could gain positive publicity, but these are especially heartfelt examples of corporate concern. And, yes, they show the company in a positive light.

Johnson & Johnson is another example of a company that offers both donations and sponsorship in areas of interest. Its giving policies support organizations that focus on improving the lives of women and children, educating those who provide health care services, and preventing disease, disabilities, and stigma in underserved communities.

FACT

One of the leading reasons for corporate donations is to improve the communities in which they do business. The hope is that, by improving the community in terms of making it cleaner, safer, and better educated, people will not move away. This is good for business.

Teaming Up

The primary ways corporations participate in fundraising efforts and activities include:

- Sponsorship of activities or fundraisers
- Forming foundations for the express purpose of philanthropy
- Grant giving
- Staff fundraising and volunteerism
- Partnering with nonprofits
- Corporate donations

If you are seeking any of these means of support from a major corporation whose mission aligns with yours, consider what, if anything, the return on the company's investment can be. In your efforts to procure funding, try to offer something in return. Determine how the company's participation can show it in a better light or help it in its fiscal goals.

For example, if you are looking for corporate sponsorship for your upcoming charity golf tournament, either through underwriting, or providing the funds for the event or direct contributions, ask yourself or your organization: Will sponsoring this golf tournament help put the company's name before the public and attract new customers? What can you do to help present the corporation in a positive way?

FACT

Studies have shown that employees feel a greater sense of pride and dedication to a company that is involved in cause-related marketing or philanthropic endeavors. Some companies have programs to match employees' charitable contributions, although these programs are sometimes limited to certain charities.

After all, the corporation is offsetting part or all of the expense of running such a tournament. Perhaps you could include the company in the tournament name, or feature its products at your pre-event luncheon or kickoff event. There are many ways you can team up with a company to promote its goods or services while also raising money for your fundraising efforts.

FACT

Some companies may not seek publicity for their contributions. These companies may choose to stay out of the spotlight because they don't want to be overwhelmed with requests for funding. They also may not want to set a precedent in giving away a certain amount one year, only to find they are unable to do so the following year.

Private Corporate Donations

It is true that some companies do not make their donations public. They work in subtle ways to do good deeds in their communities. If they are not operating through a foundation, they do not have to make such information public, which makes researching the giving policies of such companies more difficult. Yet at a time when the government is calling for increasing transparency, companies are now considering posting their charitable grants online; this transparency may become more prevalent in the pharmaceutical industry, after the Senate questioned whether drug companies were contributing only to those nonprofits that would recommend their products.

Increasingly, company executives are making charitable giving decisions rather than leaving them to the philanthropy or community relations department. These executives typically base their decisions on how they will best benefit the company.

If a company does not want to receive exposure for its donation(s), you must respect that decision by not publicizing where the funding came from. It is possible the company's leadership is concerned shareholders will think the organization is giving too much of its profits away.

Approaching Corporations

Before approaching a corporation, put together a strong proposal. Whether you are seeking a grant, sponsorship, or donation, you need to have your proposal on paper, with plenty of backup materials prepared.

Begin the process by doing careful research to determine which companies might be interested in sponsoring activities such as those you are planning. See what kinds of fundraising the company's name has appeared with in the past. Determine how sponsoring you would help its image and customer base. Look for a good match.

Who Do You Know?

With the competition among so many nonprofits to raise money, it is very important to know the right people. The higher the person ranks in the company, the more influence he will have in spending the company's money on a cause.

Start by taking a look at your board of directors and committee members. Who do they work for? Nonprofit organizations may have a number of board members who are professionals in fields such as construction, development, economic consulting, or real estate law. They may work for companies (or even own a business) that are likely to be contributors, newsletter advertisers, or event sponsors. Always remember to provide your board members with the opportunity to get their business more involved with the projects and programs of your organization.

The CEO of a major Fortune 500 corporation may sit on the board of several nonprofits, having a very limited role in the activities of each. Unless she has a personal interest in a cause, it is unlikely she will have the time to commit to hands-on activities, which is why she will seek out a well-run and well-established nonprofit. If your board does not include corporate executives or you have not yet recruited any, you should speak with board members to determine whether they have any contacts.

ALERT!

Don't try to slant your mission to fit the parameters of a company's giving policies. Approach the company honestly. Open your dialogue by saying, "I know this isn't the type of cause you usually fund, but . . ." and be ready with some hard-hitting reasons why they *should* fund you.

Create an initial list of companies that may be interested in your cause based on the connections you have from board members and other members of your organization. Again, look for the best fits, but remember the old saying, "Beggars can't be choosers." The reality is, the who-you-know factor is very significant in trying to make headway in the corporate realm. That said, it is prestigious to sit on a board, and there are corporate executives who seek these positions because they want to help solve problems in the community and meet like-minded people.

Be resourceful in your approach and try to think of a good reason why a company should partner with you. One popular strategy is to team up with a company for a special anniversary. Anniversaries are big deals to companies, and what better way to celebrate than to give back to the community in a meaningful way? Another approach is to partner with established chains opening a new unit in your region. It is not unusual for a fast food restaurant to donate proceeds to a local charity as a way of building relationships with the community. When you hear of retail or food chains establishing roots locally, get in touch with the manager about possible fundraising opportunities.

When you are dealing with a particularly large company, it is often in your best interest not to try to reach the CEO unless you have a direct contact. Instead, look for influential, up-and-coming executives whose decision to sponsor a good cause might help demonstrate to their superiors why they should continue to move up the corporate ladder.

ALERT!

Don't try to substitute who you know for what you know. Just because you know someone in the upper echelon at a major corporation does not mean you can forgo doing your homework. With every corporate opportunity, do your research and learn everything you possibly can about the company's policies. The more you know, the more likely you are to impress your contact.

Building Relationships

It may take a year to cultivate a relationship with the right person, but if he becomes a major donor, then it is worth it. Five major donors can bring in more money than several successful fundraising events, and at less cost and with fewer hours of volunteering. Of course, courting such high-end donors is difficult and requires face-to-face meetings. You need to build trust by demonstrating your organization is capable of doing what it sets out to do, and by meeting your goals.

Privately held companies are good places for nonprofits to seek supporters. It is easier to reach the CEO, and a privately held company will have fewer nonprofits approaching it. A successful individual in a privately owned company may be making $10 million a year and could easily become a major donor for your organization. You need to take the time and establish a relationship with such a company in your community. Time establishing and building relationships with top donors is well spent, since their contributions can be significant.

Giving Something Back

For more than three decades, Lincoln Center for the Performing Arts in New York has hosted its Mostly Mozart Festival. This four-week festival features the music of Mozart and his contemporaries, performed by well-known artists. Sponsorship benefits can include the opportunity to display products and offer samples. Other benefits can include credit in print and broadcast advertising as well as on collateral materials such as brochures. In addition, they can feature Lincoln Center's name in corporate advertising and enjoy additional perks, including personalized assistance in securing tickets for other Lincoln Center performances. Of course, Lincoln Center is a world-famous institution whose performances would be hard to match; however, the benefits of its sponsorship program serve as a good model for any organization seeking to attract quality sponsors.

Businesses, no matter how large or small, are seeking a return on their investment. Sponsors will differ in their needs, and you should try to accommodate them. Establish a mutually beneficial partnership, and you can work to make it an enduring long-term relationship.

Other nonprofits flourish from innovative powers of partnership. Take The Long Island Way. It is a New York–based organization, founded in 2007, that brings businesses and nonprofits together in mutually beneficial relationships. In five months, founder and CEO Donna Cariello signed thirty businesses to serve as member advocates for seventeen not-for-profit organizations. In exchange, member advocates enjoy enhanced visibility in the business and nonprofit community through networking events and free newsletter and online advertising opportunities.

Earning Money

No matter how the meeting with a major corporation is set up—through your own efforts or through contacts—be sure to learn as much as possible about the products or services it provides. This way, you can present what you can give back. There are more nonprofit organizations seeking funding than there are major corporations with funds to give. You have competition, and you need to make a strong case for why supporting your efforts is in the best interests of everyone involved in the equation. The more you know about the group, the easier it will be to find ways to show them the benefits they'll gain by supporting your organization.

ALERT!

Look for inventive ways to work with sponsors. Think of opportunities to raise the profile of your sponsors before your audience and in promoting your organization's upcoming events. Don't forget to seek out sponsorship from businesses that have supported you in some manner in the past.

Along with giving something in return, you may also consider methods of earning money. The proliferation of nonprofits has created a logjam. Some groups are not getting donations simply because they are the fifth nonprofit to seek out the same donors for the same cause. Tapping into your membership and determining the potential for a revenue-generating vehicle within your organization may help your group gain attention and differentiate itself from the competition. For example, hospitals and other nonprofit organizations often open thrift shops. Try to find a means of earning money that does not have a high cost factor on your end.

ALERT!

If you find that your goal is the same as that of other organizations, align with one of them. Many nonprofit groups seek the same funding, and there is no need for competition if you are working toward the same goal.

Developing Partnerships

Not unlike two for-profit companies developing a strategic alliance, nonprofits and for-profit corporations are working together. Pursuing corporate sponsors can be a worthwhile endeavor—studies put corporate giving at $10 billion annually.

Corporations provide money through foundations or directly through giving programs, and your goal is to build a relationship that will provide ongoing support. They usually focus on a specific problem or area of concern such as improving elementary education.

In many instances, a major corporation will set up a specific program and then work with nonprofit organizations, schools, or charities. For example, the CVS Caremark Charitable Trust funds programs that benefit diverse populations where CVS stores are located. It provides grant applications online during a specific window of time, and interested parties can learn about the process by visiting the corporate website (*www.cvscaremark.com*).

Another example comes from Kraft Foods, which has taken significant steps to combat the serious problem of obesity. Its Eat to Live Better program in Mexico City teaches educators about healthy eating habits, physical activity, and proper hygiene. These educators, in turn, teach that same message to low-income families through a network of community centers. The companies find nonprofits that are working on the issue on which they have decided to support, making their communities healthier.

Trade and Professional Associations

Consider developing relationships with trade and professional associations. For example, the Association of Home Appliance Manufacturers (AHAM), a trade association in Washington, D.C., launched a program called Home Sweet Home, in which it donated thousands of dollars in kitchen appliances and other items in 2007 to families in New Orleans whose homes had been greatly damaged during Hurricane Katrina. In donating items, AHAM partnered with Gifts In Kind International and the United Way of the Greater New Orleans Area to encourage its members to give back to communities in need. The program was mentioned in numerous industry magazines and was highlighted on the Gifts In Kind website, which also posted a video of the donation program. The Gifts In Kind website also includes content in which companies can learn how to launch similar programs.

Trade and professional associations look for publicity and can provide your organization with a rich network of contacts including professionals in various businesses. When partnering with associations, let their contacts know how they can become more active in supporting your cause.

Employee Donations

Numerous companies have employee contribution programs, many of which are in conjunction with the United Way, which serves as an umbrella group for such donations. More than 12 million people invest in the United Way annually.

Whether through the United Way or their own charitable giving program, a number of companies also match donations made by their employees, or at least a percentage thereof. If your nonprofit stands to receive such donations, you should remind your donors that their contribution might be matched by their employer and be tax deductible if you have qualified for 501(c)(3) nonprofit status.

Sit down with the person in charge of employee giving programs in your company and provide her with literature about the nonprofit to which you belong. In some cases, an employee program may not yet exist, and you may be the catalyst that jumpstarts the initiative within your company.

One major bank has a matching gift program whereby it directs money from its foundation to meet the donations of employees. The company matches donations dollar-for-dollar for up to $10,000, enabling their associates to make a positive influence in their communities. Other organizations match donations of $50 or more, up to $2,000 per year, for full-time employees who have been with the company for a specified amount of time. The donation can be made to a single organization or to several organizations as the employee sees fit. The organization must be a 501(c)(3) nonprofit. While this is typical of many such programs instituted to promote employee giving and company involvement, some companies are cutting back, citing concerns over uncertain economic conditions.

It is also in your best interest to talk with people about the companies they work for. Often, if an employee has worked for a company for several years and is involved with a nonprofit organization, the company may be interested in contributing or sponsoring some activity. Even small businesses may want to begin their involvement with fundraising efforts, and employee interests are a wonderful place to start. It helps boost employee relations and morale when a business shows an interest in the concerns of its employees.

Let your involvement in a nonprofit be known around the office, particularly to whoever is in charge of charitable contributions. This person may not be in a position to respond immediately, but should she seek to donate to or form a partnership with a nonprofit organization at a later date, yours may come to mind more quickly because of the employee connection.

The United Way

The United Way is the granddaddy of corporate giving programs. Originally known as the Charitable Organizations Society and founded in Denver in 1887, the United Way raised more than $4 billion in 2006, up by 2.3 percent from the year before. As an umbrella group, the United Way pools the contributions of thousands of employees that are made directly through payroll deductions. The dollars from annual employee workplace campaigns total $2.64 billion, making up 65 percent of the organization's total revenue, according to the most recent figures; the United Way also collects funds through foundations and targeted individual giving. The money is then distributed to numerous nonprofit organizations nationwide. Many long-established notable organizations such as the Red Cross receive a portion of their funds through United Way contributions.

Donating to the United Way can be like investing in a mutual fund, only you are not looking for a monetary return on your investment. Instead of your money going to one nonprofit, it could be going to any of a number of organizations. You can donate to the United Way and let it choose where to distribute the funds, or you can select where you want your contributions directed. By aligning with numerous organizations and corporations, the United Way has established itself as the premier organization for bringing employees and charities together. Nonprofit groups are eager to get a piece of the billions raised every year, and they apply to the United Way for such consideration.

FACT

The United Way system is now made up of 1,300 community-based United Way organizations. These organizations are each owned separately, and are governed by local volunteers. Participants include government, business, faith groups, nonprofits, the labor movement, and ordinary citizens who gather to solve community challenges.

It is recommended that you contact your local United Way to learn if it is still accepting applications for 501(c)3 nonprofits as designated recipients and what the application process entails. If your organization is accepted, you can then let your constituents know you are a participating United Way organization. They can then set up automatic payroll deductions through their employers to make regular contributions to your organization.

CHAPTER 12

Community Fundraising

Perhaps you are raising money to help renew a blighted community or soliciting funds to clean up the shoreline. The common element in both examples? Local nonprofit groups spending time and money in order to maintain their communities. Such community groups and neighborhood associations form and grow based on the common desire to maintain or improve the quality of life in a community. The goals of subsequent fundraising efforts are to meet the vital needs of everyone from preschoolers to seniors.

Involving the Whole Community

Not everyone you ask is in a position to donate money or volunteer time, but if your community-based nonprofit group studies the issues affecting your community and researches how to effect change, you can inspire much of the community to get involved in your efforts and your results have the potential to impact everyone.

Start by doing your homework. Research the issues affecting your community and look for the source of each issue. Is there a lack of funding? Has redevelopment changed the face of the neighborhood? Is there a need for more police or a community watch?

FACT

Focus on everyone, not only high-end, big-money donors. Studies show 80 percent of individual donations come from households with incomes of just $50,000 or more. Therefore, it is worthwhile to look to the middle and working class when developing your fundraising campaign.

Look at the map and determine the community boundaries. Then explore the demographics of the community. What cultural groups are represented? What are their needs and concerns? Are there abandoned buildings and boarded-up stores? Are local merchants losing business to a nearby mall in a neighboring community?

Get a feel for what retailers and business owners want and need. You may be able to help them while they, in turn, help you solve community issues and problems.

Establishing a Nucleus

Somewhere between the idea of forming a group to deal with neighborhood concerns and the actual researching of problems and input from the community, you will need to establish a group within the group. These are the core members who may have been instrumental in the formation of the ideas, who have the resources and experience to get things done, or both. This core group may be only half a dozen people, but they are key to building the organization.

Your Core Group

To form the nucleus of the group, seek out people who are committed to dealing with the cause or problem(s) at hand, able to make a time commitment, good at communicating with others, and open to various opinions. Civic leaders, community activists, business owners, government officials, philanthropists, and environmentalists may all offer valuable input. You'll also identify candidates for your core group by talking to community leaders, taking part in community activities, and looking in local newspapers for names of people who have impacted the community in other ways.

Once you have formed your core group and have begun your community-minded planning, determine which community newspaper, local groups, churches and temples, and/or government groups should know about your organization. Print some basic materials to alert them to your presence and mission; then follow up with fundraising information as it develops.

Once you have established a core group, hold meetings before opening your doors to the community at large. This way you can develop a consensus on the issues and determine a broad approach to implementing changes. While you will want input from the community, you will first want the opportunity to build a framework for running the organization effectively. For example, you may want to list some of the practical means of raising funds, such as a community fair or block party, and eliminate less practical ideas. This will give your core group a little time to address concerns such as the need for permits, should the larger group decide to organize a county fair or block party. Divide responsibilities and determine who will implement the fundraising campaign, who will be leading the promotional campaign, and so on. You can also set the agenda for the first public meetings to involve the community as a whole.

The objective is essentially to get the organization or fundraiser off the ground. By formulating a mission statement and setting goals and strategy, you establish basic parameters and build a structure from which to operate. Core group members should conduct research and become knowledgeable about the issues and the community. They should be prepared to head up committees, if need be (although your committee chairpersons don't have to be members of this nucleus group). This creates a framework the larger community-based membership can step into.

Of course, it is important the core group refrain from dotting every *i* and crossing every *t* or the general membership will not feel a sense of involvement. People are more likely to join a community organization that is, to some degree, a work in progress and not a finished product. This way, they can provide input for some of the decisions and feel a sense of ownership in the cause or problem.

The membership may comprise some very qualified individuals who are not in the core group but could step in and chair committees and handle other important functions. By not having everything completely in place prior to opening the doors to the community, you leave a little room for new members to get involved and, more significantly, present ideas that might work and generate a sense of excitement within both your organization and the population you are serving.

The Community Meetings

With your core group established, you can move on to the next phase, setting up a time and place for larger community meetings. Begin by finding a hall or auditorium to accommodate a larger group. Look at schools, churches, libraries, or community centers that have facilities available so you will not have to rent. In addition, ask your core group for donations for refreshments, or promise signage and promotion to a local bakery or coffee shop in exchange for some freebies. Remember, it's always advantageous to spread the word about the new community group to local merchants— some might want to get involved.

Making Things Happen

While some community organizations are multipurpose and deal with a number of community issues, many are formed around one central issue. For example, there may be a need to address increased drug use by teens. Such focused organizations do not need to seek out issues because they already have a pressing one. It is, however, still necessary to research the issue.

Your initial neighborhood concerns may also be the springboard for future, larger-scale projects. Start small, get people on board, and build your group's enthusiasm through incremental successes. As you establish a track record, you'll be able to tackle larger community issues. Gathering a consensus regarding the problems in your community will help you identify the issues of greatest concern. Conduct polls or surveys if necessary.

First Steps

Once you identify the issues, start seeking constructive, realistic solutions. If, for example, you determine a problem challenging the neighborhood is the lack of places for young children to play, then your goal might be to build a small park or community playground. You'll have to determine where it could be built, how much it would cost, who would build it, and how long it would take.

FACT

Conduct surveys to determine where your community interests lie. Discover the issues the public wants to tackle by distributing and collecting well-placed, easy-to-complete surveys about community concerns. If you already have a substantial database of e-mail addresses, send an e-mail blast with a link to an online poll for additional feedback.

Evaluating Potential Partners

Some organizations may already have the ear of philanthropists and partner with them to bring about positive social change. Venture philanthropists look for promising nonprofits and typically offer funding as well as financial and management guidance. For instance, Venture Philanthropy Partners in Washington, D.C., supports organizations that provide opportunities to low-income children in the region. Venture philanthropy may be the next wave in charitable giving.

Those who do not partner with a venture philanthropist must determine where the funds will come from. If fundraising is your answer, it is necessary to create a plan and, as discussed in Chapter 2, determine what methods of fundraising would be most effective. If your town, like Greensburg, Indiana, has a large corporate presence (Honda), you might go to the obvious source for a grant or donation. Know your community and the available donors and resources. In most instances, research several key sources, including merchants, residents, and the local government. Start by looking for funding from the local community, for example.

Groups can use fundraising activities to reach out and communicate with the neighborhood to make changes. Community groups and neighborhood associations publish neighborhood newsletters, organize events, and implement neighborhood improvement projects.

Working with Your Community Board

A community board is generally made up of volunteers who represent and look out for the best interests of the community at large. The members of such boards typically represent a cross section of the community's population. The board holds meetings to discuss pertinent issues. It follows set rules and procedures but is usually required to provide an open forum for the public to participate at meetings, discussions, and/ or hearings.

Involving a community board is one step in the process of building awareness of a community issue that needs to be addressed. Do your homework before approaching the community board so that you know exactly how to request its help or support.

Before you can raise money for a community issue, try to get the local governing board on your side. If you need board approval for a project or program, help its members get to know your group by bringing several people from your organization along when presenting your plans. Designate one person as the speaker and make sure he assembles a concise but effective presentation backed up with supporting facts and figures.

If, for example, your group has gathered to discuss the building of a library and you are ready and willing to do fundraising toward that goal, address the need for a library, the most suitable location (and why), and your plans for raising the necessary funds.

ALERT!

Watch for conflicts of interest when dealing with a community board. If you have members who sit on the community board and the board of your organization, they may need to dismiss themselves from taking a vote on such issues. Other people may not sit on both boards but may have ulterior motives, which are sometimes political. Full disclosure of any potential conflict is advised to minimize the risk of future problems.

Finding Local Sponsors

One way of benefiting the neighborhood might include cosponsorship of activities with local merchants and institutions. Perhaps the clothing drive can be run from the front lobby of the library or the candy sale can take place in the local mall. Community banks are often happy to sponsor an activity that supports local artists. Retailers may team with you to provide space and resources, and your promotion will help them attract more business. The advertising and promotion done by such local sponsors can also help ensure a good turnout. You can use these relationships as both a networking opportunity and a way to get in-kind donations.

By getting different sponsors on board, you can help cover the costs of your event. For additional support, contact your local chamber of commerce, business improvement district, block association, or other local merchant groups. After one strong pitch to the chamber of commerce, it can then reach out to all of its members, which is more efficient than talking to a couple of dozen merchants individually. Once a few local retailers get on board, others will also want to be included, creating a snowball effect, particularly if a major store has agreed to be a sponsor.

There are also situations in which a major store or local business may donate money to, or sponsor the activities of, local nonprofit organizations. This keeps the business highly visible in the community and is an excellent means of public relations. By spreading the word about your work and letting everyone know you have plans that are significant within the community, yours can become such an organization on their list. For example, in 2007 Whole Foods made nearly $15 million in charitable donations, supporting causes that bolstered communities and the environment.

Selecting the right fundraising activities goes a long way. Often, athons are a great way to draw community interest and utilize local businesses. For example, a bikeathon can be sponsored by a local bike shop and draw people to the downtown area on a Sunday, a boost for area store owners. A bowlathon or aerobicsathon might include sponsorship from a bowling alley or fitness center.

Local associations are generally a good place to seek funding because they represent a segment of the community. You can also look for foundations that are dedicated to providing funding for community needs and request a donation or apply for a grant.

Neighborhood banking institutions, including local branches of major-name commercial banks, often pledge to return a portion of their profits to help the communities in which they are located. You might turn to a local branch manager or other bank officer to inquire about funding options. See what type of program they have and ask for an application.

Many major retail and fast food chains such as the Gap or McDonald's are also places to turn. The manager of a local franchise can often tell you how the corporation handles donations and how to apply for grants. The Foundation Center can help you find local sources as well.

Laws and Ordinances

One of the areas of concern when planning local community-based fundraisers is making sure you know what you can and cannot do. Local laws and ordinances vary tremendously from county to county. Some are not well known, but may be enforced.

It is your responsibility to check with the county clerk's office, city hall, or any city permit offices to make sure you have all necessary licenses or permits. Permits may be required for:

- The sale of liquor, including wine or beer
- The sale of raffle tickets
- Bingo or other games of chance
- The use of rides or amusement park activities
- Soliciting of any kind

Depending on where you are holding your fundraiser, you may need additional permits. Give yourself adequate time to apply for and receive such permits. There may be a wait of several weeks or, in larger cities, even a few months before you receive the required licensing. In addition, find out how long the permit is good and if you will need to reapply if a similar fundraiser is held in six weeks, six months, or a year.

FACT

In some cases, the sale of food and beverages requires a permit from the local board of health, unless you are working with an established food provider (a caterer or restaurant) who already has the necessary permit. In other situations, you are required to use a specific vendor who is under contract to the facility you have selected.

On a broader scale, be sure to follow the latest state laws. For example, at the time of this writing, various states are making changes to their privacy laws to protect the identity of donors. In another example, states are changing laws that ease the restrictions for nonprofits in spending endowment money. One way to stay current with state and federal laws is to regularly check the website for the Association of Fundraising Professionals, at *www .afpnet.org*. Also check with legal and accounting professionals who are well versed in all areas of nonprofit organizations.

Promoting Locally

Local PR is important in promoting a community fundraiser, and good planning can result in effective media coverage. For example, the Roadrunner Food Bank of New Mexico holds an annual Souper Bowl the week before Super Bowl Sunday. Created to help stamp out hunger, the event takes place in the food bank's Albuquerque warehouse where thirty-five local chefs create and serve their best soups for the public and judges. The best chefs are awarded various prizes, and the top chef wins the Souper Bowl Championship title. To end the event on a sweet note, chefs also provide dessert. The food bank's PR push included press releases and website content that led to numerous write-ups in local papers, enabling it to attract sponsors and sell tickets. The PR push helped the food bank raise an all-time high of $70,000 in 2008. Meanwhile, the Souper Bowl concept is gaining momentum across the country, with reports of similar events taking place in Massachusetts and New York.

Postevent coverage is important. Reading about the event you attended a few days or even a few weeks ago leaves people feeling good about their participation. They feel they were part of something newsworthy, and they look forward to attending next year. Postevent coverage is also positive acknowledgment for those who sponsored your event. Coverage after the event is also important because it goes into the media/sponsor packet for next year's event and can help you when promoting other fundraisers or even soliciting for donations, grants, or sponsorship.

Don't forget to thank media representatives in a quick phone call, e-mail, or hand-written note (always a nice touch) for attending and providing press coverage for your event. It's important to maintain an ongoing relationship with the press and not forget about them once the event is over. You will need them again.

Don't forget the power of the Internet, which can work with other community groups to help you generate buzz. One New York organization e-mails a weekly electronic newsletter to supporters, with a section announcing upcoming events from other nonprofits and links to their websites. This is community building at its very best.

How far in advance should we promote our event?
Give yourself three to five months to promote your fundraiser. This will allow enough lead time for newspapers and magazines to run ads or write articles. It will also allow you to do pre-event public relations.

Becoming Established in the Community

Sometimes it's a slow process for your organization to plant firm roots in a neighborhood. By performing community service and promoting the fact that your organization is working on behalf of the neighborhood, you can establish your presence to a point where people will actually come to you when there is a problem facing the neighborhood.

In the mid 2000s, parents, environmentalists, and health advocates began to voice concern over the safety of athletic fields made of artificial turf, fearing they were exposing children to possible toxins. When one such field was planned in Nyack, New York, opponents found support in Citizens Campaign for the Environment (CCE) in nearby White Plains, which helped them inform the public about the potential exposure to toxins. Starting out as a small group of people in 1985, CCE is now 80,000 members strong, with five offices in New York and one in Connecticut. It has developed a deep presence with a strong voice, which people turn to when fighting to preserve the environment.

Rosedale

Another example of an organization firmly planting its roots in the community comes from Washington, D.C., where $12 million was raised in several months by Cleveland Park neighbors to purchase a six-acre historic estate in their neighborhood named Rosedale.

According to Andrew Hamilton, president of the community organization Friends of Rosedale, there were several tools available and in place by the time the funds were needed. The neighborhood was already organized and engaged in defining itself. Some people say the organization had unofficially begun in the 1950s when the neighbors successfully prevented an expressway from being built through their backyards. The community was clear about its shared values, particularly relating to land use. Several community and government organizations had successfully intervened together on a number of development issues impacting the neighborhood. Active community members amassed an enviable track record by utilizing existing citywide historic preservation and zoning laws to maintain the quality of life in their neighborhoods.

ESSENTIAL

Remember to promote what you have done and keep up your neighborhood profile so people will know they can turn to you for help. The Red Cross does this by keeping its name in the public eye, and when there is a hurricane or another disaster, people immediately know they can turn to the Red Cross for help.

The most recent effort originated to protect three acres of lawn and gardens on the Rosedale Estate, which includes a 1794 farmhouse listed on the National Register of Historic Places. The lawns, garden, and farmhouse were part of a six-acre tract of land that was on the market.

The Friends of Rosedale and the group of neighbors acted together to retain something the community valued. The Rosedale neighbors built trust as they worked to protect a community asset. They informed the community of their objective to preserve the land as open space for public use, showing they were working to benefit the neighborhood. As their struggle progressed, every step was explained to the community and the process created trust in their objectives.

The successful fundraising effort was the end result of building a base of support, dating back some five decades to their successful fight to prevent the expressway from coming through the neighborhood.

Social Networking

Once enjoyed solely by college and high school students, social networking sites such as Facebook and MySpace are enabling nonprofit organizations and their supporters to get the word out about their cause—and as a result, cultivate a new source of donors.

Facebook, for example, offers an application appropriately named "Causes," which enables individuals to champion a nonprofit among the site's more than 65 million members. Individuals can then invite other members to join the cause. Members who join can list themselves as a supporter of the cause on their profile, helping to raise awareness of an issue. Members can also make a secure donation to a charity or political campaign through a credit card. Experts say Facebook's Causes application can help raise the awareness of charitable giving among students. What's more, once interested, members can visit the website of the nonprofit's organization if they want to learn more. That grassroots push also provides the opportunity to engage a new audience and transition them into not just donors, but active participants with a sustained interest in your cause.

ESSENTIAL

Social networking sites that support nonprofits are constantly adding new applications to make their venues more effective and enjoyable for members. Take advantage by posting videos and adding blog updates and testimonials and trying other new features as they become available.

MySpace offers an application called "Impact," where nonprofit organizations and political campaigns can raise funds from donors who contribute using PayPal. Members who support a cause earn badges that are featured on their profile, generating buzz among their MySpace friends and raising awareness and additional funds. As of this writing, nonprofits that want to be listed can contact impact@myspace.com for more information.

As fundraising through social networking increases in popularity, new online opportunities will become available. For instance, Change.org is another online venue dedicated to supporting more than 1 million causes around the world. The site offers the ability to post testimonials, blogs, and videos highlighting the work of each nonprofit and tracking fundraising progress. Karma411.com is another website where users can champion a cause, write a description of why the cause is meaningful to them, and invite friends to donate. Like Change.org, the site includes a feature that demonstrates how much money each cause has raised to date. Karma411.com even measures users' karma based on their philanthropic activity on the site. Social networking sites are gaining traction because users find them entertaining, and they spend time making connections and seeing what other members are doing. The partnership between social networking and philanthropy is just getting started, so keep an eye out for new online possibilities.

Giving Circles

A new trend has emerged in the philanthropy landscape: giving circles. These organized groups of individuals meet regularly and pool their resources to support nonprofits that interest them. This method enables individuals—who are often young and female—to make a bigger difference collectively than they could on their own. And they are making an impact. Research shows that giving circles distribute tens of millions of dollars to causes that participants research and believe are worthwhile. One giving circle in Washington, D.C. donated $60,000 to an organization that mentors girls who live in public housing so they can establish good relationships with adults.

ALERT!

If you want to attract a giving circle, it is important to establish relationships in the community. Networking and public relations will go a long way toward building those important connections. After all, if no one knows about your good work, how can you expect to get noticed by a giving circle?

According to a study by the Association of Fundraising Professionals, members of small giving circles donate anywhere from $50 to $5,000 each. Before distributing the money, they meet to discuss which charities to support. They may also ask prospective charities to complete an application process, which can also include a site visit. Typically, it is the giving circle that seeks out the charity, not the other way around.

If your organization is approached by a giving circle, be prepared to make a presentation about your organization and invite the members in for a tour. This way they can learn more about you and the good work that you do.

Partnering with a giving circle may provide some idiosyncratic challenges, which were highlighted in the AFP study. For instance, rather than working with just one liaison, as one would with the community relations person at a corporate sponsor, you may have to deal with several members of the group. In addition, giving circles do not necessarily fund the same organization every year, due to changing membership and interests. However, they are another possibility to consider and are another example of how visibility in your community can help you raise funds.

CHAPTER 13

Grassroots Fundraising

Even those who are not involved in a nonprofit group or other organized group are often passionate about a cause. Small groups of people can effectively raise funds to help their community in a variety of ways. This chapter addresses the specific needs of these groups of grassroots activists who are simply people trying to help raise money in their neighborhoods.

13

Small-Scale Efforts, Big Results

No, you won't be approaching major corporations, writing up bylaws, or making large-scale plans. You have no plans to elect officers, file for 501(c)(3) status, or even establish yourselves as an ongoing organization. Yours is simply an effort of five concerned friends to raise money to keep the local boys and girls after-school program afloat for the coming year. Your goals are simple—get some money together to help someone in need. You do not want to work with complex budgets, just a basic outlay of funds, if necessary. Nonetheless, planning is key to your success.

Set some basic parameters before you start brainstorming so ideas aren't totally off the mark. For example, you may want to consider your group's limitations—its size or resources—before you start throwing out ideas that sound great but are unrealistic.

Brainstorming

First and foremost, this type of grassroots fundraising requires a meeting of the minds to discuss what you can do as individuals and how you can combine your efforts to maximize results and solve the problem at hand.

Benefits

One way to utilize the collective intelligence and experience of everyone involved is to brainstorm ideas. Businesses and organizations use this method of generating ideas, so why shouldn't you? You benefit by having input from a variety of sources. The person who called the meeting might be considered in charge by default or simple courtesy.

To brainstorm ideas, everyone will need to understand the basic problem or issues. They also need to remember five things in brainstorming:

1. Everyone's opinions and ideas are equal in value.
2. Ideas, not individuals, are to be discussed or criticized.

3. No one should be married to their ideas.
4. It is not a competition to see who provides the best ideas.
5. A simple democratic vote should be available at all times to resolve deadlocks.

While brainstorming works at all levels, it is particularly effective in a small group situation because you can generate a large number of ideas without being overwhelmed. You can then list every idea as it is presented.

Procedures

To begin, write down all ideas on a master list, making sure everyone has had the opportunity to contribute. Then evaluate the logistics and practicality of the plan based on manpower needed, cost, time frame, and so on.

Eliminate ideas as you go, based on logical reasons. If the group is split on whether an idea should be taken off the board, vote on it. You add positive elements to ideas that stay on the board and eliminate ideas that are considered impractical. You then repeat the cycle as many times as you choose until you settle on the best idea.

Because there is no hierarchy in a newly formed group, there is no political agenda and no one should feel too intimidated to participate. It is a process that allows everyone to feel included, appreciated, and valued. In fact, the small, intimate setting is often ideal for stimulating the kinds of discussions that bring out true inspiration. Brainstorming creates an environment to foster raw ideas and mold them into profitable outcomes.

Dividing Responsibilities

Unlike a large organization with committees, a small group will have to throw the various tasks onto the table and see who wants to handle them. Most often, a person will take on the tasks she feels most confident performing. Each person needs to make a personal pledge to do the job because there is no formal structure, no board members, and no bylaws. In this kind of situation, everyone holds each other accountable for the responsibilities they pledge to take on. Failure to do a task can strain relationships and friendships.

If someone does a job as they see fit, everyone should either accept the outcome or politely make suggestions on how to improve it. This can be a touchy area. It is important to make and accept critiques in the spirit of achieving a greater good. Critiques shouldn't undermine another member, or you risk compromising your entire mission. Planning is important, but each person should agree not to make any unilateral decisions.

FACT

While you may turn the money you raise over to a qualified 501(c)(3) charity, you cannot advertise donations are tax deductible because you yourself are not officially a nonprofit organization. Nonetheless, you should provide individuals with a statement of receipt for their records that says you sold them an item or provided a service.

While many tasks will be divided, everyone will be involved in the overall job of raising funds though selling, performing a service, or asking for money. Carefully determine your plan of action and decide where you will each be soliciting funds. If you are soliciting for contributions, you do not want all participants contacting the same people. Similarly, if you are selling candy bars, divide the territory, decide where the group will convene, and who will collect and be responsible for depositing the money.

How Much Should You Do?

A critical aspect of your fundraising efforts is determining the appropriate scope of your efforts. Nonprofit fundraising organizations generally have a system in place for raising money and distributing funds or goods.

Do your responsibilities include raising money to give to the director of a community center who will buy toys, sporting equipment, and books? Or will you raise the money, buy the goods and then donate them to the community center? Determine where your efforts begin and end. Does the storeowner for whom you are raising funds to rebuild after a fire have a staff that will rebuild the facility, or is he in need of money and builders? Can your volunteers help?

The responsibility of handling the money once you raise it is also a major one. You do not have a treasurer in place, so you'll need to appoint someone as the trusted individual who collects the funds. It is also very important that you have confidence that the money you raise will be spent as intended. Therefore, you must pose to the group the following questions:

- Should we give the money to an established nonprofit organization (such as the Red Cross or the Salvation Army) to handle it?
- Do we have a source (such as the director of a senior citizens center) to give the money directly to?
- Should we utilize the funding ourselves to achieve the goal?

In answer to the first question, make sure the nonprofit organization you are giving the money to is in agreement with the funds being used to help the intended cause. If you raise money for library books in the local grade school, you may feel very comfortable handing the money to the PTO with an explanation of how you expect the group to spend this money.

FACT

Following the September 11 terrorist attacks, nonorganizational fundraising pulled together millions of dollars thanks to the efforts of schoolchildren nationwide, who took it upon themselves to raise money or simply ask for contributions. The money was then sent to several major charities spearheading the fundraising efforts.

In government-run agencies, a bureaucratic process may filter funds to certain groups. To circumvent this, you may be able to buy tangible goods and donate them instead of money. For example, a government-run boys and girls club in a small city, affiliated with six other such clubs, couldn't accept monetary donations; all money had to be filtered through the main office. The process was slow and the money was divided among all of the facilities. It was, however, permissible for the director of an individual club to accept donated items. Therefore, a local grassroots fundraising group raised $600 and bought equipment to donate.

In answer to the second question, you need to feel a sense of trust in a person involved in the cause or with the facility you are helping. Often, it is this person who initially came to you with the problem. It is a judgment call—will the individual handle the money responsibly and as you believe he should?

In the third case, you need to make sure you are achieving the goal in the proper manner. In fact, you may need to hire professionals. For example, if the five of you are not skilled in building, you should take the money you raise and hire a builder to repair the store destroyed in the fire rather than trying to do it yourself and doing a poor job. Of course, you can do this only with the permission of the storeowner. Don't try to surprise people with a huge undertaking they weren't expecting.

Maintaining Focus

Usually, a completely grassroots fundraising effort comes about to serve a local and immediate need. Therefore, the time factor is short and the focus remains fairly consistent. However, it is up to at least one person in the group to keep the members focused on why they are getting together, particularly if you will meet several times at private homes and are prone to going off on tangents.

FACT

Hub events are a great choice for grassroots fundraisers. They typically have several methods of raising money. For example, plan a picnic and hold an auction, sell desserts, or play games to bring in funds. Through these various activities, each person contributes a little here and a little there as she enjoys the entire event.

At meetings, allow for socializing and plan for refreshments of some type. Have each person pitch in or volunteer to bring refreshments to the next meeting. Set aside an hour and a half to two hours to talk business, and appoint someone as the leader to enforce this rule and keep the discussion on topic. You may want to assign this task to a different person for each meeting or to one person whom everyone feels comfortable with as the leader. This leader needs to be flexible and take the role as more of a guide to keep the project on track. No leader should make unilateral decisions.

Credibility

Let's face it, anyone can ask you for money and you have no way of knowing if the person asking represents a legitimate charity or organization. The question of credibility is even more important when you have no specific organization to back you up. For this reason, performing a service, such as walking dogs or washing cars, can help convince others to spend their money on your fundraiser, because the contributor receives something for her dollar regardless of what you do with the money. The same holds true for selling items at a garage sale or flea market.

Making Connections

Credibility comes from your standing in the community. If no one in your group has made any particular impact on the community, then you might want to seek out someone who is trusted and respected by the core group of potential donors whom you hope to attract.

QUESTION?

Is there one key element that makes the difference in getting a donor to contribute?
Probably the most significant element is personal appeal. If you build a relationship and talk to people on a personal level, they are more likely to donate even if they are not as passionate about the actual cause as you are. This is because they have gained a sense of trust in you and believe in your dedication to the cause.

Parents of children attending a school in North Carolina launched a grassroots fundraising campaign to help the school after a former employee was caught misappropriating funds. Parents launched an e-mail campaign and within days raised $30,000 to help the school meet its payroll. The effort gained further momentum by generating positive press coverage. Local celebrities, community members, merchants, or political figures can be drawn into what you are working on and are often interested in the new grassroots group.

Some grassroots groups raise their credibility by individual associations within the community, which might be with a school, religious institution, or business. Even though the fundraising effort is separate from the institution, people may see you in a credible light if you hold a respected place in the community. For example, a teacher may have the goal of raising money to help a family in need. His credibility as a teacher will prompt more people to give money. Of course, he needs to obtain permission from the school to take on this outside mission individually. Whenever there is a possibility of a conflict of interest, full disclosure is advisable.

Be Visual

A picture is indeed worth a thousand words when dealing with a pressing issue others are not familiar with. For example, months after the intense media coverage had subsided over Hurricane Katrina activists took photos of mangled rooftops in New Orleans to remind the rest of the country the Big Easy still needed help. Grassroots groups lacking a long track record may need that kind of visual presentation to drive home their point and emphasize the kind of work they are trying to accomplish.

There are plenty of variables affecting success in raising funds. The awareness of your issue is obviously a key factor. If you are raising money to help your community recover from recent storms and tornadoes, people in your community will see your cause all around them. In a case like this, you may not need to prove to them your cause is a worthy one.

Your Secret Weapon: The Warm Fuzzies

It doesn't matter how good you are at selling cookie dough. The biggest reason people are buying your items or services—or simply donating money—is that it's for a good cause. Giving to a friend or neighbor is self-satisfying—especially when they are doing good work.

Why does someone help you when you're struggling to change a flat tire on the highway? In general, people do not sit idly by when others are in need. This phenomenon is what sparks the abundance of fundraising organizations and volunteer groups around today. Still, not everyone you reach out to will be able to commit the time to attend meetings or follow a plan of action. You'll find more than 50 percent perform some kind of activity to help others, beyond donating money through an employee plan at work or writing a check.

No matter how much calculating and profiling an organization may do to find the ideal donor or how much time corporate executives may spend determining how their charitable efforts will best portray their businesses, there is no underestimating the basic power of the warm fuzzies. It is simply giving for no other reason than the sake of giving.

CHAPTER 14

Fundraising with Kids and Teens

Increasingly, fundraising and volunteerism are becoming part of the real-world curriculum shaping America's youth. In conjunction with their schools and religious institutions, young children and teens are joining the fundraising community and finding satisfaction in making an impact. This chapter looks at the role children and families play in fundraising.

Getting Kids Started

Many children today first discover fundraising through the various candy, wrapping paper, and magazine sales drives in their schools. They can also learn about the world of fundraising and volunteering through their parents. Most fundraising projects include tasks that even young children can do.

Teaching the Principles

Children are very receptive to learning about why we raise funds and the need to help others. Books, films, and television shows are filled with simple lessons in which a character struggles with a problem and then figures out how to solve it. So when teaching children about fundraising, the only element you need to introduce is the notion of needing to buy something—hence the requirement for funds.

Sally the sea lion lost her favorite dolly and can't afford a new one. Can we help her get a new dolly? "Where can she get one?" you might ask a young child. At some point, a child will usually respond, "At the store" or "At the toy store." Then you can explain she must pay the storekeeper for it but doesn't have enough money. Because it is hard for a sea lion to get a job, perhaps we could do something to help her earn the money. The basic point is to nudge children gently and encourage them to help. From analogies and play activities at an early age, schoolchildren—usually as early as the first grade—will progress toward understanding real needs and real situations where they will want to help other people.

Helping in Times of Tragedy

The devastation Hurricane Katrina wrought made the need to help people very real, and many children were inspired to get involved in helping others. The images on TV were frightening, and the notion of wanting to do something to help was a healthy way of working through the horrors for children as well as adults.

Kids from every part of the country pitched in and raised money and goods for the victims and rescue crews. In Port Washington, New York, an entire school district embarked on a multiyear campaign to raise funds for a mobile medical unit that would help children and their families when a disaster struck; fundraising efforts included fashion shows, lemonade sales, battle of the band events, and a basketball game between the village's fire and police departments. Garage sales, toy and clothing drives, and many other creative fundraising ideas were not only incorporated into the school calendar that year, but retained their place in community youth groups and other organizations several years after Hurricane Katrina.

Teens and Community Service

Increasingly, teenagers look for opportunities to perform community service. Because many of them want to list community service activities on their applications for college and honor roll societies, their reasons for getting involved may not be entirely altruistic. Still, for the most part, they enjoy the satisfaction of knowing they are doing good work in helping a worthy organization support a cause. This trend can provide a good opportunity to recruit interested volunteers and in the process teach the next generation the importance of fundraising.

QUESTION?

How can I interest teens to participate in my fundraiser?
Spread the word about your event in places where teens congregate. Ask the local school and library if you can post flyers describing your event and your organization on their bulletin boards. Or see if you can place an ad in the school's newspaper or programs. Don't forget to ask your local eateries to post your flyers as well.

In general, the more novel and fun the event, the more likely teens will be to participate. For example, the American Cancer Society organizes annual Relay For Life events, where teams of people gather overnight in places such as parks, schools, or fairgrounds and take turns walking or running laps. These teams recruit sponsors for their participation, and the event typically finishes at dawn. It is the kind of social happening many teens like to experience.

Teaching Kids the Ropes

No, a youngster won't get the gist of a grant proposal, but she will understand the idea that raising money means having a good product or service to entice people into giving a donation.

Get your children involved by working together as a group in order to come up with and implement an effective plan for raising funds. Show them encouragement by emphasizing the fun aspect of FUNdraising.

Children can learn teamwork and responsibility by planning and implementing a project in a group setting, and they can have a good time doing so. By showing kids how to divide tasks and involve everyone in the project, they learn how a fundraising project operates. Everyone takes part and holds up his end of the project.

The actual task of asking for money is hard for many adults and, depending on her nature, may be difficult for a child as well. However, kids can make great salespeople. If they are determined to sell a product, they will provide enthusiasm and an honest sales approach. Of course, you will need to remind them they must be polite, accept no for an answer, and write down orders clearly when they make a sale. Too often, schools put children in the awkward position of selling candy, wrapping paper, or some other item without teaching them the responsibilities that go with the job. Flashing an incentive and telling kids to go out and sell teaches them more about competition and less about the meaning of fundraising and responsibility.

Teach children how to make sales presentations to friends, family, and relatives. From a song to a skit, kids can have fun creating their own means of selling a product. If they're having fun, they should need no greater incentive. It is important to remind children that if they are selling to strangers, they should have an adult present or be on school grounds within the assigned location where the activity is taking place. Sometimes schools will combine the fundraising effort with another school activity, such as selling candy for charity at the varsity basketball game or the choir's annual holiday recital.

When a PTA or PTO is planning a fundraising activity that will involve the children, take one afternoon and teach them why they are selling candy and how to keep track of orders.

Among other lessons, fundraising can help children learn the following skills:

- Decision making
- Recordkeeping
- Following instructions carefully
- Managing time

ALERT!

Make sure you have a plan of action for distribution. Some fundraising programs will send the product directly to the buyer, whereas others will send the product to the school. If 500 rolls of wrapping paper are going to show up soon at your school, make sure you have a place to put them and an easy means of distributing them to students.

A vast number of schools are adding community service to their curriculums. Fundraising is an aspect of public service and volunteering. There are, however, differences that need to be taught. Community service in the form of helping people in need by reading to the blind or visiting children in a hospital are valuable lessons at any age. Fundraising, however, is stepping away from the actual people in need. It requires the added step of approaching others to say, "Let's help them" or "Let's do something to make a change in the neighborhood." Children need to be taught to volunteer to help others directly and raise money to help through funding community programs and other initiatives.

There are also school-based lessons in subjects such as math that come from fundraising activities. Teachers in many schools incorporate a number of lesson plans into their fundraising. For example, students learn to tally daily and weekly sales totals and multiply the number of items sold by a dollar amount to get a total amount of profit. Students in higher grades can learn what percentages of people are buying items, and they can use the concepts of mean, median, and average in real situations. Weight and other measurement skills can also be taught by hands-on examples of selling products.

Kid-Friendly Possibilities

Among the many possibilities for fundraising with kids, in schools or with other organizations, are:

- Auctions—silent, traditional, or Chinese style
- Community service, including car washes and dog walking
- Dances, including raves, disco nights, barn dances, and retro nights
- Fairs, carnivals, bazaars, picnics, or barbecues
- Cookbooks compiled by students, teachers, and/or people in the community
- Sales of hand-knit items such as scarves, hats, gloves, mittens, and socks
- Competitions such as hot dog eating, dancing, and basketball shooting
- Student-teacher sporting events or school Olympics
- Exhibitions, including photography, art, and crafts
- Bake sales, book sales, and DVD sales
- Garage sales, flea markets, and antiques fairs
- Holiday parties or Easter egg hunts
- Talent shows or karaoke nights

Selecting the activities should be based partly on the suggestions of the kids involved and partly on the practical realities of what the group can do with the finances and resources it has. Parents, teachers, school administrators, or group leaders will need to be involved in making sure the plan is realistic and practical.

The kids should also be involved in selecting the date, location, and other aspects of the overall strategy. It should be up to everyone involved to pitch in and help make the idea a reality. Various plans help spice up fundraising. A carnival in the summer and wrapping paper sales in the fall give children two diverse types of fundraisers—one that presents activities and one that focuses on selling, taking, and fulfilling orders. Introduce new fundraising ideas and try to vary the kind of activities from season to season.

When working with children, it helps to bring back a perennial favorite. Kids look forward to certain activities and can aim for a higher level of success than the previous year. Girl Scout cookie sales are perhaps the most famous example of a fundraising effort that never dies—it's been a tradition since 1917.

FACT

Girl Scout cookies are one of the best-known fundraising products. All revenues earned from cookie sales go directly to the local Girl Scout council, with a portion (roughly 15 percent) going to the individual troop. The cookies' ingredients have changed to meet new health standards, packaging has been updated, and order-tallying methods have been revised, but the tradition has not changed.

Many schools and youth organizations try to maintain some of the same fundraisers from year to year while introducing something new for specific projects that come up during the year. For example, there may be an annual school supply and bake sale every spring at the parent-teacher conference to raise money for the elementary school. However, a sudden one-time need to build a new playground may be an opportunity to try a new fundraiser. Mix up the old and the new.

You may find that using similar fundraising approaches to introduce new projects is helpful from a learning perspective. For example, a first-time holiday plant drive might use the same tally forms and order-taking system as the annual candy drive.

School Fundraisers

Grade schools, middle schools, and high schools coast to coast have fundraisers involving their students. Hurricanes, floods, and other natural disasters have brought schoolchildren together in an effort to help their communities.

However, schools also have a need to raise money for their own purposes. The PTA or PTO will initiate projects that are parent-run, student-run, or a combination of the two.

FACT

The difference between PTA and PTO is national versus local. There is a national PTA, and school organizations that belong to it pay dues to the national organization. A PTO is an independent group formed in a single school or representing a few schools in a single community. Home School Associations (HAS) and Parent Communication Councils (PCCs) are part of the PTO.

Schoolchildren today raise more than $1.7 billion by selling items to friends, family, and neighbors. On average, an organization supporting a school can raise $2,500 through a product fundraiser, and some groups raise as much as $10,000 per fundraiser. Research shows that nine out of ten parents of school-age children support these fundraisers. Many will buy to support their own children or children of colleagues, relatives, or friends. The best way to get kids involved in social action is to engage them. For this reason, it is important to come up with venues that will entice kids, particularly teens.

Teachers and a parent activist at one high school teamed up to run Fi(red) Up for Fashion, a charity fashion show that raised $5,000 for the Global Fund, an organization that provides resources to fight AIDS, HIV, tuberculosis, and malaria in Africa. Teams of students and teachers (and their young children) signed up for the chance to participate in fashion shows. Local boutiques donated outfits and a local television sportscaster gave his time as the evening's master of ceremonies, giving the show press coverage, not to mention a professional edge. The event also featured food and live music from the school's musicians. Students had the chance to have fun, support a cause, and learn about fundraising through the event.

Selecting a Fundraising Company

There are more than 1,200 companies in the United States and Canada that are set up to help schools organize fundraising events. They sell items in bulk and provide order forms and other tools of the trade. Some offer incentive programs, and others provide fundraising advice.

How do you select the right fundraising company to work with? First, remember it is not necessary to work with a fundraising company. You can have a successful flea market if you ask students and their families to contribute items for sale. Nonetheless, if you choose to rely on a fundraising supplier, you can find tons of them on the Internet or by looking in a business directory at your local library.

FACT

The Association of Fundraising Distributors and Suppliers is an international association with more than 650 member companies that manufacture, supply, and/or distribute products that will be resold by nonprofit organizations. Member companies must conduct business on a professional level and adhere to a code of standards and ethics.

References

Whenever you commit yourself to an outside vendor or company, you should always get references. The last thing you want to do is get involved with an outside vendor who shortchanges you and puts your group in the uncomfortable position of having to defend yourself to your supporters. To avoid such a scenario, start off on the right foot. Ask the company for references and call them or contact other PTOs or nonprofit organizations and ask what companies they've used and been satisfied with. Make sure to ask the following questions:

- Did the company deliver on all of its promises and meet all of your expectations?
- Did you have a good relationship with the company representative? Did the representative take an interest in your organization's needs and was he helpful in answering questions or solving problems?
- Did the company tailor the program to meet your needs, or was it a boilerplate program?

Percentages

Find out how much of a percentage the company takes and how promptly the merchandise will be delivered. Inquire about the quality and condition of the merchandise. Keep in mind that just because one company may give you a greater percentage of the money raised, it does not mean it is the best company for your fundraiser. If the material is not delivered on time or if there are complaints about the quality of the product, you could wind up with a worse deal by taking the higher percentage. The most important information for your purposes is the reliability, financial stability, and reputation of the company.

Services

You will also want to find out what services are provided. Does the company help with tallying or meeting specific orders? Ask how it handles sales tax laws. Inquire about its return policy, and find out how long it has been in business. Also, inquire how the products are shipped. Does the company fill each individual order or deliver one huge order to your front door? It makes a big difference. You'll have a lot more work to do if you need to divide boxes of cookies or rolls of paper.

Look for a company that is easily reachable, preferably by phone as well as e-mail. If you find a company on the Internet, look for an address and phone number. This allows you to check on the status of the company with the Better Business Bureau (look for any complaints) and provides multiple ways of reaching them. This is becoming a general rule of thumb, as fewer people are doing business with Internet companies that provide no address or phone number for checking their business status.

Licensing

You can, and probably should, check to see that a fundraising company is a licensed business in the area where it claims to be located. Don't forget, someone with 500 candy bars in his basement can build a nice website and try to pawn them off on you even if they are stale. Again, look for an affiliation with the Association of Fund-Raising Distributors and Supplies (AFRDS) and double-check that the company is a member.

Good fundraising distributors and suppliers know most schools will do annual or semiannual fundraising campaigns and would be eager for you to turn to them again and again for your fundraising needs. They will do what they can to win your business and keep you coming back year after year.

FACT

One common complaint about working with fundraising companies or vendors is surprise costs. Inquire about all possible costs when working with a fundraising company. You don't want hidden costs for freight, prizes, tally sheets, or anything else to cut into your anticipated profits. Get everything in writing to avoid such surprises.

The Products

Look over the company's selection of products carefully and see if it has something your group is interested in selling. Besides wrapping paper and candy, other popular sales items include cookie dough, candles, cheesecake, scratch cards, and holiday decorations. Magazine subscription drives are also very popular.

Look at the age of the sellers and the target audience and determine what item is best for your group. For example, young children may not understand how scratch cards work and will be more enthusiastic about selling candy, since they can endorse the product with great enthusiasm. Just make sure they don't eat into your profits—literally.

Along with having the right products for your sales force and your neighborhood, you want to get a feel for what other schools are doing in your area. Some neighborhoods are besieged by schools selling magazine subscriptions or wrapping paper, and people can only buy so much.

It is also important to make sure order forms and tallying are kid-friendly so the kids can handle their own paperwork. While parents may want to check the math and make sure orders are filled and money is handed in properly, the children should play a significant role in all aspects of the fundraising process.

QUESTION?

How will I know what the products are really like if I've only seen them on the company's website?
Ask for a product sample kit, some sample product, or at least a copy of the catalog from which people will be ordering. Don't just take the company's word for it—get more information on each product before you sell it.

Rewarding a Job Well Done

Incentives are nice if they are kept small. Announcing the names of all of the helpers on the project and having them come onstage at an assembly is an easy way to show gratitude. Getting the school newspaper to write about the volunteers or publishing a small article in the neighborhood paper does wonders for morale and self-satisfaction. It can also inspire others to get involved in future events. The bottom line is that children will feel good about fundraising and will embrace the meaning of what it is all about if they feel appreciated.

In addition, you should show children the fruits of their efforts. For example, if the funding was used to clean up the neighborhood, take a tour of the neighborhood before and after the project to show the difference. Sometimes a newspaper or magazine article about their efforts will be sufficient. It creates a more realistic understanding of what fundraising is all about when children can see the results.

The same holds true for the parents and teachers who took part in the hard work. Let them feel appreciated. While the reason for fundraising is to help others, everyone likes the pat on the back, hearing the words "thank you," and seeing the fruits of her labor.

ALERT!

Be careful with incentives for children. While you want to motivate them to sell, you don't want them to lose the valuable lesson that comes from selling to help raise money for a good cause. Keep incentives small enough to avoid making it seem like a competition but interesting enough to encourage kids to sell more. Have many prizes so that many—or all—of the children feel rewarded.

CHAPTER 15

Political Fundraising

Anyone running for political office knows it takes a strong campaign to make a successful run for office, and now more than ever it takes money to campaign. With Internet strategies enabling candidates to rake in big bucks in a matter of hours, a strong online presence is crucial. This chapter looks at some of the online and other basic how-to's from a practical and process-driven approach.

The Campaign Fundraising Plan

Because the candidate who spends the most money often wins the election, it is not surprising that candidates invest so much of their time fundraising. They must spend time in their campaign rallying support in their quest to ultimately secure votes. For this reason, they must put together a detailed plan for fundraising prior to announcing their candidacy for office.

A campaign fundraising plan, not unlike other fundraising plans, should include the amount of money that must be raised, the time frame in which the money is needed, and how the funds will be used. The plan should also include the manner(s) in which the funds will be raised.

One common means of campaign fundraising is a kickoff dinner or party to launch the campaign. This should be prepared prior to the campaign announcement and included in the initial plan of action. It is a way of gathering initial support for the candidate. The launch party should include:

- All of the people who endorsed the candidate
- The candidate's family and friends
- People from the local business community
- Local politicians

In addition to kicking off the campaign, the launch party will help raise some initial funding.

Various Approaches

It is nowhere more evident than in political fundraising that there is a need for different kinds of fundraising activities. A politician is seeking a cross section of voters and will need to reach this diverse audience with a fundraising plan that covers a broad range of interests and reaches supporters at various financial levels.

Big-ticket-only dinner parties at $500 a plate are not likely to attract the nine-to-five working crowd. Therefore, small-ticket fundraisers, such as a picnic for $25 per family, will bring in another realm of constituents. Online donations can make small contributions add up very quickly. While the majority of funding may still come from a minority of people, a campaign needs a majority of people to get out and vote in favor of the candidate.

Therefore, fundraising and campaigning go hand in hand. Events will bring in money while selling the politician's platform.

In addition, a politician will need to plan fundraisers that draw a multicultural audience, which creates a wider diversity of supporters and garners votes from various ethnic groups.

ALERT!

Stay in close contact with the media—they can make or break an election. The public relations team will be in charge of handling inevitable media snafus, but you can utilize positive media stories to your advantage. Play up all positive stories by posting them on a website, and use them to help generate funds.

Political fundraising includes e-mails, phone solicitation, special events, and direct mail. However, because the goal is to raise money *and* generate votes, the approach is slightly different than fundraising for other causes. Unlike ongoing nonprofit groups that may be wooing major donors over the course of years or waiting for months for a grant proposal to be accepted, supporters need to get onboard in a short time frame, and donations need to come in quickly. Among the many tools commonly used in political fundraising are:

- The fundraising letter
- The house party
- Personal appearances
- E-mail campaigns
- Big-name support

You'll read more about these tools later in this chapter.

Establishing a Finance Committee

The fundraising plan for a campaign is usually the work of the campaign manager, the candidate, and the staff they have assembled. A finance committee, however, is made up of a group of supporters who work hard to find donors. Each member of the committee is expected to support the candidate with his own contribution and then turn to his contacts and connections to get other donors. Such committees often include people who are prominent in the community. This committee helps build the donor base and works in conjunction with the campaign staffers to build a donor list.

The Donor List

Most fundraising efforts need to utilize a list of potential donors. Political fundraising is no exception. Whether you intend to raise money from events, direct mail, personal solicitation, e-mails, or a combination of all four, a list of potential givers is always necessary. In all fundraising efforts, you need to have that core group of givers who will be motivated by your message. Your list for upcoming mailings should begin with party supporters. You can start by contacting other politicians in your party and getting hold of their lists of contributors and/or volunteers who worked on their campaigns. You can also get a list of local party delegates and contact them.

Candidates who are independently wealthy have an advantage because they are not as reliant on fundraising as their less affluent opponents. Combating the multimillionaire candidate is sometimes a matter of pointing out the fact that your candidate is financed by the people. Use the concept of working hard to raise funds as a campaign point.

Finding a Receptive Audience

In addition, you'll find Democratic and Republican organizations as well as other groups that support your campaign. A third-party or independent candidate may need to rely more heavily on such nonparty lists from like-minded supporters of specific causes. For example, an independent candidate supporting many environmental issues may cull names for her mailing list from local environmental groups. Similarly, a candidate that supports the Family Leave Act and universal health care would likely get support from the Working Families Party.

Depending on the size of the town or city, you can use research and demographic data to determine where party pockets are located. There are generally areas within a city that vote for a certain party. Don't make assumptions. Look at previous data and get a feel for which areas are already leaning in your direction.

Working the Donor List

Political campaigns are both ongoing and time sensitive. Therefore, contacting names on the donor list at key times during the campaign is usually part of the plan. While a major donor giving a lump sum of thousands of dollars may be maxed out in terms of how much he can give by law, smaller donors can pitch in as the campaign builds. Therefore, a push for funding when the campaign kicks off is only one of the times to tap donors. This is where the initial enthusiasm is high and the initial platform is first revealed. Backers are gung ho and ready to talk about their candidate to whoever will listen. The first wave of funding should come from the initial campaign launch party and the first pitch to the donors.

FACT

Knowing where the money is centered in your town or region and understanding the party demographics are keys to making the most of your fundraising efforts. New York is the strongest magnet for politicians. In 2004, 2,899 people living in Manhattan gave more than $5 million to Democrats, while 575 people gave in excess of $1 million to Republicans.

Once the early numbers are in and the campaign gains some steam, you may want to tap your donors again as you reach the midpoint of the campaign. Now you can show the candidate has gained momentum and generated attention. She should have answered some tough questions and established her name around the community.

The third and final time to tap into your donors is when the campaign is nearing the homestretch and the candidate is making a serious bid. The pitch now is that with the last-ditch fundraising, she can get over the final hurdle and win.

It's also worth mentioning that the candidate, no matter how much he dislikes seeking out campaign funding (and many politicians do not like this part of the job), should tap into the major contributors personally. The candidate should talk directly to the people with the money in his region.

ESSENTIAL

Keep donors informed. A regular newsletter, e-mail, or a mailing of some type to supporters should keep them informed of how the campaign is going. The more engaged donors feel with the process, the more likely they will be to donate again.

Don't Ignore the Smaller Donations

Minor donors can be very valuable to your efforts because they can give money at different times in the campaign. This is important because you will need continuous funding throughout the campaign. It takes strong budget-management skills to handle the budget for a political campaign, because the size and scope of the campaign will grow as it picks up steam, and funding is needed at each turn. The initial 200 people who came to the kickoff party may be more than 2,000 by the time the election approaches. It is an ongoing process.

Legal Issues

Campaign funding has become a very hotly debated issue. Therefore, contributions to political campaigns are watched closely.

The federal government, all states, and even most counties and towns have their own laws regarding campaign financing. These laws detail who can contribute, how much they can contribute, what the money must be spent on, and how contributions and expenditures need to be reported.

Before the campaign gets started, it is imperative that everyone involved in fundraising efforts understands the laws and regulations that will affect the campaign. You can be sure your opponents will immediately jump on any missteps you make.

ALERT!

If you have someone with a legal background involved as a volunteer or supporter in any manner, this may be the person to ask about following up on such laws. It is important to appoint at least one person to check and make sure each aspect of fundraising follows the letter of the law.

In 2002, a new set of campaign finance laws, the Bipartisan Campaign Reform Act, was enacted. National political parties cannot use soft money to run campaigns. Soft money is the term used to describe contributions that are not regulated by federal election laws. The original exemption was made to encourage party-building activities, which benefit the political parties in general but not specific candidates. The money was supposed to be used for political activities to support the party platforms, from bumper stickers to ads encouraging more people to vote. The result, however, allowed very wealthy donors (who could only contribute a limited amount to a single campaign) to contribute heavily to a party, and the money would then filter into high-tech office equipment and other means of helping a specific candidate. Parties also used it to back candidates in key states during the midterm year elections.

Unlimited contributions to the national political parties are no longer allowed. In addition, contributions from corporate or union treasuries are outlawed in federal elections. This will have a major effect on the financing of the Democratic and Republican parties. The contribution limits for individuals giving to federal candidates and political parties were also increased. Individuals can now give $2,300 (up from $2,000 when the law was first enacted) to a candidate for an election, which is more than twice the previous limit under the old law.

The Internet

Without question, the Internet plays a tremendous role in political campaigns and fundraising. Never before have advocates been able to mobilize their efforts, build communities of like-minded thinkers, and solicit donors. Some even say online fundraising is so empowering, it allows candidates to campaign across wider territories.

Studies show that in 2007, presidential candidates raised nearly $552 million, more than double the amount candidates raised in 2003 gearing up for the 2004 presidential election. Candidates were able to boost their fundraising efforts largely because of the Internet. Small contributions garnered through Internet fundraising made up 22 percent of all individual fundraising in 2003. The number jumped to 26 percent in 2007.

Of course, Internet fundraising benefited some candidates more than others. Ron Paul in 2007 and Howard Dean in 2003 were Internet stars, yet neither of them were able to win enough delegates to secure their party's nomination. How effective can one be with Internet fundraising? Ron Paul reportedly earned $6 million in one day in 2007, while Barack Obama raised $28 million in one month.

A report from the Pew Internet & American Life Project found that in 2008, 42 percent of people eighteen to twenty-nine learned about the issues in the presidential campaign on social networking sites, up from 20 percent in 2004. Through their websites, politicians can collect e-mail addresses and update their supporters with nuances of their campaign, asking for solicitations at key moments to inspire others to help them meet their fundraising goals.

Political groups also use websites to generate support around candidates or raise money for political ads in quick response to the ever-changing political landscape. Through e-mail, grassroots organizations can organize supporters to throw house parties or start rallies to get a message across. As experts continue to marry data with technology, the power of online campaigning and fundraising will only get stronger.

Take advantage of online sites such as MySpace and Facebook. Design a website and make it easy for supporters to provide their contact information and make one-time or recurring donations online with a credit card. Post important announcements and video clips of key speeches. Include a blog. These online tools help candidates build a strong following.

The Fundraising Letter

One of the most important tools of your campaign fundraising activities is a good fundraising letter. The candidate should be ready to reach out to all those whom she knows, from friends and neighbors to doctors and store owners.

Party politics aside, people are often drawn into supporting someone they actually know. The candidate needs to tap into as many individuals as he can, and a letter is a strong way of starting the process. Your letter should explain why the candidate is running, what he hopes to do if elected, how much money is required for an effective campaign, how the money will be spent, and how soon it is needed. Finally, two or three suggested donation amounts should be provided.

The letter should be heartfelt, sincere, and to the point—a couple of pages with short paragraphs that are reader-friendly. A personalized letter will be better received, and it is even recommended to use live stamps instead of a printed indicia. This is not the place to go into details about political reforms, only to generate interest and give people a broad overview of the campaign.

The letter should be accompanied by a self-addressed stamped envelope. The return address can be that of the candidate or the person sending out the letters on behalf of the candidate. Keep it personal. Not unlike a wedding invitation, someone should hand address the outside envelopes (unless the candidate is running for office in a major city) and include a reply card to return in the envelope.

It is important to seek money as early as possible. In politics, most vendors, including printers, will want money up front because of the volatile nature of political campaigns. Campaigns end abruptly if a candidate drops out or runs out of money. If you are planning to do mailings to get the vote, be sure to get the funding before approaching the printer.

The House Party

The banquet dinner is commonly thought of as a way to attract major donors and raise big money for a campaign. However, house parties are smaller and more easily manageable at the community level. These are simply get-togethers in the home of a supporter to help generate some much-needed cash. Weekday evenings are often the best times to hold a simple reception, but a weekend gathering may also work. The determination will be based on the makeup of the guest list and the availability of the candidate, who should certainly be present.

Generally, a committee helps make the arrangements for a house party. Someone needs to open her home to such an event. It is best if this is someone who is centrally located and has the space to host the party. It is important to print and send out professional-looking invitations. Include directions to the party, a reply card, and the host's return address. Or, send out an e-mail inviting supporters to sign up online if they want to attend or even host a house party in their community.

You should request various levels of support so you fulfill the objective of such a party—raising funds. The candidate should make an appearance and speak to the gathering briefly. He should mingle and shake hands with as many guests as possible. In larger towns or cities, such house parties may become impractical, so receptions move into larger venues. The principal idea is the same, but the scale is much larger.

FACT

Signs, stickers, banners, and bumper stickers are all part of the political campaign. Use funds early on to get these basic sources of promotion printed before you launch the campaign. Lawn signs are popular and should be present outside a house party and in supportive neighborhoods. Have plenty of items with the candidate's name on them ready to distribute to supporters.

Personal Appearances

Campaigning requires a lot of personal appearances, which gives you extra routes for obtaining funding. Supporters of the candidate should set up a means of donating money to the campaign wherever possible and allowable by law. The trick in these situations is not to detract from the quest for votes. Campaign staffers do not want to draw attention away from the candidate, but they do need to be taking contributions.

A personal appearance schedule for a candidate can be rigorous, especially in a larger town or a city. She needs to be focused on making a positive impression and gathering votes. If nothing else, each visit can help promote an upcoming fundraising event that will be open to the audience in attendance.

Big-Name Support

Perhaps the biggest fundraising tool of all is support by the right people. In politics, having significant party members on your side for campaigning and fundraising is extremely helpful. It lends credibility to the candidate and links him with a party member who has garnered the support of the constituents.

Celebrities, whether local or national, are also a big plus at fundraising events for politicians. Politicians or celebrities can make speeches on behalf of the candidate, shake hands, sign autographs, or simply smile and make their presence felt. The bottom line is that they are endorsing the candidate, and you can use this to raise funds.

However, don't let the celebrity or well-known politician take the spotlight away from the candidate. If the candidate is overshadowed, people may give money because they are caught up in the frenzy of support. However, the donors may be less enthusiastic the next time around when the well-known politician or celebrity is not present. The focus needs to remain on the candidate.

Image Is Everything

In politics, image is almost everything. Yes, it helps to have a good platform, but image is still the key ingredient for voters who often have little time to fully digest the issues. Image building, ripe with consultants and the right photo ops, requires funding, and this is also part of the fundraising package. The candidate needs to project the right image to ascertain funding, and then turn around and use such funding to improve on that image and promote the platform.

Fundraising efforts need to focus on a cost-effective means of image building in conjunction with the ongoing campaign. In addition, public relations and the flip side of image building, damage control, are key parts of the fundraising plan. It's more than bumper stickers, lawn signs, and rallies; fundraising also lends itself to hiring the right political publicists.

CHAPTER 16

Odds and Ends

Whether your fundraising campaign is large or small, you will find there are plenty of little details associated with the success of the project. Some are tangible, such as ordering nametags, and others are learning experiences, such as honing your skills in asking for and collecting money. This chapter covers all of those particulars—and then some.

The Art of Collecting Money

Almost anything you read about fundraising emphasizes one key point: You have to ask for money. It is unlikely that donors will simply give unless they have a personal reason and seek you out. Therefore, you must ask for a donation, and asking for money is not easy for most people. In addition, fundraising adds a new wrinkle; you may have to ask for payment of money that has already been pledged.

There is an art to asking for money. It starts with the firm belief in your cause—the very reason you are asking. The words get stuck in your throat if you don't honestly believe people should give their hard-earned money for your cause. If you are willing to put your own money in, then you will feel it is easier to ask others to do the same.

Practice your approach, and if you're reading from a script for phone solicitation, work on the inflection and the timing and try to sound as confident as possible. Sometimes it helps to role-play with someone you trust so you can become more comfortable presenting the information to another person.

If you are trying to collect money from friends and the situation is awkward, keep the discussion on the organization. While you want them to know you are a member, you can always approach from the organizational point of view, saying, "They are collecting" or "We are collecting" as opposed to "I am collecting." This kind of phrasing is accurate, because it is the organization conducting the fundraiser, and it takes the attention and awkwardness away from you personally asking someone you know for money.

Owed Money

Requesting money and actually collecting it can be two different animals. You may need to contact people who have pledged money and gently remind them you are required to hand in the funds and you haven't yet received their payment. If people continue to owe you money, you can politely become more persistent with reminders. However, you should also realize they may be unable to pay or may have pledged money they only thought they could afford to pay. In this case, you should assume the money is not forthcoming and just let it go.

You should treat collecting money for your fundraiser as you would treat any business. However, because you cannot hold people responsible for a promise, be reasonable when ascertaining whether a collection seems attainable. You don't want to waste time chasing down a $50 donation when you could just as easily find other contributors.

Auction Prizes

Many people find it hard to ask for auction prizes or sponsorship of activities for their fundraising event. The easy way to get the ball rolling is to start by sending an e-mail or letter (this can work for all fundraising activities). This way, the person you are asking has a point of reference, and you don't have to start from the beginning.

The conversation can be structured around the auction or similar activity, and you can include some of the other prizes you have received or suggestions of the kinds of prizes you are hoping to get. The more you already have, the easier it may be to get more people on board. After all, people get inspired when they see how others are contributing, and they don't necessarily want to be the first one to step up to the plate. You might ask for a donation without specifying a specific item. That allows the individual to think of the price level at which she wants to donate, and provides an opportunity for her to be creative. For example, rather than a gift certificate to a food boutique, the owner might surprise you with a fabulous basket of goodies to auction off.

Ordering from Vendors

Whether it's items to resell or party supplies to make your dinner party a political hit, you need to work professionally with vendors. You should:

- Check to see that a vendor is licensed.
- Get referrals.
- Ask about additional costs above and beyond the product or item, such as shipping and handling.

- Inquire about a return policy if you need to send something back because it is broken or does not work.
- Find out the method(s) of payment in advance.
- Make sure to let vendors know you are a nonprofit organization. You won't have to pay sales tax if you are tax exempt and have your 501(c)(3) letter to prove it.

One of the biggest problems organizations run into is the issue of timing. It's not the vendor's fault if he clearly explains it takes two weeks to ship and you have not given yourself adequate time. You're always better off having things delivered too early than too late, so it is highly advisable to shop around and compare vendors well in advance.

ALERT!

Make sure to see what you're buying. It's too easy to get inferior products. Get a sample, or at least a good picture with the dimensions of the items clearly listed. This way, you are not in for a surprise when the dresses you ordered for young girls turn out to fit American Girl dolls instead.

Also, look for vendor closeouts or seasonal discount rates. For example, one school group took advantage of the week-after-Christmas half-price sale on holiday cards and ordered 500 boxes of cards at the discount rate. In fact, when they explained they were ordering for fundraising purposes, the card manufacturer gave them an additional 20 percent off. This amounted to a 70 percent discount on cards that normally ran about $10 per box. The group stored the cards in the assistant principal's office closet for about nine months, and then sold them as the following holiday season approached. They were able to sell the cards at close to full price, thus making almost $7 per box of cards, roughly $3,500, for the school. Had they ordered the cards a few months in advance, the cards would only have brought them a $3-per-box profit, and they would have made only $1,500.

Shipping

Don't overlook the need to establish how everything will come together to make your fundraiser work. If you are ordering items that must arrive by the date of your fundraiser, make sure to prepare well in advance and have a contingency plan ready in case the items you ordered do not arrive by a certain date.

Shipping costs can add up. When researching vendors or fundraising companies, make sure to inquire about shipping costs and price breaks. Many companies provide free shipping if you order more than x amount of goods. You can also try to negotiate if your need does not meet that magic number.

Printed materials need to be delivered with sufficient time to send out invitations or post signage. You need to establish a calendar specifically detailing the date you will receive what you ordered, a follow-up date, and a last "must have" date, after which time you will no longer accept the delivery because you've spent more money to get a rush order from another printer or company.

It is very important that you provide explicit shipping details. You need to take the following steps:

- Secure in writing exactly what date the items will ship out.
- Secure in writing by what date the items will arrive.
- Provide a shipping address and backup address if necessary.
- Line up someone ready to accept the shipping order(s).
- Get explicit details as to whom you can contact if the order is wrong or late.

Don't rely on someone's good word when the success of all of your hard work depends on that individual delivering the products on time and to the right place. Make a detailed plan and have it in writing.

If you are taking orders for wrapping paper or magazine subscriptions, the orders will either be delivered to one location for you to distribute or sent directly to the individuals who bought them. In the first scenario, make sure you have a central location where someone can receive the shipment, organize it, and store it. Volunteers may say it's fine to deliver to their house because they know they will be home during the day. However, when 800 rolls of wrapping paper show up, these volunteers might wish they had not signed up to receive the goods. Make sure there is some storage space available.

Utilizing all Available Resources

The premise of the play *Six Degrees of Separation* centered on the idea that everyone is connected to each other in some manner by no more than six links. The same theory holds true for resources. Anything you need to locate can probably be found through six connections or less. The trick is making lists of the people you know who might know people who have what you need.

FACT

When reviewing contacts or researching for major donors in any manner, *Who's Who in America* and the *Standard & Poor's Directory* can be valuable resources for finding information on high-profile business donors. You can also utilize software or the library to help locate public records for top executives and CEOs of major corporations.

Making connections is easier than ever with social networking. For example, on LinkedIn (*www.linkedin.com*), a social networking site for professionals, members often peruse the connections of others, and they can even ask for introductions if they see potential for a positive relationship. Members can also pose questions to their connections, asking for assistance in whatever area they see fit. Facebook similarly allows members to ask friends to join causes. The potential for rallying others to pitch in are virtually limitless.

Still, in general, people tend to give up too easily. Remember that your chains of connection can come up with remarkable results; this is something you need to emphasize to your organization. Auctions have brought in celebrities and raised thousands of dollars for schools because one child's father's boss was good friends with a TV celebrity.

As for available resources, there are usually items in the school, church, temple, community center, or homes of your members or volunteers (or their friends or families) that can help make a fundraiser work. It's not necessary to go out and buy or rent everything. The key is to make a scavenger hunt kind of plan and send everyone on a mission to look for what is necessary in advance. Too often groups realize they need supplies at the last second and have no choice but to buy them at retail price, only because no one took the time to make a detailed list well in advance. From paper clips to pickup trucks, if you search for most items, you'll find them.

Successful fundraising organizations report that upward of 75 percent of their resources, including manpower, goods and services, and venues, come from sources within the organization. The most common resource needed from the outside is entertainment.

Mergers and Partnerships

Running any organization can be costly, and it's no different with nonprofits. By the late 2000s, when economists began talking of recession while energy and health care costs continued to spiral upward, many nonprofits looked for ways to pare down expenses. During economic downturns, charities also find that donations tend to dwindle. This can put organizations at risk. They are faced with weighty decisions that may include cutting personnel, cutting back hours, or diminishing services to people in need.

ESSENTIAL

Get creative. Look to see how your organization can partner with another. Perhaps you can join forces to host a fundraising event or share expenses in building a website that provides separate web pages for each organization. Conduct an analysis first to ensure you are really paring down expenses while continuing to fulfill your mission.

For this reason, organizations look to partner where they can, enabling them to optimize their dollars for real estate, programming, and event planning. Some also look to merge with like-minded organizations.

Through mergers and partnerships, organizations can maximize their effectiveness and reach a broader audience. In California, two organizations that provided small business development expertise to low-income residents merged to form the Bay Area Business Hub, widening the territory of the communities served and offering more services. However, mergers can be costly, often requiring consultants to bring two organizations together. It can take time to blend the cultures of two organizations. In addition, it is critical that the two organizations—including their staff, board, and volunteers—believe in the same mission.

Babysitting and Child Care

Volunteers need to put in plenty of time making a fundraising project a success. This can include attending meetings at night and on weekends. In addition, you may get a larger turnout at a dinner or other activity if you can provide some help with child care. If parents bring young children along to meetings or other activities, they need to be responsible for them. By having kids present, you run the risk of an injury or accident, which can result in a lawsuit. Therefore, you should not try to provide a child care facility. The best you can do is to simply make your environment child-friendly.

If you are having an event in the winter, make sure there is an adequate coatroom for your guests. Most attendees will appreciate the opportunity to take off their bulky winter coats. This can also serve as part of the strategy of extending people's stay at your event.

One organization had extra space at its monthly meetings and invited people to bring their children, who did craft projects for the two hours of the meeting. The adults took turns overseeing the children's activity and it was understood in advance that the parents were responsible for their children.

When group babysitting is not possible, programs and activities for kids accompanied by their parent(s) makes your event more family friendly and attractive to more people. One health fair geared toward new parents at a public library provided plenty of activities and snacks for children while also providing parents with important information about immunization and nutrition. Their children were entertained and the parents learned where to turn for resources they may need in the future. Likewise, a school event filled with children's activities might have something for the adults to do, which might simply be a place set up to have coffee or to read. Always consider your primary audience and then consider others who may also be present.

Security Concerns

Far from being a little detail, security is something that needs to be carefully considered from several standpoints. First, you need to make sure attendees are safe and security is on hand in the event of a problem. Second, you need to make sure the funds you have raised so diligently are secure. Unless you are working on a political fundraiser where security will be more prevalent, try to maintain a low level of security that is discreet, yet present at all times.

ALERT!

Not all of your events and programs will be held at easily identifiable locations. Make sure people know where to park and how to find the entrance to the event. Good signage is important if the entrance to your event is not obvious. If parking is an insurmountable problem, a valet service may be a good solution.

Note fire regulations and other potential crowding situations when you do a walk-through of your site. Make sure there is always a path to fire exits and a smooth traffic flow so potentially dangerous overcrowding situations do not arise.

CHAPTER 17

All about Grants

Grants do not provide the bulk of financial support; most charities still turn to individual donations when they try to raise money. Still, grants can serve as a great potential source of the funds you need. You will need to do your research to target the right foundation and prepare a winning proposal that generates results. This chapter provides the essentials to successfully find and apply for grants.

Finding Grants

A grant is a financial donation to support a person, program, or organization. In the world of fundraising, it is a much-welcomed gift of endowment usually bestowed by a foundation. The big question is where does one get such a generous subsidy?

Do Your Research

Procuring a grant will take some investigation on your part. The best strategy is to narrow down a large list of foundations to those that best match the goals and mission of your organization. Apply to a select number rather than blitzing every foundation you can find. Selectively targeting the most suitable foundations will almost always yield a better response and increase your chances of finding a good match.

ESSENTIAL

When researching foundations, look for the geographic area(s) in which they bestow grants, the kinds of grants they give, and the areas of interest of the foundation. Also, be sure to follow their guidelines so your proposal receives the serious consideration it deserves.

There are more than 40,000 foundations you can apply to for a grant—and there's a lot of money to be awarded. In 2006 alone, foundations awarded more than $36.5 billion, up by more than 12 percent from the previous year, according to *Giving USA*, a publication of Giving USA Foundation. However, only a small percentage of foundations will even consider your proposal. In fact, one Michigan foundation reported rejecting as many as 80 percent of the applications it received.

How can you separate yourself from the pack? Do your homework. Foundations have guidelines and criteria. Some may serve only the greater San Francisco area whereas others fund only scientific research projects. Some may insist your nonprofit have at least a three-year track record, and others will fund newly founded nonprofits. Narrowing down your list prevents you from wasting time and money sending grant proposals to foundations whose mission and goals are vastly different from yours.

The Internet and the library are two primary sources of information on foundations and grant possibilities. The Foundation Center, now more than fifty years old, has five main libraries and more than 340 cooperating collections throughout the United States, all of which can help you research foundations. The organization, considered the most highly recognized source of foundation information, also has a comprehensive website at *www.foundationcenter.org.* Other sources for grant research can be found in Appendix A.

What to Look For

First, consider geographic restrictions. Many foundations operate in areas close to home, so you are best off starting with foundations nearest to your home base; explore the ones in your community first. The Foundation Center and other online grant research websites are designed so you can easily search by geographic region. Be sure to visit your local library so you can learn about the foundations that are either not yet on the web or that maintain a low profile. The *Guide to U.S. Foundations* and the *Foundation Directory* are valuable sources for locating foundations.

Next, you need to consider the guidelines of the foundation. What types of projects do they fund? What are their areas of interest? If you read about a foundation that funds science and technology and you are looking for a grant to help maintain a children's day-care program, don't waste your time applying.

You should also take a moment to consider what the grantor looks for in an organization. Along with looking at the need for funding, they want to see that your organization is well known in the community and that it addresses an existing need. Sound fiscal management, a strong and involved board, committed volunteers, qualified staff, and a realistic budget are all very important considerations.

There are public and private foundations. A private foundation is an organization whose support is usually from one source—an individual, family, or business—and provides funding through grants to other nonprofit organizations. It is subject to more restrictive rules than a public foundation. Still, those seeking grants may find that private foundations provide a more personal, less formal grant application process, and a less bureaucratic approach to giving than public foundations. Public foundations receive one-third of their support from contributions from the general public. Because they are public, their materials are a matter of public record, including the accepted grant proposals, which anyone can examine—with the distinct advantage of seeing what kind of applications succeed.

Visit *www.nozasearch.com* for critical information regarding grants written by foundations in a particular tax year, as well as those grants that have been approved for future payments. In addition, you will find detailed information about grant application criteria, deadlines, and geographical relationships. You can also learn about recent foundation grants by contacting an organization and requesting a copy of its annual report.

Some foundations offer support on a general basis by providing operating grants for the day-to-day operations of the nonprofit, believing these grants make a bigger impact on an organization overall. Yet many other foundations prefer to fund particular projects or activities. This makes it easier for them to monitor the results of a grant and to know the money is being used as intended.

Policies of Foundations and Grant Providers

The funding goals of many foundations change from year to year. The most current information on the foundation's giving policies may be available through research on the web, but it might be best to get it from a program officer. To learn more about a foundation, call its program officers and ask questions, such as:

- What are your key areas of interest for this year's funding?
- What are your geographic preferences, if any?

- What kinds of restrictions do you have?
- How many grant awards do you plan to make this year?
- What are your application deadlines?
- When will the awards be announced?
- Can you explain the overall evaluation process and criteria?

Ask to receive a copy of the foundation's guidelines, which may also provide answers to many of the questions listed above. Read them several times to understand how the foundation wants the grant application to be submitted. Follow their instructions to the letter. Otherwise, your application will likely be discarded, no matter how aligned your mission is with the foundation and how worthy your cause.

QUESTION?

Can foundations provide grants to organizations that have not applied for 501(c)(3) nonprofit public charity status with the IRS?
Yes. According to federal law, public schools, libraries, other government and nongovernment organizations, as well as individuals, can receive grants provided the foundation follows specific rules detailing their expenditure responsibilities. The foundation will be required to file reports to certify the funds were spent only for the charitable purposes outlined in the grant.

Renewal Grants

You might also look for foundations that provide renewal grants, which means they will offer the same grant for the same project(s) next year. If you think you will be running the same project on an ongoing basis, keep the renewal grant in mind. However, just because a foundation offers ongoing grants doesn't mean that by receiving a grant you automatically qualify for renewal. The renewal is based on the performance of the organization and how the initial grant money has been spent. Also, keep in mind that most foundations do not want you to be solely dependent on their grant for funding. They will usually want to see that you are seeking funding from other sources. In addition, some foundations may only renew a grant for a set period of years, and then want to spread the wealth to other worthy organizations, no matter how well prepared your application or how worthy your cause.

ALERT!

You can save time and money applying for a grant by co-applying with a like-minded entity. Granting agencies like to see collaborative projects, believing two partnering entities can be more efficient and may serve a broader audience. Partner only with agencies that share your objectives and goals; you want to make the case that together you can better help your cause.

The Application Process

To apply for a grant, you must write a proposal in accordance with the guidelines of the foundation. The proposal, typically around five pages, will be the cornerstone of your application. The other materials you will need to fill out are primarily for administrative purposes. Remember, follow instructions carefully.

The Data

You will need to do advance preparation for your proposal. This includes gathering your backup support materials and making sure the data you are about to include is factual and up to date. While many people labor over the wording of their grants and may hire professional grant writers, even the most carefully worded, professionally written grant proposal will be unsuccessful if the data are incorrect or the claims that are made are unsubstantiated.

Your proposal should make key points in a clear and compelling manner. Your objective is not to dazzle prospective grantors with vocabulary words, nor is it to try to tug at their emotional heartstrings. It is to make sure that whoever makes the funding decision understands the significance of your cause or mission and the need for funding at this juncture. You must also explain in specific and practical terms how their funding will help.

When writing a grant proposal, don't make the common mistake of focusing more heavily on the wording than the credibility. Putting the right substance into a concise and attention-grabbing package is the key.

The Specifics

Include the specifics regarding your mission first. Then include some facts about your organization, followed by the specifics of your program, such as how long it will run and other pertinent information. Be realistic in what you feel can be accomplished within a set time frame.

Make sure you have both backup information and clearance from whoever needs to approve such activities before you put anything in writing. Don't assume your organization or school board will go along with whatever you ask for. You should also explain the various tasks that will be carried out in the project and the experience of the people who are slated to handle these tasks.

The Guidelines

While working on the proposal, have the funding requirements and guidelines open at your side and follow them closely. If the foundation provides research grants, don't claim that a building grant will be a research grant just because the building may be used for research. Likewise, don't decide your project is so important you can take ten pages to explain it when the requirement is five. Remember, if the foundation is going to provide five grants this year and they have 200 proposals sitting in front of them, you can be sure that one manner of narrowing down the huge pile is to eliminate the proposals that do not adhere to the guidelines—without even reading them.

Also keep in mind that the application may request a copy of the IRS letter regarding your organization's 501(c)(3) tax-exempt status. This is not optional. You must provide a copy.

ALERT!

If your grant proposal is requesting seed money for the startup of a project, the foundation will be interested in how the program will be funded in the years after the funding it has provided has been spent. Be as detailed as possible; demonstrate that you've thought it through completely.

Support and Endorsements

You may also seek support for your proposal from outside sources. Individuals in academic, medical, or political positions who believe in your work can help by adding a letter of support to your proposal package. Endorsements from government or other agencies, organizations, or influential individuals can help promote your cause.

Grant application reviewers will also look for a division of responsibility if you are collaborating with other organizations. In your grant application process, you will need to present a schedule of meetings for the project and display a clear division of responsibility. Show that the project deliverables (or tasks that make up your fundraising effort) are being produced by more than one entity.

Presentation

While the validity of the mission is the most important part of the equation, presentation is also a factor. Your proposal should look good and be user-friendly. Many foundations now request that applicants use a standard format application, which may vary by region. Some foundations participate in regional associations, such as in southeastern Pennsylvania, where the Delaware Valley Grantmakers has developed a standard format that many foundations in the metropolitan Philadelphia area use.

Some pointers:

- Use a popular and easy-to-read font, no smaller than 12-point.
- Use the headings from the grant application.
- Don't crowd your pages or try to cram nine pages of material into five.
- Use words and phrases that say what you mean.
- Use a cover page and keep it simple.
- Include all necessary documents and signatures.
- Include tables, charts, and graphics that are clearly labeled and explained.
- Include all contact information.
- Don't use clip art, cutesy pictures, or plastic covers.
- Recheck your work several times.
- Ask several people who are known to produce meticulous work to proofread the application to help ensure the text is cohesive and there are no typos.
- Use FedEx, UPS, or another shipping provider that allows you to track the proposal so you can be sure it was received before the proposal deadline.

While presentation is not the deciding factor, it will often help keep your proposal in the "To be read" pile. Neatness counts. Edit, spell-check, and proofread.

Take pride in the details of your presentation. Never deliver a handwritten application or one presented on notebook or loose-leaf paper or that includes cross-outs. Make sure to address the application to the correct person (check the spelling of the person's name!) at the correct department. Never submit a proposal late.

Increasingly, foundations now include online grant applications. The process requires some transition, as grant seekers must adapt to telling their stories in a paperless format and often within a limited amount of space.

It can also have its share of glitches, such as servers going down, preventing an applicant from accessing the site and meeting the foundation's deadline. Yet because online applications allow foundations to streamline processes, experts predict the paperless format will become progressively more prevalent.

Timing and Follow Up

Give yourself sufficient time to research and compose an A-list of foundations you most want to approach. Factor in the time it will take to write the proposal and run it past board members and other key people in your group or organization. Make sure you are aware of the time frame in which the foundation is looking to read grant proposals. Then prepare to wait.

It can take from several weeks to several months before you receive a response. Competing for grants is competitive, and it is unlikely all of your grant requests will yield funds for your organization. Don't fret when you get rejection letters; even the best grant writers in the business receive numerous rejection letters. Like finding a job or selling your novel, receiving rejections is part of the process. The good news is you may get more than one positive response. In fact, the more you receive the better. Foundations that see you are receiving grants from other foundations may look more closely at your proposal.

ALERT!

If you hire a professional grant writer, make sure he is knowledgeable about your organization and your mission. Spend time explaining your organization's goals. Too often, professionals come in and use all the buzz words but do not include the right substance because they are unfamiliar with the organization.

There's nothing wrong with calling a foundation if you are unclear about its guidelines or need to request information. It helps to be prepared, sound professional, and ask specific questions, but do not call often or become a pest. Also, when you call, be prepared to provide details in the event someone asks you about your organization or project. If you need to follow up with additional information to properly answer a question, do so in a timely manner.

Corporate Grants

Large corporations may have foundations set up to allocate funding through grants to organizations such as yours. This may come from an endowment or through the earnings of the company.

The corporation is very likely providing funding for the sake of good public relations, a positive image within the overall community, as well as the opportunity to give back and make the community stronger. Since they need to justify to stockholders why they are giving away money, they may request they be clearly recognized for their efforts. You can do this in an announcement at your event or with their name on your literature.

A clear distinction must be made between the for-profit corporation and the nonprofit organization. Does the fact that the corporation's name is associated with your organization change the image or alter the work being done by your organization in any manner? Does it alter the public perception of the organization?

If an organization that helps and supports families and children receives a grant from a company that manufactures alcoholic beverages, could that be seen as a conflict or an improper sponsorship? Consider your sources carefully.

Consider which companies do and do not serve as a good match for your organization. If the public perception will be more focused on the corporate sponsor than on your cause, or if the company is asking to have a say in how you proceed with your fundraising agenda, then they may not be right for you. Money with strings attached can end up costing you more in the long run. Most companies won't ask to be involved, just apprised of the progress made by your organization. The public relations goal of the company usually means simply acknowledging it in some manner that puts its name in front of the public but does not interfere with your mission.

Keep in mind that corporations may change their grant formula. Those that have historically supported the arts may opt instead to award grants to organizations that foster leadership to the underprivileged. Stay current with your research, and try not to become reliant on any one corporate foundation.

Federal Grants

If you are seeking a grant from the federal government, visit *www.grants.gov*, the online site to find and apply for federal grants and track your application over the Internet. In addition, be sure to look at the *Catalog of Federal Domestic Assistance* in a library or on the Internet at *www.cfda.gov*. Federal agencies provide various kinds of grants as well as other kinds of assistance in the form of loans, insurance, and federal relief, in the case of disasters. You can search the website for federal assistance by subject.

There are fifteen kinds of government subsidy assistance, each of which includes a number of programs. Among these are:

- Formula grants, allocated by law for activities of a continuing nature not confined to a specific project
- Project grants, allocated for specific projects, including research, training, or planning grants
- Direct payment for specialized use, which means federal assistance is provided directly to individuals, private firms, and other private institutions to encourage or subsidize a particular activity
- Direct payment of unrestricted use, which is federal funding to recipients who qualify, without restrictions on how the money is to be spent
- Direct loans, which may or may not require the payment of interest

As is always the situation when dealing with the government, the process can be time consuming, especially if this is the first time you are applying for a federal grant. The website *www.grant.gov* enables applicants to search for grants by keyword or by agency and download pages of grant opportunities. You can also find out about new grant opportunities by signing up for e-mail alerts. You might try to strike up a conversation with support staff on the phone to help you sort through what many find to be a complex, confusing process. If your budget allows, work with a proposal-writing consultant who is experienced in applying for federal grants. The more people who can provide suggestions and feedback for your ideas the better able you will be to structure the grant to conform to the agency's requirements.

FACT

Most grant applications are scored using a point system. Ask for a written evaluation so you can learn where you need to improve. Talk with or write to the program officer to learn what was missing if your grant was not accepted.

Tailor your proposals to the individual foundations as opposed to writing a blanket proposal for all foundations. Chapter 18 focuses on the actual writing of proposals and what you need to include.

Grant Writing 101

Like any other kind of writing, grant writing takes some practice, so don't be concerned if your first attempt doesn't sound quite right. Your goal is to create a proposal that will entice grant givers to provide you with funding. In this chapter, we look at the elements that must be included in your grant proposal. Remember, you can—and should—use other grant proposals as examples.

Overview of a Proposal

When you write your grant proposal, keep your goals and objectives in mind. Your goal is whatever it is you plan to do with the grant award; for example, increase the number of retail businesses in the Main Street district.

Your objective is how you are going to achieve your goal. How will you increase the number of retail businesses? Include all the activities or action steps you can take to realize the goal. For example, you can increase consumer interest in the district by designing an Internet forum in which 20,000 employees working for neighboring corporations within a ten-mile radius can go online and view menus from dozens of restaurants.

Writing a grant proposal is like writing a business plan. Outline your goals in a manner that will attract someone to fund your venture. The inclination is to jump right into your need for funding up front and make an impassioned plea. Don't do this. You need to first state a compelling problem, not unlike the way a narrative sets up the intriguing story line of a novel. You must reach a point where the reader will wonder how to resolve the significant dilemma you present. The meat and potatoes of the proposal will then explain how you will set goals to tackle this problem. This section will also detail how your organization is capable of doing the work necessary to complete this mission. Finally, you will detail the manner in which a grant award will resolve the issues. This is a very broad overview, but it explains the basics of what a grant proposal should do.

FACT

Grant proposals need to identify expected outcomes. These outcomes are also known as measurable objectives, which need to be clearly defined in your proposal and must be achievable.

The topics covered in your proposal should usually include:

- A project summary
- Information about your organization
- A problem statement
- Your goals, objectives, and desired outcomes

- Your plan of action or methodology
- How you will analyze or evaluate your results
- The budget

Sometimes a wrap-up page or two will follow and, in many instances, you will have additional pages of data, which we'll discuss in the final section of the proposal.

The Project Summary

A project summary should appear at the beginning of your proposal. It should consist of two to five paragraphs outlining the fundraising project in very basic terms. Even though it appears in the beginning, the summary is often written after the rest of the proposal has been prepared to ensure you include what is actually in the proposal. This also lets you be sure you haven't locked yourself into trying to write a proposal to fit the summary.

Make sure the summary is worded carefully and encompasses your key ideas in brief. The summary must include the overview of the project, the key issues that will be detailed in the rest of the proposal, and how the funding will impact the community in question.

Keep the interests and ideals of the foundation in mind when you write the summary. Do not include any extraneous information about areas that are not covered within the proposal. It will likely serve you best to write the summary last because you may wind up with changes to other parts of the proposal that need to be reflected in the summary.

About Your Organization

Whether you are a longstanding nonprofit organization, a fledgling newcomer, or a university or high school, you will need to introduce or present your organization to the foundation. Include a brief organizational history, perhaps short biographies of the board members (or key staffers), and your goals, philosophy, and success stories. In addition, mention programs you currently provide.

Sometimes, biographical and other aspects of this organizational data can be moved to the end of the proposal. The idea here is to present the credibility of the organization. Keep in mind, this section should be the condensed *Reader's Digest* version of how marvelous your organization is, not a full three-act play.

FACT

Grant givers will find merit in your organization's accomplishments, so be sure to highlight them. If your organization has won awards or if you've received mention in the press, you should point out such honors. You may attach clippings at the end of the proposal. If you are filling out an electronic application, include a link to the media coverage; if the application allows attachments, include a PDF file.

The Problem Statement

Also called the needs assessment, this section requires a well-crafted statement of the problem that needs to be addressed. Explain what the problem is, who is at risk, and how your organization became aware of this need. Mention how this problem is currently being handled and how addressing this issue in greater depth can rectify the problem.

Be factual in your statements, cite sources wherever possible, and include information about how the issue is affecting economics, social well-being, the environment, or other key areas. Match the needs and interests of the foundation whenever possible without stretching your own limits.

By the end of this section, you should have drawn the reader into the problem at hand. If you are appealing to a foundation that is interested in your cause (which you would know from your research), a well-crafted problem statement should have the decision-makers' undivided attention.

Goals and Objectives

This section follows the introduction of the problem. It takes the reader from wondering what will happen to potential solutions to the problem.

It is important to note the objectives and goals of your program and the related activities in the proposal. The desired outcome is the result you hope to see from your organization's hard work. This section is not defining your actual plan of action but presenting a broader view of the program, including measurable results, which the foundation or organization funding the program will want to see.

This section is often the hardest part of the proposal to write because you do not want to state objectives or goals that cannot be clearly met. Be sure to maintain a level of objectivity and not let your dreams of overwhelming success get the better of you.

Your Plan of Action

In this section, explain your methodology and show in detail how you will achieve your goal. Describe the specific tasks that will take place, how they relate to each other, and who will handle each of them.

ALERT! If you use supporting data, do not overdo it. Too often, grant writers believe that if they load up the proposal with tons of graphs, charts, bios, and other documents, it will help get the grant request accepted. It won't. Include only a few pages of the most pertinent information.

While you may have all the details in place, the trick is to present a sound plan while keeping the reader intrigued. Try to make the section flow smoothly as you take the reader on a tour of your plan. Remember to illustrate the logic and reasoning behind your ideas, so it is clear why your plan will allow you to meet your goals. Highlight all of the aspects of your program, including how you will promote your activities or event, any technology necessary, and any new personnel you may need to hire.

Use supporting data to substantiate what you are claiming will take place. If you feel supporting material will interfere with the flow of the narrative, then place such materials at the back of the proposal in an appendix.

If you are applying electronically, see if the format allows you to attach supporting materials. If the answer is not obvious, read through the frequently asked questions or contact the foundation and ask.

You may also differentiate why your program will work as opposed to other programs or methods that have been used to address this particular problem in the past. Most issues are not brand new and other attempts may have been made to solve the problem. Your proposal should not belittle other efforts, but should state how this plan is unique or how it compares to other successful plans that have worked in the past.

Evaluating the Program

In this section, explain how the success of the program will be measured. First, describe how the evaluations will be conducted and who will handle the process. Also, include the method of measurement. Besides evaluating the results of the project itself, you will want to evaluate the process by which you achieved the results. Grant givers will ask how the project will follow the plan of action. Explain how you will determine the answer to this question.

Federal agencies and foundations will want to see the kind of evaluation you plan to use and at what junctures during the project you will conduct your evaluations or analysis.

You want to show you are prepared to determine whether the project served the anticipated number of people. You also need to evaluate whether the fundraising project stayed within the initial budget and how it impacted the community, neighborhood, or other affected group(s).

Your Budget

You are asking for a foundation's money as an investment in your project. The program officer needs to know how the money will be spent. Along with a strong narrative, you need to include a budget.

A carefully prepared budget should justify all of your expenses and be consistent with the activities listed within the proposal. There should be no surprise items entered on the budget that aren't mentioned in your plan of action. Some common budget areas include rental of building(s), equipment and resources, transportation, publicity, insurance, and food/refreshments. Personnel costs are also included and subtitled.

Remember to include only the costs that relate to this particular program and not ongoing administration costs that are not part of this grant proposal (unless you are applying for a general operating grant). In fact, you might even explain what will become of equipment after the project terminates. Will it be donated or put to good use for future projects?

FACT

Often, pro bono and in-kind services will be accepted as a source of a funding match. If your proposal states you'll match a grant with money or donations from other sources, you may be able to use volunteered services as part of your other donations. The value of volunteered services may need to be substantiated in the proposal by using average wages or a figure agreed upon in writing.

Indicate where the project will take place. Are the project personnel working out of an office? Are they using typical office equipment, such as copiers and telephones? If so, do the budget guidelines of the funder allow for space and usage of equipment to be considered as eligible project costs? Will meeting rooms, auditoriums, and audiovisual equipment need to be rented to complete the tasks of the project? These are legitimate project costs. Include them in your budget.

Make sure you list the various sources of income, including sponsors, donors, sales, grants, and so on. Foundations will want to know where other funding will come from. The foundation providing the grant will not usually be your primary source of funding but one of several. Many grant applications require that the applicant show matching funds and additional resources. Be sure to check the grant maker's guidelines so you know which expenses are eligible and which are not.

In the End

To complete your proposal, you may include a formal wrap up, or conclusion, but it is not essential. You may simply want to reiterate some of the key points of your proposal so the last item the person reading it sees is something other than the budget. Whatever you choose to conclude with, keep it brief.

In addition, all accompanying documents will be attached in the appendix at the end of your proposal. This should include the bios of your board of directors, your nonprofit status, and the previous year's financial statements. You might also include press releases of your organization's activities, major grants received in recent years, and letters of support for the project goals.

There are many classes and seminars on grant writing. Look for ones in your area. You are usually better off taking a course and improving your own skills than hiring someone who doesn't know about your organization to write a grant. However, if you are more comfortable hiring a professional, make sure she is a grant writer and not another type of scribe. Also, look at work she has accomplished previously and make sure to provide her with all the data she will need to capture the essence of your goals and needs. In short, make sure the grant writer is on the same page as your organization.

Sample Grant Application

Here is the written portion of a sample grant application presented by a historical preservation committee to an urban preservation foundation. Most of the above-mentioned areas were requested in the questions and guidelines and are included in the grant application. You'll note that this particular application lumped goals and results with plan of action in part three. Remember, each grant proposal is slightly different, and you will need to follow the application carefully.

1. Project Summary

The Northwood Downtown Historic District (NDHD) seeks funding to create a comprehensive plan that complements the overall framework of the region's historic area. This project will help us achieve our goal of economic viability and revitalization of the Northwood Historic District.

The infrastructure, facades and signage, mercantile issues and streetscape, including parks and public art, will be addressed. Current and future zoning issues will be examined with the intent of safeguarding this plan. The results will be described both visually and verbally for use by the community in its negotiations and dealings with the district government including the departments of Public Works, Parks and Recreation.

The procedure for producing this plan will incorporate significant input from area residents, business owners, clergy, civic leaders, and village officials prior to and during a two-day neighborhood design workshop. Local experts in urban design, historic preservation, retail marketing, and business development will donate their services. All relevant technical information including maps, photographs, historic guidelines, and zoning and scale drawings will be prepared, updated, and analyzed. Two weeks after the neighborhood design workshop the final project report will be presented at a community-wide meeting in Northwood.

The NDHD will implement this project with the assistance of a planning group known as Design Unlimited, an organization sponsored by the state commission on the arts and humanities, funded in part by the National Endowment for the Arts and supported by the American Institute of Architects.

2. Description of the Need for Funding from the Urban Preservation Foundation

Funding is being requested because the neighborhood referred to as the Historic District is in need of revitalization. Business and shop owners have reported a decline in customers of nearly 40 percent over the past five years. Tourist traffic in the area is also down significantly. In addition, several of the buildings have been reported to have minor structural damage as determined by the City Buildings Safety Commission. The loss of revenue for the Northwood community resulting from the lessened tourist traffic and business conducted in this area is projected at nearly $1 million annually over the next two years.

There is also a cultural and historic obligation to the city to maintain the historic buildings that were the cornerstones of the Northwood community.

This is the first time the community has sought funding from outside the neighborhood to support a project regarding historic preservation. The Island Architectural Bureau has agreed to pledge $5,000. Additional funding of $5,000 is requested from the Northwood Preservation Foundation to be used specifically for this project.

3. About the Organization

The NDHD was founded in 1984 as a privately endowed, independent institution devoted to collecting, interpreting, and presenting the rich multicultural history of the community and the state to the public through exhibitions, programs, research collections, and publications.

In addition, the committee also works to establish historical status for select buildings in Northwood, and works to maintain and preserve its twenty-four structures that are already listed as historical landmarks.

4. Describe your goals and future plans for the project or activity beyond the scope of this grant proposal (that is, how the consultant's recommendations will be implemented, how educational programs will be institutionalized, and so on).

The goals and subsequent results of this project will be to:

- Encourage compatibility of building rehabilitation and new construction with protection of the historic district
- Enhance pedestrian activity and tourism in the area
- Strengthen and identify the character and attractiveness of the area
- Improve and increase retail business activity

The project will include a major overhaul of the sidewalks, curbs, streets, lighting, landscaping, and village green in the downtown historic district of Northwood. This work, scheduled to begin during the spring of 2010, will work with the already pledged support of the local municipal organizations and the Department of Public Works.

The work is expected to take six months and will include the historic district's seven-square-block area. To accommodate residents and merchants, work will be completed in three parts. See attached work schedule. Our committee also recently negotiated with the Business Improvement District and Department of Public Works to take responsibility for special projects to improve the district's village green. This work will begin in the fall of 2010 and include planting, new lighting, and a new public walkway.

In addition, the proposed urban redesign and historic preservation plan of the Northwood Historic District will be the foundation for the Northwood traffic calming project, scheduled to begin in the fall of 2010. This additional project is expected to take five months and is not part of this specific project and will be separately funded.

5. Evaluating the Project

The NDHD is seeking project funding, with the average grant in the range of $1,500 to $2,000. In the evaluation process, the NDHD will confirm the proposed project, an urban design plan for the neighborhood's commercial district, and show continual building progress on a monthly basis as well as accounting for the project expenses. Committee reports will also be provided monthly from the fundraising, planning, and project committees.

The "Urban Design Plan" for the Historic District will be completed with information gathered from a two-day community workshop to be held in May. Approximately 125 residents and planning professionals will be invited to participate in the workshop. A report, with drawings prepared by architects, urban planners, and landscape architects will be distributed in July through a community newspaper. A copy of the report will also be provided to all funders.

A search for funding to implement some of the recommendations has already begun. One local foundation has publicly expressed interest in funding projects in this neighborhood, and an introductory meeting has already been scheduled.

6. Budget
   Estimated total of this project/activity: $25,000
   Amount requested from the (name of grantor): $5,000

PROJECT ACTIVITY/INCOME

Source of Cash (specify)

Urban Services Fund Grant (request submitted)	$5,000
Preservation Foundation (grant requested)	$5,000
Local business contributions	$1,000
Direct mail solicitation in neighborhood	$1,500
Neighborhood bazaar and flea market	$1,500
Raffle	$1,000
Barbecue picnic dinner	$1,500
Total	**$16,500**

Source of Donated Services and Materials (specify)

Printing and reproduction donated by Inkwell Shop	$300
Food donated by area restaurants and supermarkets	$750
Room for workshop donated by St. Peter's Church	$500
Audiovisual equipment donated by Northwood Audiovisual Co.	$400
Mika Architects' donation of drafting services	$570
Donation of services of six design professionals (architects, urban planners, and landscape architects) for two days @ $700 per day	$6,000
Total	**$8,250**

Cost Category	Description	Cost	Applicant Share	UPF Share
Consultant (cash)	Preparing technical/ structural reports	$2,250	$750	$1,500
Salaries/ honoraria (cash)	Facilitator, administration, and staff coordinator	$10,020	$10,020	——
Donated services (in-kind)	Professional design team	$6,000	$6,000	——
Printed materials	Technical materials, report, and raffles	$3,000	$300	$2,700
Supplies	Office, drafting, and two fundraising events (bazaar and picnic)	$1,200	$1,200	——
Space/equipment rentals	Meetings	$900	$900	——
Food and beverages		$700	$700	——
Mailing and postage		$130	$130	——
Other	Preparing technical data	$800	——	$800
Total project expenses		**$25,000**	**$20,000**	**$5,000**

Note that in the sample budget, under expenses, it indicates exactly what the applicant (the organization requesting the grant) will pay for and how the funds from the specific grant will be used. This grant proposal is a sample of the kind of information that may be requested and how it might be presented. Remember, grants alone will not save the day, but they can help you in your quest to complete a successful fundraising project.

CHAPTER 19

Taxes and Accounting

Wherever income and funding are involved, taxes must be addressed. As a nonprofit organization, determine your tax status and set up your bookkeeping methods in a manner that will help your organization remain financially accountable. Tax regulations vary from state to state, but this chapter introduces you to the basics.

Your Tax Status

If you are a nonprofit organization, you can apply for federal tax exemption by filing with the IRS. Churches, synagogues, mosques, schools, hospitals, nonprofit old-age homes, and certain other organizations automatically qualify for nonprofit status because they are considered public charities. However, they must meet certain criteria. For example, a school has to provide ongoing instruction, have a student population, and have faculty members. A hospital must meet health requirements and have a regular medical staff. You cannot simply call yourself a school or hospital and expect to be recognized as such. For information on which tax-exempt status is right for your organization, you can look at IRS Publication 557, which can be obtained from the IRS or found on its website at *www.irs.ustreas.gov*.

FACT

The fee for filing Form 1023 depends on your organization's gross receipts. As of this writing, if your income has exceeded $10,000 annually over a four-year period, the fee is $750. However, these fees are subject to change, so be sure to visit *www.irs.gov* and search for the term "user fee."

Operating as a nonprofit organization, company, or association, you can obtain tax-exempt status under section 501(c)(3) of the Internal Revenue Code if your purpose is charitable, educational, cultural, scientific, literary, or religious or if it tests for public safety, fosters amateur athletic competition, or prevents cruelty to children or animals. The benefit of having this status is that contributors can take a tax deduction on their federal income taxes when they give to your organization.

Applying for Nonprofit Status

To apply for 501(c)(3) status, you will need to file IRS Form 1023 and attach Form 8718 (User Fee for Exempt Organization Determination Letter Request). To make filing easy, you can download Form 1023 from the IRS website or call 1-800-Tax-Form and request a copy or order a CD ROM.

You will need to fill out several parts of this form, which asks for administrative information, a description of the activities of your organization, financial statements, and so on. A twelve-page document, Form 1023, will take a while to complete, so proceed slowly and carefully. Then attach all requested accompanying documents and remember to attach a check for the fee.

Not all groups need to file Form 1023. If your organization is part of a larger parent organization that already qualifies for 501(c)(3) status, you do not have to apply. For example, if you are a chapter or branch of a national charity or your state PTA has secured from the IRS federal income tax exemption, you would not have to file the 1023 form. It is important to check with your umbrella organization. Public charities that have gross receipts totaling less than $5,000 a year also need not apply.

If your organization is not a corporation, you will need to submit your constitution, articles of association, or other governing documents besides your bylaws. These materials should include at least two signatures by officers or leaders of the organization. You also need to send financial data, including an income statement (if you have already had some income) and a two-year projected budget. If you are incorporated, submit the articles of incorporation, including the secretary of state's stamp.

ESSENTIAL

It is recommended for most independent nonprofits to apply for tax-exempt status. Achieving this status is the only way to be assured that the IRS views the corporation as a 501(c)(3) tax-exempt group and, therefore, you can confidently let contributors know that they can take a deduction on their personal income taxes for any contributions.

If you are a corporation, you will need to have your 1023 application filed and postmarked within fifteen months after the end of the month in which your articles of incorporation were filed. If you file on time, the tax-exemption status is effective retroactively to the date on which your articles were filed.

You will then receive your 501(c)(3) status letter from the IRS determining that you qualify for tax-exempt status. Copies of this letter will come in handy when:

- Sending grant proposals
- Purchasing equipment for the organization
- Dealing with government agencies
- Applying for a bulk mail permit
- Placing classified ads (you can get lower rates)
- Recording public service announcements

Keep copies of the letter handy for other situations that may arise.

Incorporating

You may wish to become a nonprofit corporation. To do so, you will first have to incorporate in your state. Keep in mind that each state has its own guidelines for incorporating. Depending on state laws, you may need to incorporate in each state separately if you are doing business in multiple places.

You will need to follow the guidelines of incorporating, which include establishing bylaws and holding annual meetings of members and directors. Incorporating, however, does not automatically qualify you for tax-exempt status. You will still need to file for your 501(c)(3).

Despite a lot of additional paperwork, incorporating has some important benefits. As a nonprofit 501(c)(3), your corporation will be exempt from federal corporate income taxes. In addition, you will be able to apply for public and federal grants. As a corporation, you get increased protection against liability. This means board members and others involved in the corporation are protected from being held personally responsible should the corporation incur debts or liabilities.

Donor Contributions

Contributions to nonprofits with 501(c)(3) tax-exempt status are tax deductible. This encourages people to donate money as well as goods and services. The fair market value of donated goods or services is also deductible.

If you provide goods or services in exchange for someone's contribution, that person can deduct only the amount of the payment that is more than the value of the goods or services received. If, for example, someone donates an item that is worth $50 to your auction and you sell it for $200, the buyer can deduct only the $150 difference between the amount he spent (the contribution) and the actual value of the item. If the value of the goods or services is greater than $75, your nonprofit organization must be ready to provide a statement to the contributor stating such information.

Should you receive a gift in kind, look for some third party to provide you with an approximate value of the item unless the donor provides you with an amount. You need to know the value of the gift for your own income records.

ALERT!

A 501(c)(3) qualified nonprofit organization is not allowed to be involved in politics, so steer clear. Political nonprofit groups operate separately from this classification. Organizations that either support or oppose political candidates may face an excise tax or may even risk losing their tax-exempt status. The Internal Revenue Service offers guidelines at *www .irs.gov/charities*.

Pledges are a unique kind of contribution. In effect, a pledge is a promise (written or verbal) of a contribution to be given in the future. A pledge is usually monetary and may be based on an activity at your fundraising event, such as money pledged for each mile a participant at a walkathon completes. A pledge can also be a nonmonetary item.

According to the Financial Accounting Standards Board, a binding pledge should be entered as revenue—and this practice is especially pertinent at a time when nonprofits are expected to be accountable. There are times, however, when donors fail to honor a pledge. While some nonprofits choose to sue in those circumstances, others opt not to, fearing the move would portray the organization unfavorably. Most pledges are unconditional, but if there is a condition the organization must meet, such as matching a contribution, that is part of the binding agreement. Once the condition is met, the pledge becomes binding.

It is worth noting that pledges can present a misleading picture of your income, much in the way that technology and Internet stocks made a lot of people look wealthy on paper in the late 1990s. A total of $30,000 in outstanding pledges needs to be clearly differentiated from $30,000 in actual income for your organization. An organization that is frequently reporting far more money in pledges than it is seeing in income may look suspicious to the state charity commission.

FACT

Contributors can donate up to 50 percent of their annual gross income to qualified 501(c)(3) nonprofit organizations and be eligible for full tax deductions. There are some items that do not qualify for tax deductions. Raffle tickets, for example, are not considered tax deductible. A tax professional can help contributors determine the exceptions to the rule.

Filing with the IRS

A nonprofit organization is required to file a Form 990 with the IRS. You must also have copies of the past three 990s that you have filed available for the public to read.

When filing, you will use a fiscal year in the same manner as a for-profit business. You can use either the regular calendar year or a variation. Some organizations may base their fiscal year around the nature of seasonal activities. For example, if you are very busy with fundraising activities from September through March, you might have your fiscal year from July 1 through June 30. This way, the preparations and other work that needs to be done before filing your tax return can be done during a quiet time for your organization. Whatever your fiscal calendar year, make sure to file by the fifteenth day of the fifth month following the end of the fiscal year, or request an extension in advance of the filing date.

Churches and organizations that receive less than $25,000 in gross receipts do not have to file Form 990 by federal law. However, they must submit an annual electronic notice using Form 990-N, *Electronic Notice (e-Postcard) for Tax-Exempt Organizations not Required To File Form 990 or 990-EZ*, also known as the e-Postcard. The e-Postcard can only be filed electronically; there is no paper version. For more information about the e-Postcard, go to *www.irs.gov*. In addition, there may be state laws requiring you to file. Double-check state filing requirements.

Bookkeeping Practices

Keep a careful watch over your books. You want accurate data regarding your income and expenses as they relate to each activity or event you run. This will help you when it's time to file taxes or you need to show financial information to an auditor, a government agency, or a foundation from which you are seeking a grant.

It is imperative that someone in your organization has basic bookkeeping and financial management skills. If not, you may need to hire someone to handle your accounting. Board members and directors need to address this key aspect of an organization. In small groups, one person may find himself wearing many hats, including those of the bookkeeper and accountant. Cash management and bookkeeping need to be done carefully and with utmost integrity.

If you are in a management position for a nonprofit organization or are running a fundraiser, you should have a basic understanding of how to read financial statements and your organization's books to better comprehend the financial status of the organization. Brush up on basic accounting skills.

Whether you or someone you trust is handling the bookkeeping activities, it is crucial to record all financial transactions in a clear manner. The work needs to be easy to decipher in case there is cause to review your books. Remember, each organization will have its own policies and guidelines for handling financial transactions. Once such a working system is established, it should be carefully maintained.

It is common for nonprofit organizations to authorize two or three people to sign checks. In some cases, two signatures may be required for every transaction. Some organizations, however, may feel this is unnecessary because it may be difficult to get the check signed by two people when it needs to be mailed out quickly. Whatever system you use, be consistent and only give signing privileges to a limited number of responsible people.

ALERT!

Because members of the organization do not see each other regularly, checks are often presigned to be used when necessary. This practice should be avoided whenever possible. It can lead to serious problems if the checkbook falls into the wrong hands.

Your Accounting System

When handling the accounting for your organization, you can use either a cash-based system or an accrual-based system. The cash-based system is similar to the manner in which you maintain your checkbook, except you'll be using a ledger and posting cash receipts into the cash receipts journal and cash disbursements into the cash disbursements journal. The system, which is more common in smaller to mid-sized organizations, is based on cash transactions.

An accrual basis is one where entries are posted when money is earned and owed. This is usually more common in larger organizations. Utilize this system when filling out financial statements where you need to list what income is due you and what expenses are owed. Larger organizations that handle more money can afford to have more money owed, while a small organization will need to have its money readily available at all times.

Methods of Tracking Funds

Depending on the size of your organization or fundraising effort and the computer comfort level of your treasurer, you can work in anything from a basic ledger to an advanced accounting software program. Many people have used a simple Excel program to create spreadsheets and QuickBooks or Peachtree software to handle the accounting for a small nonprofit group. Both QuickBooks and Peachtree also offer online programs whose features include grant and donor tracking, as well as the ability to run reports for board members.

Nonprofit organizations must report account activity for program transactions that relate specifically to services provided. They also need to report supporting transactions, which are more general transactions that are common to all ongoing programs and activities, such as administrative costs.

An audit can provide you with a financial overview. It is generally done by an experienced professional accountant and provides an all-inclusive report of the financial procedures and activities of your organization. An audit will provide you with a document detailing the manner in which your organization is handling its finances. Some nonprofits are required by their own boards to have audits done periodically. In fact, it is a good idea to track state laws to ensure that they do not require audits, as some experts believe this is trend that will gain traction in local legislatures. Even if you are not required to have an audit completed, it is a good idea to conduct one because the document can prove beneficial when you are seeking grants, sponsorship, and corporate funding. The only drawback is that an audit can be costly. Smaller organizations generally cannot afford to have one done until they have built up significant funding and can justify the need for an audit.

Cash Flow

Often, your cash flow will depend on seasonal activities, including your fundraising campaigns. Membership drives or renewals may provide income at certain times of the year, and your special fundraising events will help you maintain a positive cash flow. You will need to plan in advance to have sufficient cash on hand during the rest of the year to cover operating expenses.

Plan accordingly when buying equipment for your office or beginning a public relations campaign. However, situations—or even emergencies—may arise where you will need to spend some of your funds. For example, one group dedicated to preserving the ecology of a particular region suddenly found it needed to help when an oil spill threatened to destroy a nearby lake.

Make sure your organization has procedures dictating how and when to use emergency funds. This may include a vote of the board or other means of determining the use of such funds. The policies should be spelled out in advance so you can act quickly when necessary.

Many organizations set aside a portion of their funding for such emergency use. The larger the organization, the more it can put into this special pool of funds. In any case, keep money in reserve and have cash available at all times.

Reviewing Your Financial Picture

Watch your finances as you proceed through operations, and especially through fundraising activities and special events preparation.

Planning Ahead

It is important to examine how much you can dip into your funding and still have enough to continue operations. Plan ahead and never expect the next fundraiser to solve your financial woes, even if the last three years have proven a particular event to be a major success. Ultimately, look for a balance in maintaining enough funding to keep your organization running smoothly to meet your goals and further your mission for years to come. Depending on the needs of the organization, nonprofits report they spend 20 to 50 percent of their money on fundraising.

Organizations do not want to build up excessive amounts of money. If you find that you are operating with significantly more money in reserve than your anticipated needs, you should sit down with your board or key members of your group and decide how to put the money into programs that better serve the community and further your goals as an organization.

FACT

A nonprofit can show money in reserve above and beyond its operating expenses, but this money cannot be used to benefit any individual in the organization or to back a political candidate or a commercial venture. It must be used for the designated mission of the organization.

The Numbers

To get a good feeling of where your organization stands financially, you need to review your financial statements. Ask yourself:

- Are you sticking to your budget?
- Are there extra expenses beyond those for which you had planned?
- Are you keeping administrative costs down?
- Are contributions being used for their intended purposes?

These are among the questions you will need to ponder to get an adequate assessment of where you stand financially. If, for example, you find the percentage of money going toward administrative costs is too high, you will know where to make adjustments. Naturally, the nature of the organization and the size and scope of the fundraising activities will factor into your analysis.

Also, consider the age of your organization. In the first year, the setup of the office and establishing of the presence of the organization will likely require more money than after you are up and running. It's important to monitor and analyze the finances of any nonprofit organization or grassroots fundraising activity on a frequent basis. Organizations with monthly or bimonthly board meetings often require a financial report at each meeting.

Financial Accountability

Besides having your past three Form 990s available to the public, you should also check all state and local government regulations to determine what other documents you are required to have available to donors and other stakeholders.

Related Income

You will need to be financially accountable and be able to show that income is related to the purposes of the organization. If, for example, the IRS determines that income is unrelated to the purpose of your nonprofit organization, you may be liable for taxes even if you have tax-exempt status. One charity dedicated to raising money for the treatment of a serious illness also owns a building from which it performs its administrative activities. It utilizes only two of the three floors in the building and rents the third floor to another company. This rental income is taxable because it does not relate to the organization's main function. If, however, the floors were rented to a research team that was working on medical issues relating to the same illness, this could possibly be considered related income.

FACT

Organizations that maintain nonprofit status as public charities typically obtain less than 33 percent of their backing from gross investment earnings and more than 33 percent of their funding from membership fees, contributions, and gross receipts from purists that are an integral part of their tax-exempt function.

What is and is not considered advertising is also a question that has many answers. If, for example, Bob's Meat Market purchased uniforms for a Little League team, the value of the uniforms would not be considered unrelated income, but an advertising expense. However, if Bob took out an ad in a journal for his meat market, it would depend on the organization and the content of the ad as to whether this was or was not considered advertising and thus unrelated income. Journal ads can be a gray area. Talk with a tax specialist and don't be surprised if she needs to refer to her tax books to give you answers.

Unrelated business income can be tricky, and it is advisable to sit down with an accountant and review what falls under that classification and is considered taxable income. When you pay taxes in this situation you will pay under the corporate rate if you incorporated prior to receiving your 501(c)(3) status.

Being financially accountable for a nonprofit organization means maintaining integrity and making sure all income and expenses are clearly accounted for. It also means upholding the nonprofit status of the organization and being accountable to the IRS in the case of an audit or review of the tax-exempt status. You will maintain your nonprofit status, provided your organization:

- Does not engage in for-profit business activities
- Does not have board members or other nonstaff individuals benefiting monetarily from the activities of the organization
- Is not conducting any kind of income-generating activity that is not in keeping with the purposes of the organization

With the rapid increase in nonprofit groups in recent years, the government is now watching very closely to make sure such groups follow the IRS guidelines.

Substantiation and Disclosure Requirements

According to the IRS, a donor is responsible for obtaining a written acknowledgment from a charity for any single contribution of $250 or more before he can claim a charitable contribution on his federal income tax return. This means you are required to provide such written acknowledgment.

You are also required to provide a written disclosure to a donor who receives goods or services in exchange for any single payment of $75 or more. This includes buying tickets to a fundraising dinner or auction. The fair market value of the ticket must be determined and provided to the contributor so he can deduct this amount from the amount spent to purchase the ticket. The remaining total can then be deducted on his income tax return. Keep in mind, just because your organization may have received a discount on tickets that were $25 each, does not affect the fair market value, which may be $50 each.

ALERT!

While you are required to provide the fair market value of goods or services greater than $75, you are not required to advise the donor how she should deduct this amount from her taxes. Do not provide financial advice that can get your organization into trouble.

Sometimes it is difficult to gauge fair market value, but you need to come up with a system and a number you can justify should the IRS ask you to do so. An estimated amount can be printed on the ticket or provided on a separate document, such as a thank-you letter.

Statement of Acknowledgment

A simple statement of acknowledgement requires only the name of the organization, amount of the contribution, description of a noncash contribution or statement of goods or services provided, and a good faith estimate of the value of such goods or services. Avoid using a small font because the type should be large enough to come to the attention of the donor. Also, make sure the date is included. This can be sent in a letter, computer printout, or any other clear manner. You should send these acknowledgments out by mid-January (no later than January 31) of the following year so people have them for their tax returns. Save a copy for your organization's files.

Be diligent about sending out statements acknowledging donations. When people do their income tax returns, they generally look for tax deductions. If you have 501(c)(3) status, they are anxious to receive a letter from you.

CHAPTER 20

Measuring Success

After your fundraiser is over, meet with your committee members, volunteers, and board members to evaluate your fundraising campaign. Did you raise as much money as you had originally hoped? Did everything go as planned? Evaluating your results and looking at ways to improve on them next year are important parts of any fundraiser.

Evaluating Your Efforts

The obvious measurement of your success will be whether you raised the funds you originally hoped to raise. This is easy to evaluate because it's a finite number. However, there is more to your success or failure than a dollar figure.

Evaluating Funds

First and foremost, assess whether you spent the funds on the fundraiser or your intended mission. Major fundraising organizations always track the money they receive and make sure it goes to the right place.

While organizations try hard to filter their money to the appropriate channels, expenses do add up, and unexpected ones often deplete the raised funds. Many small nonprofits find the costs of staying afloat eat into their profits on a regular basis.

Post-event evaluations are a worthwhile planning and learning tool. To maximize the process, take a sheet of paper and create two columns. Title one column "What Worked" and list each of the major components whose practices you'd like to reinforce and continue. Title the other "What Needs Improvement." Use this format to stay focused on the goal of improving the event.

Your evaluation must go hand in hand with the various components mentioned throughout the book. Pose the following questions:

- Was the original budget a fair assessment of our projected income and ultimately our expenses?
- Did everyone involved in the fundraising campaign act responsibly? Is all the money we raised accounted for?
- Were there surprise expenses? Were they completely unpredictable or did we overlook something in our calculations?

By answering these questions, you will be better able to determine whether you raised sufficient money and fulfilled the goal of your organization's fundraising plan.

Committees, Board Members, and Volunteers

Along with evaluating your overall fundraising effort, look at the various committees and board members involved. Assess efforts of each committee and review final reports, which should be submitted in a timely fashion after the fundraising campaign is over. Make sure all evaluations are conducted in the same manner and are available for others to read. Fairness and consistency are very important when evaluating the work of individuals. You will also want to review how the board responded to the needs of the fundraising committee and the manner in which it helped raise funds through contacts and resources.

In addition, you should review how the volunteers performed their various tasks. This is in many ways the most difficult evaluation because volunteering itself is already a positive. It's tough to say the volunteers should have conducted additional tasks. Nonetheless, you can determine which plans of action worked, who really excelled at their particular tasks, and who would be better suited for a different task next year.

Personal Evaluation

You might also take time to look at the results of your fundraising efforts on a personal level. After all, no one is forcing you into fundraising. Was the work worthwhile? Do you feel you accomplished the goals you set out to achieve from an organizational and personal standpoint? Did you learn anything new? Perhaps you made new connections or built stronger bonds with people you've known in the organization but never worked with before.

If you led the fundraiser, you might want to ask yourself several questions:

- Did I work well with the volunteers?
- How well did I communicate my ideas?
- Did I keep board members and key parties abreast of the progress of the fundraiser?

- Did we stay on schedule?
- Did we reach our goals?
- Was I able to manage conflicts?
- Would I do it again?

Take your time and think it through. Fundraising can be rewarding, tiring, and enlightening. You can learn about both the process and yourself.

Evaluation Standards

An evaluation is worthwhile only if you have some set of standards to measure the work against. If, for example, your goal of reaching $50,000 in a school fundraiser was grossly unrealistic, you are setting an unattainable standard. Conversely, you may set a goal of $5,000 and bring in $12,000. It's always better from a morale standpoint to keep your goals on the low side and bring in more than double your target amount. Does this mean you did very well, or did you set a goal that was too easily attainable?

What Should You Measure?

Begin by researching what a group of your size, working within the same time frame and in similar conditions—area demographics, geographical location, and so on—should do. Remember, no plan should seek the "perfect" results—you'd just be setting yourself up for disappointment. Along with setting proper standards comes objectivity, which is often difficult to obtain if you are working close to the project.

One of the major problems with any kind of evaluation is that it will inevitably become subjective. Someone is doing the evaluating and using an arbitrary system to make a judgment. Therefore, factors such as personalities and preconceptions can factor into the equation. If someone thought he should have handled the event's promotion, that person might be more critical of the person who was actually given the responsibility.

A school having its first fundraiser may measure its results against the success of another school in the district. The other school, however, might have more students, a larger PTO membership, or more funding, or it might have received $10,000 in donated computer equipment from a parent who just happens to own a computer company. The technology may have made it much easier to run the fundraising campaign.

Look outside the organization to get a feeling for what people thought about how well the fundraiser worked. Distribute brief questionnaires as people exit, or perhaps place them in the organization's newsletter or next mailing. The responses can help you better understand what people thought of your efforts, but take everything with a grain of salt. Remember, more people will respond with negatives than with praise. People who thought everything was terrific aren't as quick to express themselves as those who have complaints.

ALERT!

It's natural to want to compare this fundraiser to a previous year's event, but be careful. There are numerous factors—including the overall economy, accessibility of the venue, and even the weather—that make it difficult to conduct a straight comparison from one year to the next.

Did You Make the Right Choices?

Okay, so Super Bowl Sunday was not the time to hold the carnival. If your fundraiser fell short, you'll need to review your choice of time, place, activity, promotion, and other variables. Was it the wrong fundraiser for your demographic group? Did you neglect to check on what other schools were doing? Were you the ninth school in the community to sell candy in the last six months? Did you pick a venue that was too small for the party or started too late at night for families to attend? Consider all the possibilities and examine your efforts.

Each fundraising effort your organization holds will be a learning and growing experience. You can have successes even without making money. Positive, nonmonetary outcomes may include the following:

- Discovering new talents in membership
- Spreading the word about your group to more people
- Building your presence in the neighborhood or community

- Developing a working system for conducting a future fundraising project

You should take some time to consider these outcomes, which may be hard to measure but are important for the future of the organization.

Common Evaluation Errors

Several types of errors are commonly made when evaluating a fundraising project. Some of these include:

- Evaluating only the final results and not how results were achieved. Numbers don't always tell the whole story.
- Failing to get a broad view. If the fundraiser can affect your whole community, evaluations from three people may not be enough.
- Taking poor notes. If you don't document the results of your efforts, how can you evaluate them fairly? How can you repeat them next year?
- Allowing evaluations to become too complicated. If you've ever been handed a ten-page form to evaluate a twenty-minute lecture, you'll understand the need to keep evaluations within the scope of the project.
- Looking only at the negative and neglecting to review the positives and leverage the best aspects of the event in future endeavors.
- Allowing too much time to elapse between your fundraiser and your review. People may not remember the details of the bake sale six months later. Hold evaluation meetings shortly after your fundraiser.

While no evaluation is foolproof, try to take some time and step back so you can evaluate the efforts of your organization and the overall event using a broad view.

Making Improvements

During your evaluation(s), review which methods worked and why. Look at the manner in which tasks were completed and determine if the best approaches were used. If the process was one the organization found to be most effective, carefully review the process in order to replicate it in the future. If a task succeeded but the manner in which it was handled needs improvement, list exactly which aspects of this task need revamping for the future. Determine why this new and improved version would be more effective and what the implications would be if you use it during the next fundraising project.

If you are asking patrons or contributors for their evaluations in written form, make sure your questions are simple and to the point. Request direct feedback to specific questions regarding the fundraiser and don't overwhelm them with wordy text.

Naturally, it's important to look at the big picture to determine how close the final results were to your expectations. Most completed projects are rarely identical to the original concept. Trial and feedback can lead to testing and tinkering, and the numerous obstacles you confronted along the way tend to change the course and alter the outcome of any project—sometimes for better and sometimes for worse.

The learning process is twofold. Not only will future project teams learn from your detailed accounts, you will also improve your own skills for future projects.

Judging Weak Points

There are many aspects involved in the success or failure of your fundraising effort. Factors may include the environment, scheduling, budget, promotion, products, services rendered, and even the weather. Before you determine what you could do better next time, differentiate between those factors that were within your control and those that were not.

If the fundraiser failed because there was a major storm, obviously the fate of your event was out of your hands. Try to pinpoint each source of success or failure within the project. Ask yourself and everyone involved in the fundraising activities to assess the various elements that made up the overall project. Consider the following:

- Was the initial plan too complex?
- Were you missing certain expertise?
- Were there too many or too few people involved?
- Was the communications system effective?
- Was there a conflict that went unresolved and slowed down the project?
- Did an outside fundraising company come through or disappoint?
- Were outside experts or consultants effective?
- Should key decisions have been made sooner?

These are just some of the many questions to consider when evaluating how the fundraiser went and how to make it better next year.

FACT

One of the most common post-project determinations is a need for more test marketing. If, for example, you had mailed (or test marketed) a fundraising letter to fifty people before sending it to all 15,000 families in the community, you might have been able to improve the letter's phrasing and garner better results. Now you'll know for next time.

Look at the Positives

Keep in mind that evaluating does not mean looking only at what went wrong. Take ample time to applaud the positive aspects of staging your fundraising campaign or activity. Incorporate those aspects in the future. For example, if the raffle was a big hit, perhaps next year you'll seek out bigger prizes and sell tickets a month in advance instead of only a week. Build on your successes!

Lasting Effects

You may not be able to determine the overall results of your efforts at the end of a fundraising project. If you raised money to beautify a neighborhood, keep in mind that the results may not be obvious for some time. A year later, you will see if the work helped revamp the neighborhood. However, if you immediately put the money to use to help maintain a community garden, then you've taken a meaningful role in making a difference where you live.

UESTION?

Are there any benefits from supporting a political candidate even if he does not win?
Yes. A losing candidate can help rally support for other party candidates by building up his profile. He can also run in the next election and have a higher profile. A candidate may also lose the campaign but score a different victory by drawing attention to specific problems or issues.

Sometimes progress takes years. Merck Pharmaceuticals donates a medicine called Mectizan to people suffering from river blindness in the most remote parts of Africa. The medication is administered once annually. Over the twenty-plus years of the unique Mectizan donation program, the number of people suffering from this serious, debilitating disease has decreased. The program is slated to continue for many more years, and the results may not fully be seen for another decade. This is also the case when raising money to fight a disease such as HIV; progress is very slow. Conversely, a response to a local disaster or political fundraiser will have more obvious short-term outcomes.

It's worth noting that most fundraising projects have a carryover effect. Rarely does a project end without a discernable trace. Even a small-scale school fundraising project resulting in a few new textbooks may mean a dozen more children will make it into college in the future. There are both tangible and intangible results that will come from your fundraising project.

Wrapping Up and Moving On

After a major fundraising drive, most organizations require time to regroup. People often need to step back and detach themselves for a while to catch up with friends and family. The larger the project, the more downtime your organization may find necessary. Take time to pat yourselves on the back regardless of whether you raised your projected total.

If you are planning a conference, party, book sale, auction, picnic, or seminar, make sure you account for the cleanup process. It's important to plan who will clean up, break down, or disassemble in the end. Put this in your initial plan along with other closing activities such as a final evaluation.

A wrap party is often a good way to conclude your busy fundraising efforts. You might choose to wait a week or two before celebrating to give everyone a chance to recover. The party should be simple and come from the organization's ongoing budget, not from the project.

Maintain a computer file or log detailing the efforts and resources for your event so they are at the ready when you plan future fundraisers. There's no need to reinvent the wheel every time you run a fundraising activity.

Preparing for the Future

Make sure everything is in order for the future. For example, do you have a file for each donor, complete with contact information and amount contributed? Do you have the names and contact information for each person who volunteered and worked on the project? Software programs can make this kind of database management easy. Be sure to file all vendor numbers and those of any fundraising experts so their information is easily accessible for future reference. Also, make arrangements to return any items borrowed from friends or neighbors, as well as rentals and leased equipment.

Reporting Results

Post your results in some manner. For example, you might publish a story in your monthly or quarterly newsletter about the success of the fundraiser. In addition, you might write a press release, detailing the highlights of your event, whether it was meeting your fundraising goals or attracting 500 people to the auction. No matter how your fundraiser turned out, put a positive spin on the final results.

Board members should meet to hear a final report that includes the budgetary details, number of attendees, and so on. Inform stakeholders, sponsors, and anyone else who was involved in your fundraiser about the details of your event. After all, if sponsors are pleased with the results, they will be eager for you to call on them in the future.

ALERT!

When your fundraiser is completed, don't leave a lot of materials behind. While you are cleaning up, determine what may be used for ongoing operations or future fundraising projects. Also, be sure to collect necessary information from volunteers, such as the password they used on the computer and the location of certain files.

Paperwork

Finish off all accounting procedures, which will include payment of any outstanding bills and fulfilling any contractual obligations. Make sure all bookkeeping is up to date and all information is accessible for the board members or other stakeholders who will review the figures. Have 1099 forms ready for the people you hired to work on the project. In addition, you may need to file reports with local government offices or follow up on any grants you received.

In short, there are plenty of loose ends to tie up after your fundraiser is completed. Plan for these activities ahead of time. Generally, this occupies the time and efforts of only a few key people, particularly whoever was handling the books, budget, and accounting procedures.

Saying Thank You

This concept is worth repeating. Thank everyone who made your carnival, walkathon, or golf tournament actually happen. Whether you raised the money you hoped to or not, you still must recognize the efforts of those who helped. Nearly all nonprofit groups agree that cards, notes, or even just saying thank you are the top ways to bring volunteers back for your next fundraiser. Appreciation goes a long way.

From a simple thank-you note to a token gift to acknowledgment in front of a group of peers, a thank you means a lot. Make sure everyone who was involved feels appreciated when your fundraiser is completed, and promptly send out thank yous to donors and vendors. This way you can count on their efforts in the future!

Fundraising Resources

Organizations and Associations

The Aspen Institute

One Dupont Circle NW, Suite 700
Washington, D.C. 20036-1133
☎ 202-736-5800
✍ *www.aspeninstitute.org*

The fund aims to advance the quantity and quality of nonprofit research.
It has awarded more than $9 million to support more than 350 research
projects since 1991.

Association of Fundraising Distributors and Suppliers

5775-G Peachtree-Dunwoody Road
Atlanta, GA 30342
☎ 404-252-3663
✍ *www.afrds.org*

The association features more than 650 member companies that
manufacture, supply, and distribute products that not-for-profit organizations
and schools can sell to raise money.

Association of Fundraising Professionals

1101 King Street, Suite 700
Alexandria, VA 22314
☏ 703-684-0410
✐ www.afpnet.org

In more than forty years of operation, this association has provided publications, an electronic database, and the latest information on relevant policies, salaries, endowments, ethics, and so on.

Association for Research on Nonprofit Organizations and Voluntary Action (ARNOVA)

550 West North Street, Suite 301
Indianapolis, IN 46202-3272
☏ 317-684-2120
✐ www.arnova.org

ARNOVA provides substantial research on voluntary action, nonprofit organizations, and philanthropy. Additional resources include an annual conference, several publications, and electronic discussions and seminars.

Association of Small Foundations

4905 Del Ray Avenue, Suite 308
Bethesda, MD 20814
☏ 301-907-3337 or 888-212-9922
✐ www.smallfoundations.org

This association provides programs to foundations with little, if any, staff. Members have access to newsletters, national and regional meetings, and more.

BoardSource

1828 L Street NW, Suite 900
Washington, DC 20036-5114
☏ 202-452-6262 or 800-883-6262
✐ www.boardsource.org

A go-to resource for nonprofit board governance once known as the National Center for Nonprofit Boards, BoardSource provides tools, training, leadership development, and other information for nonprofit board members.

The Campaign Finance Institute

1990 M Street NW, Suite 380
Washington, DC 20036
☎ 202-969-8890
✍ www.cfinst.org

Affiliated with George Washington University, this nonpartisan, nonprofit institute conducts objective research and provides education.

Council on Foundations

1828 L Street NW
Washington, DC 20036
☎ 202-466-6512
✍ www.cof.org

This organization promotes and aims to improve philanthropy.

The Foundation Center

79 Fifth Avenue
New York, NY 10003
☎ 212-620-4230
✍ www.fdncenter.org

This organization aims to enhance institutional philanthropy, in part by assisting those requesting grants. It offers ample research, which is available at five libraries across the United States, and other resources.

GuideStar Customer Service

427 Scotland Street
Williamsburg, VA 23185
☎ 757-229-4631
✍ www.guidestar.org

GuideStar is an organization dedicated to transforming philanthropy and nonprofit practice by offering a wealth of information.

Pfau Englund Nonprofit Law, P.C.

1451 Juliana Place
Alexandria, VA 22304-1516
✆ 703-751-8203
✉ *www.nonprofitlaw.com*

This organization provides ample legal information about fundraising and creating a nonprofit, as well as tools to carry out nonprofit research.

Women's Philanthropy Institute

134 West University, Suite 105
Rochester, MI 48307
✆ 248-651-3552
✉ *www.philanthropy.iupui.edu/PhilanthropicServices/WPI/*

This resource provides periodicals, books, software, and additional tools for nonprofits.

Websites

Charity Channel

✉ *www.charitychannel.com*

This site features reviews of nonprofit periodicals, books, and software and provides a resource guide, newsletter, discussion groups, and other materials to the nonprofit community.

FundRaising.com

✉ *www.fundraising.com*

FundRaising.com sells cookie dough, lollipops, and smoothies to nonprofits for fundraising, as well as wristbands and donation cards. It also provides fundraising tips, special promotions, and a newsletter.

Fundraising Ideas and Products Center

✎ www.fundraising-ideas.org

This site includes fundraising ideas, information, news, and a product directory from LarMar Enterprises, Inc.

Fundsnet Online Services

✎ www.fundsnetservices.com

Fundsnet provides nonprofit organizations, colleges, and universities with information on financial resources. It also features fundraising programs, resources, information on grant writing, and an online foundation directory.

Give.org

✎ www.give.org

Give.org, the website of the BBB Wise Giving Alliance, provides operational standards and guidelines that BBB created for nonprofit 501(c)(3) organizations.

idealist.org

✎ www.idealist.org

The online site for Action Without Borders, this resource is dedicated to bring together people, organizations, and resources to help develop a better world for all.

Nonprofit Resource Center

✎ www.not-for-profit.org

This site provides numerous web addresses that may be of benefit to nonprofits, and concentrates on resources regarding finance and accounting, fundraising, governance, and more.

Schoolpop Inc.
✑ www.schoolpop.com

Schoolpop has assisted more than 30,000 schools and nonprofits nationwide raise money by providing access to hundreds of stores, catalogs, and online merchants that deliver a percentage of revenue generated to the nonprofits.

Grant Information

The Grant Advisor
✑ www.grantadvisor.com

Grant Advisor features a newsletter providing grant information for grant writers and faculty in higher education.

The Grantsmanship Center
✑ www.tgci.com

The Grantsmanship Center provides training and low-cost publications for nonprofit organizations and government agencies. It has trained more than 110,000 nonprofit leaders.

Prominent Charitable Organizations

American Cancer Society
✑ www.cancer.org

American Heart Association
National Center
7272 Greenville Avenue
Dallas, TX 75231
✆ 800-242-8721
✑ www.americanheart.org

American Red Cross

American Red Cross National Headquarters
2025 E Street NW
Washington, DC 20006
✆ 800-REDCROSS
✐ *www.redcross.org*

Americares

88 Hamilton Ave.
Stamford, CT 06902
✆ 800-486-4357
✐ *www.americares.org*

Boys & Girls Clubs of America

1275 Peachtree Street NE
Atlanta, GA 30309-3506
✆ 404-487-5700
✐ *www.bgca.org*

Catholic Charities

66 Canal Center Plaza
Alexandria, VA 22314
✆ 703-549-1390
✐ *www.catholiccharitiesusa.org*

Family Violence Prevention Fund

383 Rhode Island Street, Suite 304
San Francisco, CA 94103-5133
✆ 415-252-8900
✐ *www.endabuse.org*

Girl Scouts of the USA

420 Fifth Avenue
New York, NY 10018-2798
✆ 800-478-7248 or 212-852-8000
✐ *www.girlscouts.org*

Humane Society of the United States

2100 L Street NW
Washington DC 20037
☎ 202-452-1100
✎ *www.hsus.org*

National Conservancy

4245 North Fairfax Drive, Suite 100
Arlington, VA 22203-1606
☎ 703-841-5300
✎ *www.nature.org*

Salvation Army

615 Slaters Lane
P.O. Box 269
Alexandria, VA 22313
✎ *www.salvationarmyusa.org*

United Way of America

701 N. Fairfax Street
Alexandria, VA 22314-2045
✎ *www.unitedway.org*

World Wildlife Fund

1250 24th Street NW
P.O. Box 97180
Washington, DC 20037
☎ 202-293-4800
✎ *www.worldwildlife.org*

YMCA of USA

101 North Wacker Drive
Chicago, IL 60606
✎ *www.ymca.net*

Major Foundations

Bill & Melinda Gates Foundation
P.O. Box 23350
Seattle, WA 98102
✆ 206-709-3140 (Reception)
✆ 206-709-3140 (Grant Inquiries)
✐ www.gatesfoundation.org

The David and Lucille Packard Foundation

300 Second Street, Suite 200
Los Altos, CA 94022
✆ 650-948-7658
✐ www.packard.org

The Ford Foundation

320 East 43rd Street
New York, NY 10017
✆ 212-573-5000
✐ www.fordfound.org

The Foundation Center

79 Fifth Avenue/16th Street
New York, NY 10003-3076
✆ 212-620-423
✐ www.fdncenter.org

J. Paul Getty Trust

The Getty Center
1200 Getty Center Drive
Los Angeles, CA 90049-1679
✐ www.getty.edu/grant

The Robert Wood Johnson Foundation

P.O. Box 2316
College Road East and Route 1
Princeton, NJ 08543-2316
☎877-843-RWJF
✉ *www.rwjf.org*

W. K. Kellogg Foundation

One Michigan Avenue East
Battle Creek, MI 49017-4058
☎269-968-1611
✉ *www.wkkf.org*

Major Fundraising Companies

American Publishers, Inc.

One North Superior Street
Sandusky, OH 44870
☎800-284-9711
✉ *www.apifund.com*

This provider of magazine drive fundraisers offers a starter kit and more than 750 magazine titles, as well as fundraising programs and tips and customer service.

Cherrydale Farms

☎800-333-4525
✉ *www.cherrydale.com*

Assisting thousands of schools with fundraising programs that include candy, candles and more, this organization provides a website that offers fundraising ideas, promotions, features, and tracking information.

Entertainment Fundraising

☎800-933-2605

✉www.entertainment.com

A provider of entertainment coupon books, this firm assists schools in raising more than $90 million annually. It also offers fundraising ideas and products on its website.

Hershey's Fundraising

☎800-803-6932

✉www.hersheysfundraising.com

Hershey's has enabled school groups, teams, and bands to raise more than $40 million selling Hershey products.

Innisbrook Wraps

✉www.innisbrook.com

This provider of school gift-wrapping drives serves schools nationwide.

M&M/Mars Fundraising

☎800-964-6663

✉www.mmmarsfundraising.com

The company offers fundraising programs where dollar variety packs of Snickers, Skittles, M&Ms, and more are sold.

Scholastic Book Fairs

1080 Greenwood Boulevard
Lake Mary, FL 32746

☎800-242-7737

✉www.scholastic.com/bookfairs

A leader in children's books, Scholastic's Book Fairs department assists in creating fairs that feature hardcover and paperback bestsellers for kids and adults, raising funds for schools with the help of PTO volunteers.

PBS: Forty Years of Successful Fundraising

The Public Broadcasting Service (PBS) features a wide range of programming, from the classic *Masterpiece* and favorites like *Antiques Roadshow* to educational children's programs such as *Curious George* and *Wordgirl*. Without commercials, the majority of public television is supported by the public. It is, and has been for more than forty years, a unique public-private partnership that hinges on a variety of fundraising methods.

How PBS Works

In 1968, President Lyndon Johnson signed the Public Broadcasting Act, authorizing federal operating aid to public broadcasting stations through a newly created agency, the Corporation for Public Broadcasting (CPB). On average, the annual grant from CPB comprises about 15 percent of a station's budget, making outside fundraising a necessity. Stations then leverage their federal support through revenue-generating activities and a variety of development methods.

PBS was created in 1970 as a nonprofit membership organization charged with distributing quality educational programming. Today, 355 noncommercial public television stations, all individually owned and operated, are part of the public service media enterprise. These stations have autonomy in scheduling decisions and may acquire programming from sources outside PBS, as well as produce their own. Each week, PBS content reaches more than 73 million people in all fifty states, Puerto Rico, Guam, the U.S. Virgin Islands, and American Samoa, either on-air or online.

PBS Member Stations' Approach to Fundraising

While on-air membership drives (pledge), which began in the 1970s, might be the most recognizable form of PBS fundraising, it is not the sole source. PBS and its member stations continually seek to refine and strengthen fundraising, adapting as technology advances and other methods of philanthropic giving emerge.

Stations supplement the funding they receive from federal grants and CPB's allocation with several different types of fundraising, including on-air (pledge), direct mail and telemarketing, online giving, auctions, major giving, planned giving, and local corporate underwriting.

In FY 2007, nearly 4 million individuals contributed more than $400 million to PBS member stations in gifts of $1 and greater. Of gifts less than $1,000, the average donation to a PBS station is $97.

On-Air Fundraising

Unlike any other nonprofit organization, PBS stations have the capability to reach millions of people through broadcast television. Utilization of this unique ability enables them to tell their story and conduct on-air membership drives. Throughout the year, this practice, commonly called pledge, allows local viewers to make financial donations directly to the PBS station in their geographic area.

As a token of appreciation, most stations offer donors thank-you gifts designed to be an extension of a PBS program, providing the donor with an opportunity to stay connected long after the program has aired. As a service to stations, PBS researches which gifts are best suited for different audiences, saving stations time and money and preventing them from having to do the same research separately.

Research is an essential part of planning pledge drives. PBS stations generally look for times in the schedule that contrast the programming of the commercial networks. The majority of stations pledge three times a year—March, August (or September), and early December.

PBS acquires or, sometimes, commissions special programming to air on stations during the membership drives. Stations exercise complete control over which, if any, PBS programs they want to present during these periods. While much of the contributions generated through pledge are in response to programs that have been specifically designed for on-air fundraising; stations have also found success in fundraising around PBS's icon series such as *American Experience, Antiques Roadshow, Frontline, Masterpiece, Nature, NOVA, The Newshour with Jim Lehrer,* and others. PBS provides a framework, including scripts, recorded breaks, taped roll-ins, and training and counsel for on-air drives, but the diversity among the stations and their individual needs mandate they establish their own schedules and priorities.

In addition to membership drives, each PBS station employs a variety of fundraising methods. By diversifying how they raise money, stations are able to cultivate long-term relationships with their donors and reach new audiences with their individual approaches.

Direct Mail and Telemarketing

PBS member stations utilize both direct mail and telemarketing to renew existing donations acquired through on-air pledge and to gain new supporters throughout the year. Direct mail provides an opportunity to tell prospective and existing donors about the work of the station, foster relationships, and ultimately seek financial support. While telemarketing has the same goals as direct mail, it allows for a more personal experience: to speak directly with a volunteer or local station employee. Some stations also work with third-party firms to implement their telemarketing campaigns.

Online Giving

Today, PBS member stations are seizing opportunities presented by the web to engage donors online and cultivate relationships with new—and often younger—audiences. Almost all PBS member stations have secure websites that enable individuals to donate online, and many use blogs and other social media to engage with donors. While still representing a small percentage of the overall fundraising mix, online donations continue to grow. The average donation made online is generally larger than that received via direct mail.

Auctions

About sixty PBS member stations include auctions in their development efforts. The presentation of auctions continues to evolve, with stations switching from an on-air, multiday presence to an online auction supported by on-air promotion. With the move toward online auctions, stations have realized cost savings due to lower production costs associated with an on-air presence, and an opportunity to reallocate their air time from auctions to other programming priorities.

Major Giving

Through a multiyear, nationwide program called the Major Giving Initiative (MGI), led by CPB, two-thirds of all PBS member stations began or strengthened their major giving efforts during the past several years. Major gifts, or annual donations of $1,000 or more, are a relatively untapped opportunity for stations, but they are growing in importance.

PBS stations have invested in building up the resources necessary to seek and sustain major gifts. Station staff ensures that donors of major gifts understand that their contribution benefits not only their station or a specific program but the community as a whole. Through their articulation of the mission, vision, and values of public television, stations have increased the number of donors giving at the $1,000 or greater level and boosted their total revenue.

Planned Giving

Planned giving, an extension of major giving, is another option in securing large donations. PBS developed and made available to member stations a series of on-air, planned giving spots for stations to use in communicating this option to their supporters. PBS stations that have made a long-term commitment to promoting planned giving have been successful in cultivating bequeathed gifts.

Local Corporate Underwriting

PBS member stations generate revenue and strategic partnerships from corporations and foundations within their communities. This may take the shape of underwriting the local broadcast of national PBS programs, funding local productions, educational services, community outreach activities, local online content, and special events. While stations acknowledge corporate support on-air, the underwriting credits only serve as identification and are not meant to advertise the funder, its products, or its services. A number of regulations govern the approval of on-air underwriting credits—including those mandated by the Federal Communications Commission (FCC)—PBS national guidelines, and local station practices. At its best, corporate underwriting is a powerful blend of community engagement and corporate philanthropy that ultimately strengthens member stations' relationships with key sponsors and turns them into long-term supporters.

PBS Foundation

In 2004, PBS established a foundation to enlist philanthropic support of public broadcasting through special initiatives funds and a permanent endowment. These funds are dedicated to ensure PBS's continued excellence, and to promote and enhance outstanding public broadcasting programs and services. The PBS Foundation solicits funding for PBS at the national level by seeking extraordinary grants and gifts of $1 million or greater. Working cooperatively and collaboratively with PBS member stations at the local level, the PBS Foundation's fundraising efforts benefit and enhance the system as a whole by providing a source for revenue.

In all, PBS and its member stations' development structure encompasses varied fundraising methods. Stations have diversified the ways in which people can contribute to their local stations and the national organization. The collaborative relationship at the national and local levels helps both small and large stations meet their individual needs, while allowing every station the flexibility to maintain its own distinctive identity—making PBS a truly remarkable study in fundraising for nearly forty years.

INDEX